Feb 7

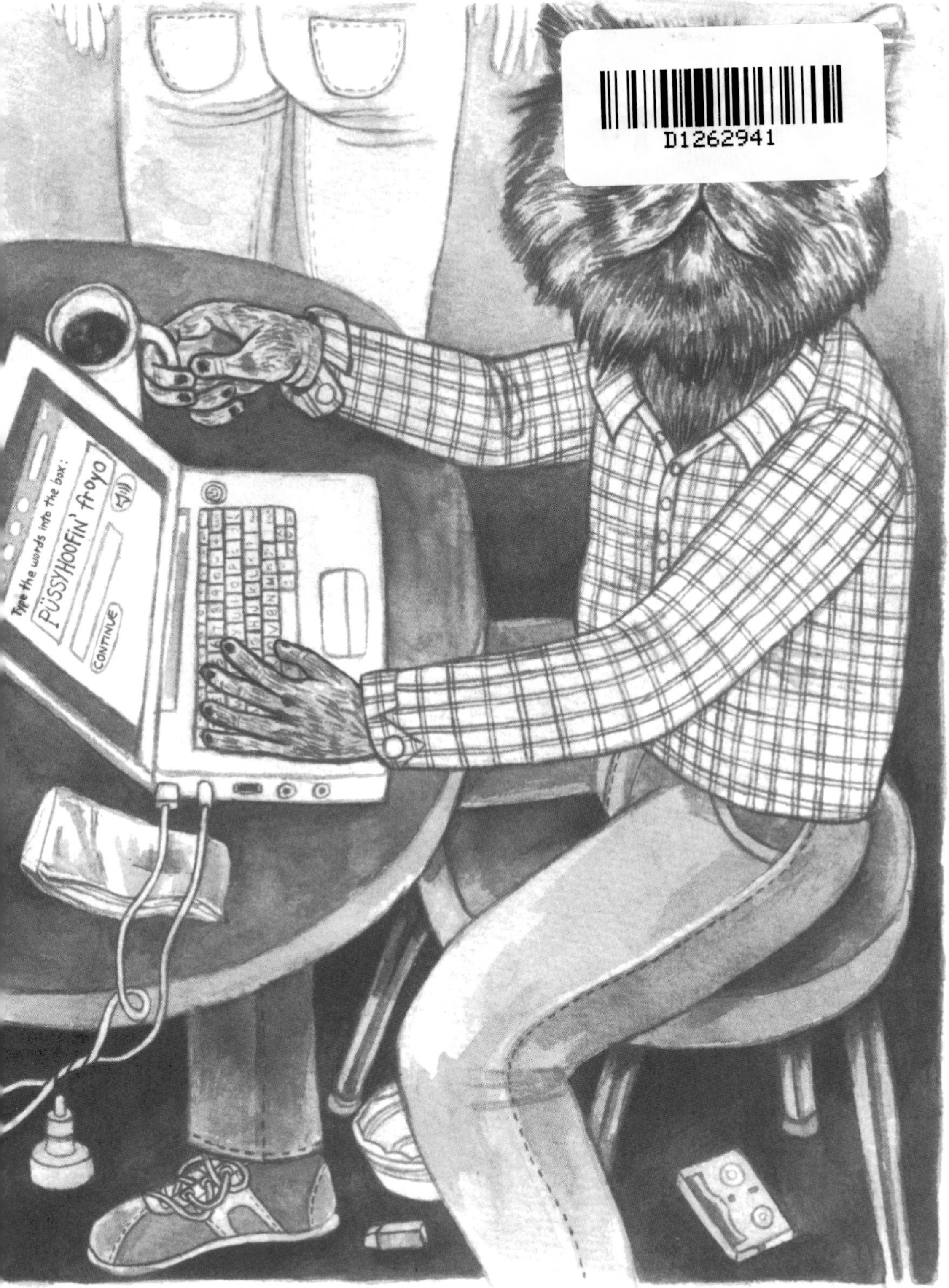
Type the words into the box:
PÜSSYHOOFIN' froyo
CONTINUE

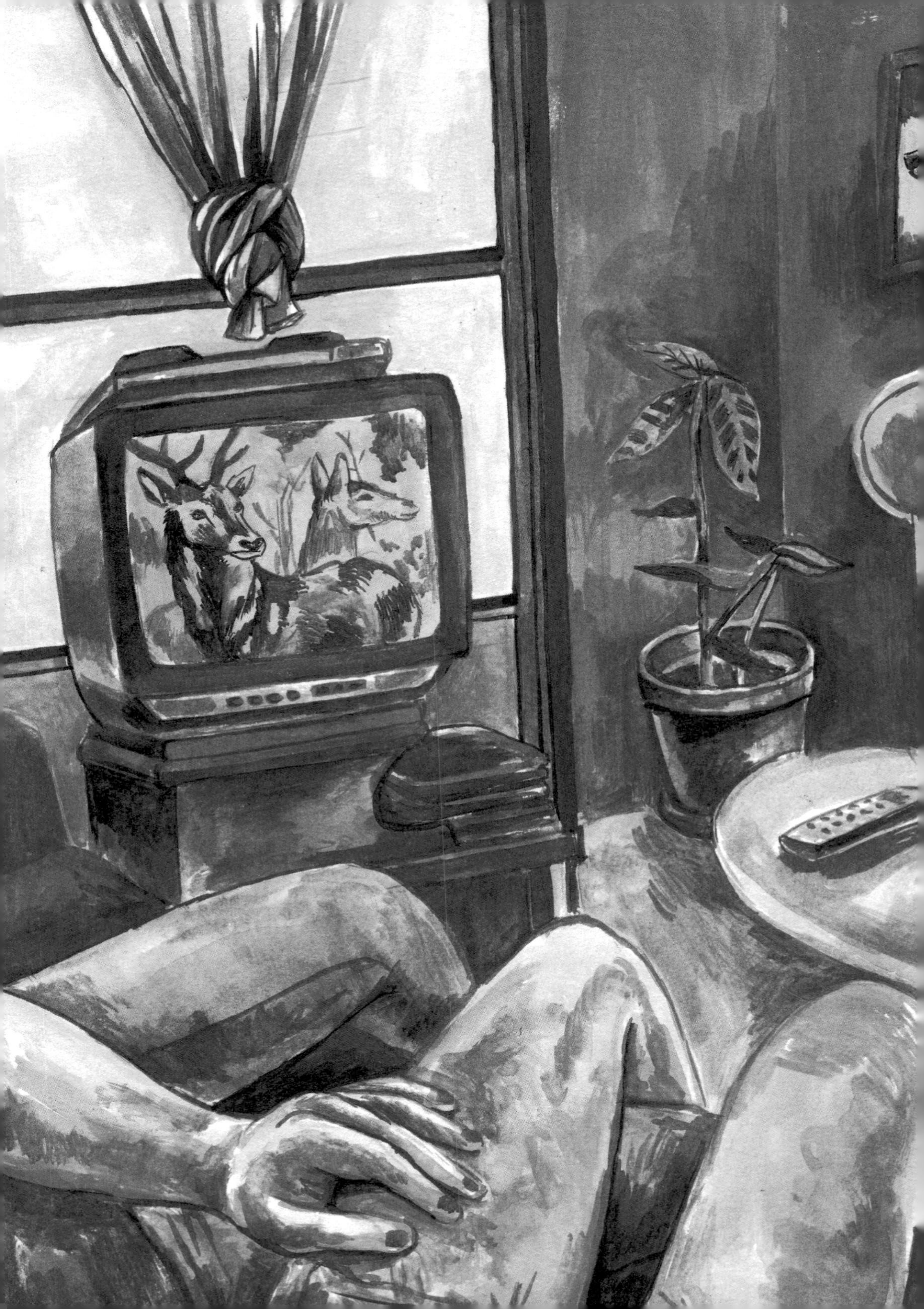

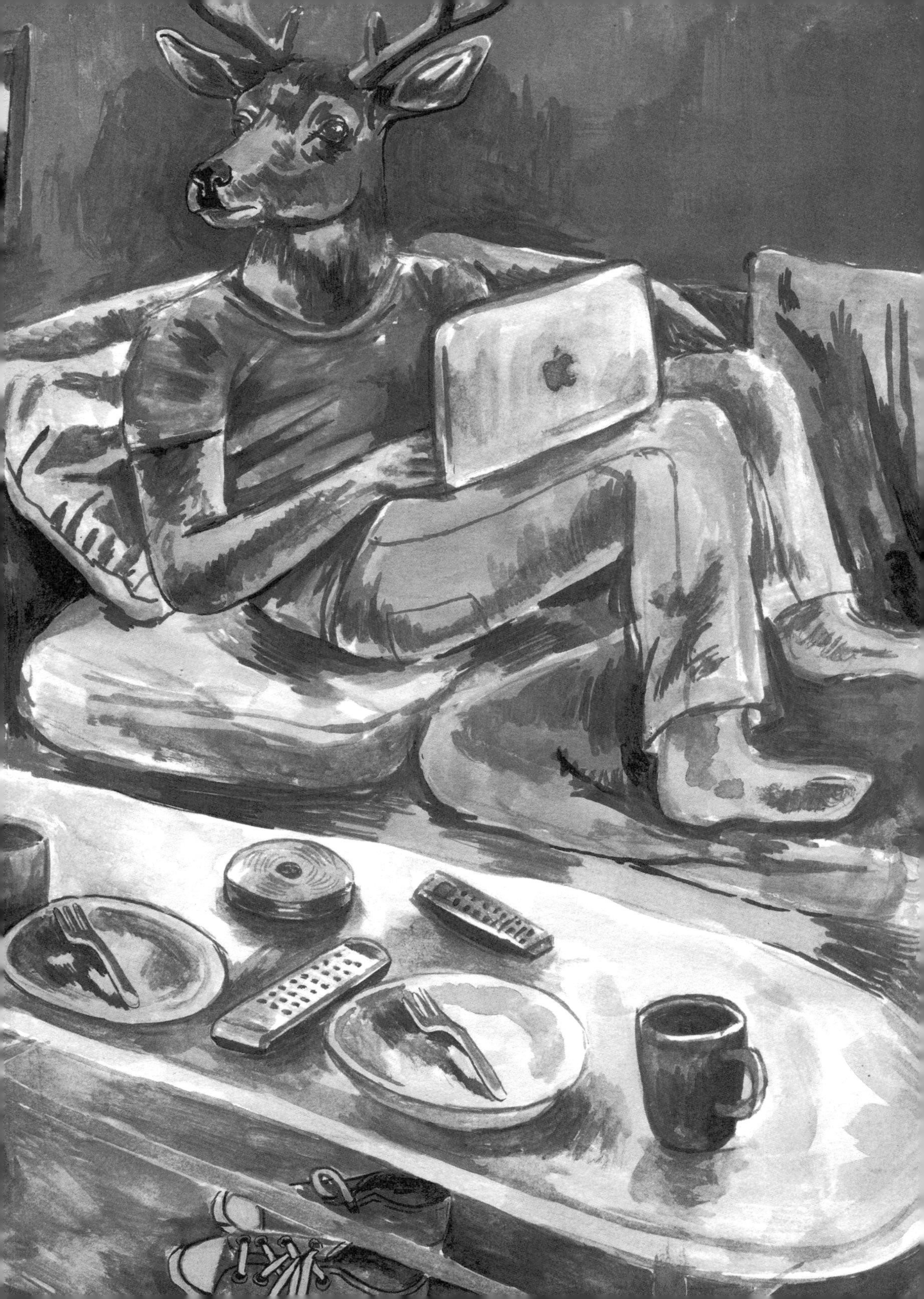

When I first made the work in this book, I learned what an
"indicia" is, and now here I am, inking an indicia for
the 5765th time. Makes ya think!

drawn and quarterly . com
lisa hanawalt . com

ISBN 978-1-77046-388-2
First edition : September 2020
Printed in Bosnia
10 9 8 7 6 5 4 3 2 1 0

It's 70 degrees outside and the sun will set in 6.25 hours.

Cataloguing data available from Library and Archives Canada

Published in the USA by Drawn & Quarterly, a client publisher
of Farrar, Straus and Giroux. Published in Canada by Drawn &
Quarterly, a client publisher of Raincoast Books. Published in
the United Kingdom by Drawn & Quarterly, a client publisher
of Publishers Group UK.

I want you

LISA HANAWALT

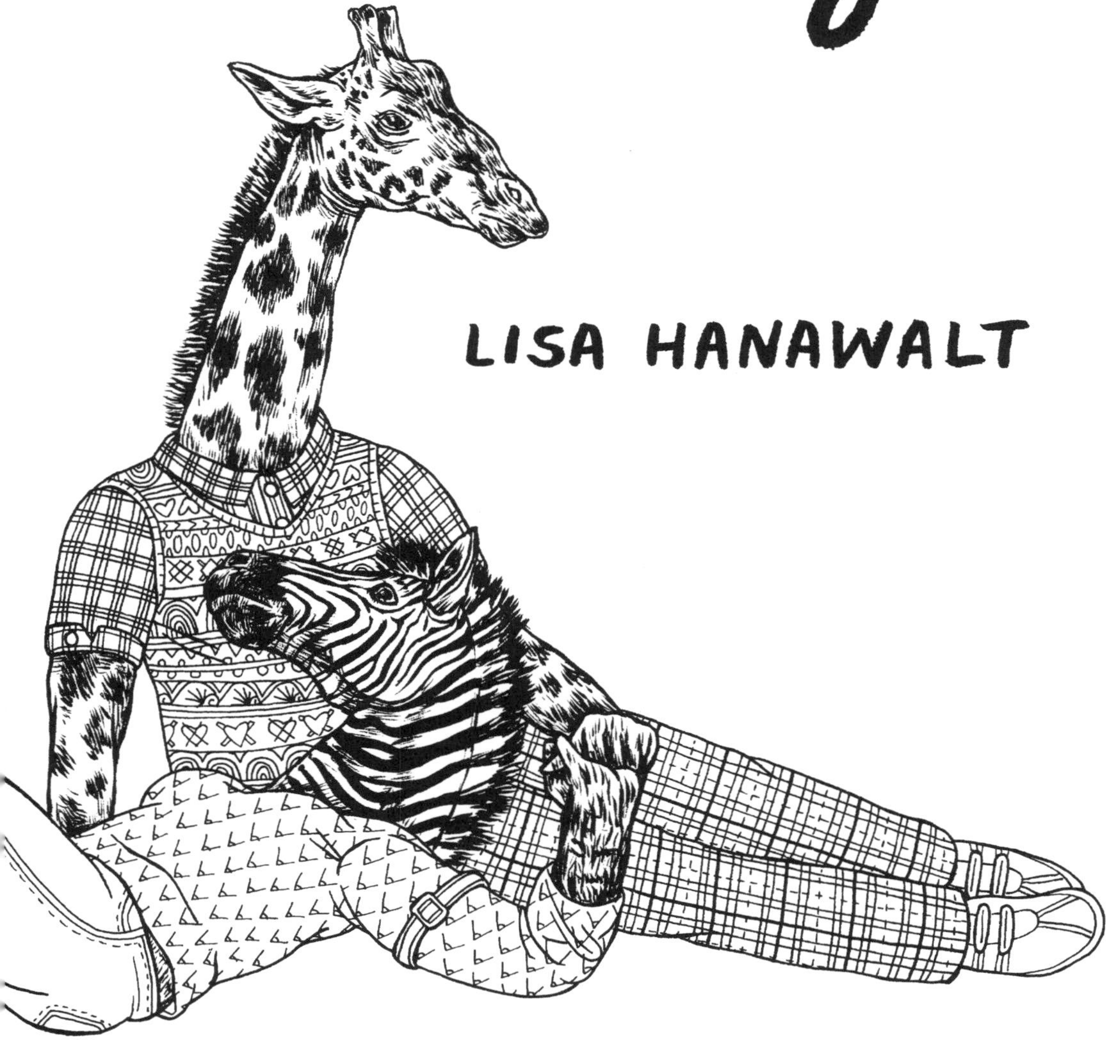

DRAWN & QUARTERLY

AN INTRODUCTION (WITH SOME THOUGHTS ON BEING *SLIGHTLY* OLDER)

WHEN I MADE THE FIRST ISSUE OF "I WANT YOU," I WAS IN MY TWENTIES, SINGLE, LIVING IN L.A., AND I SPENT TOO MUCH TIME ON THE INTERNET. I HAD A DAY JOB WORKING IN A WAREHOUSE OFFICE AND I WORKED ON COMICS EVERY EVENING.

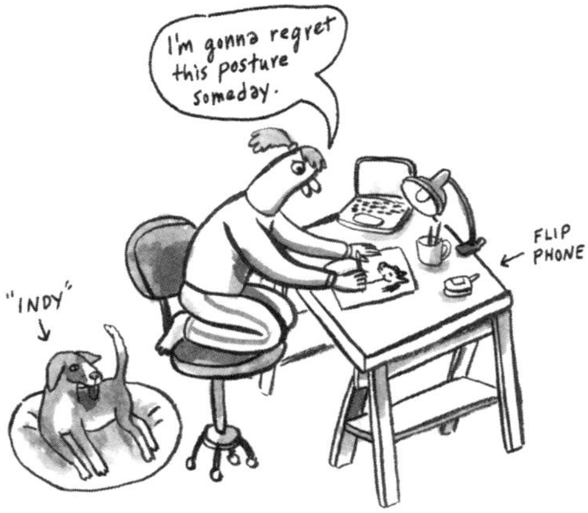
I'm gonna regret this posture someday.
"INDY"
FLIP PHONE

NOW I'M IN MY THIRTIES! I'VE BEEN WITH MY BOYFRIEND FOR OVER A DECADE, I'M BACK IN L.A., AND I STILL SPEND TOO MUCH TIME ON THE INTERNET. I'VE BEEN WORKING IN ANIMATION AND TV, AND I STILL MAKE COMICS.

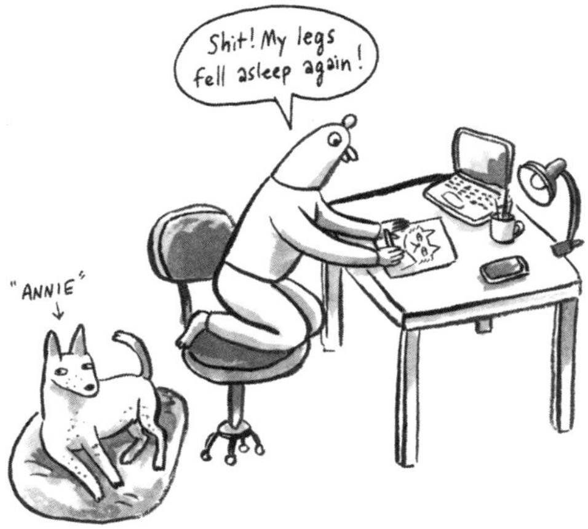
Shit! My legs fell asleep again!
"ANNIE"

I'M STILL NOT GREAT AT TAKING CARE OF MYSELF, BUT I'M TRYING. I'M A BETTER COMMUNICATOR AND I'M MORE CONFIDENT. I CAN'T WORK FOR AS LONG; MY ARM SEIZES UP IF I DON'T REST IT.

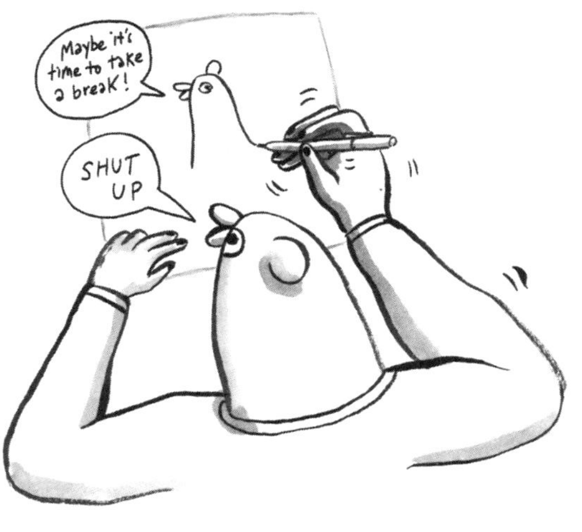
Maybe it's time to take a break!
SHUT UP

I'M ALWAYS NERVOUS ABOUT THE FUTURE. I HOPE IT DOESN'T LOOK TOO DIFFERENT.

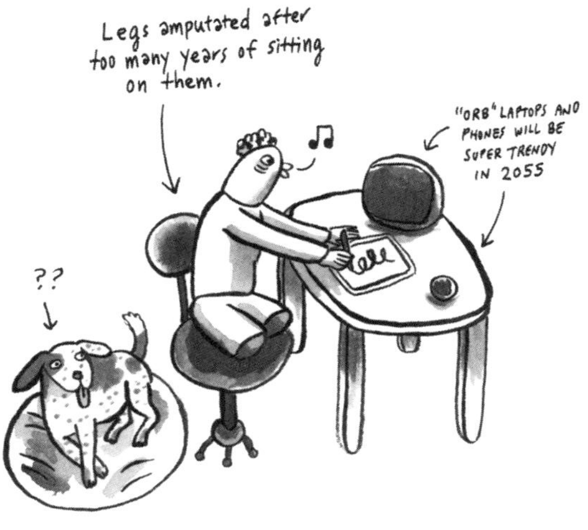
Legs amputated after too many years of sitting on them.
"ORB" LAPTOPS AND PHONES WILL BE SUPER TRENDY IN 2055
??

I TRY TO AVOID LOOKING BACK AT OLD WORK. IT FEELS LIKE TAKING A SHIT AND NOT FLUSHING IT. I'M SORRY THAT'S SO RUDE, BUT IT'S TRUE!

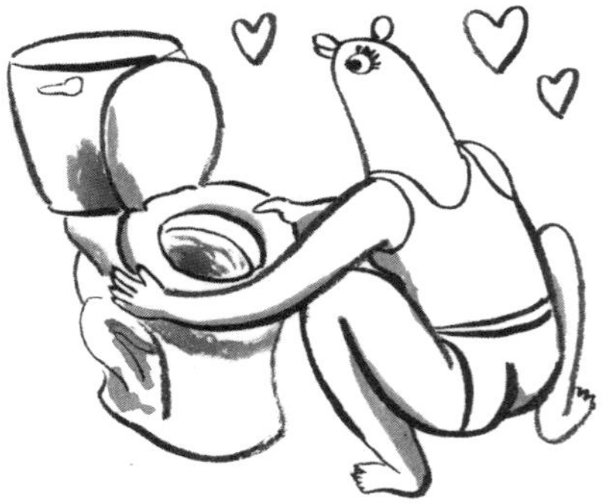

I NEEDED TO EXPRESS SOMETHING AND NOW THAT IT'S OUT OF ME, I WANT TO LEAVE IT IN THE PAST. (THIS FEELS HEALTHY AND NORMAL TO ME).

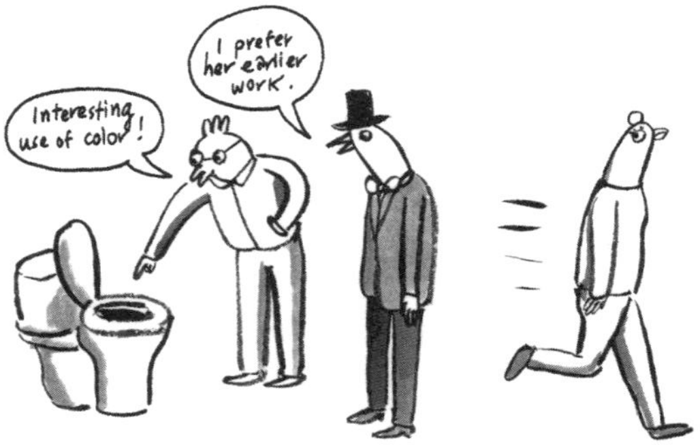

Interesting use of color!
I prefer her earlier work.

I WORRY READING MY OLD COMICS WILL BRING BACK PAINFUL MEMORIES AND REGRETS.

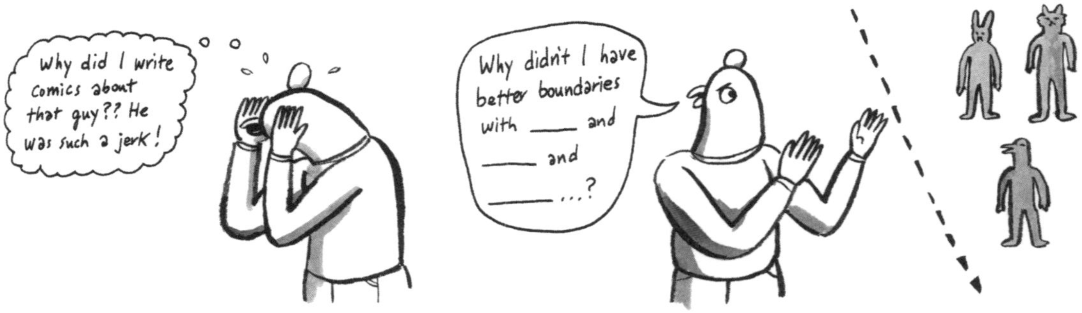

Why did I write comics about that guy?? He was such a jerk!
Why didn't I have better boundaries with ____ and ____ and ______...?

WHEN I WAS IN MY TWENTIES, I WANTED SO BADLY TO BE LIKED AND ACCEPTED THAT I DIDN'T NOTICE WHEN I WAS TREATED POORLY. I THOUGHT I WAS IN CONTROL, BUT I WAS A BIT NAÏVE.

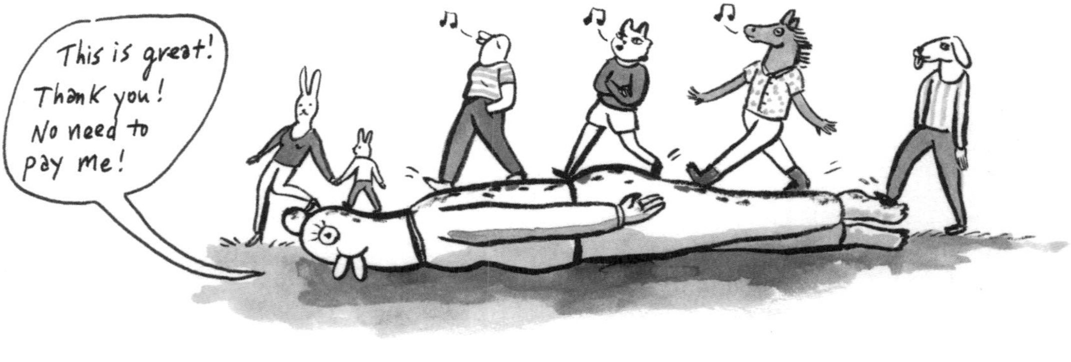

This is great! Thank you! No need to pay me!

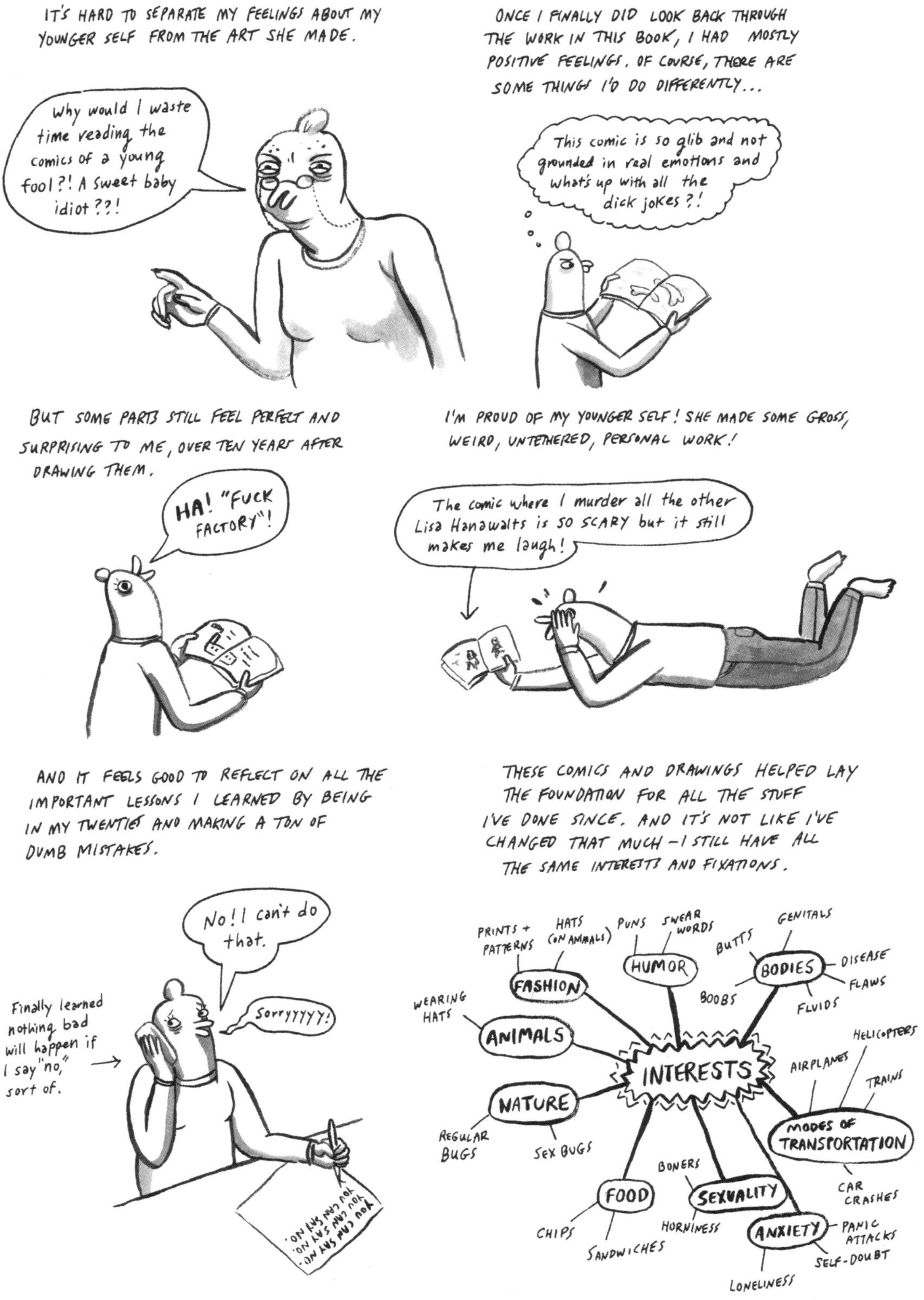
IT'S HARD TO SEPARATE MY FEELINGS ABOUT MY YOUNGER SELF FROM THE ART SHE MADE.
Why would I waste time reading the comics of a young fool?! A sweet baby idiot??!
ONCE I FINALLY DID LOOK BACK THROUGH THE WORK IN THIS BOOK, I HAD MOSTLY POSITIVE FEELINGS. OF COURSE, THERE ARE SOME THINGS I'D DO DIFFERENTLY...
This comic is so glib and not grounded in real emotions and what's up with all the dick jokes?!
BUT SOME PARTS STILL FEEL PERFECT AND SURPRISING TO ME, OVER TEN YEARS AFTER DRAWING THEM.
HA! "FUCK FACTORY"!
I'M PROUD OF MY YOUNGER SELF! SHE MADE SOME GROSS, WEIRD, UNTETHERED, PERSONAL WORK!
The comic where I murder all the other Lisa Hanawalts is so SCARY but it still makes me laugh!
AND IT FEELS GOOD TO REFLECT ON ALL THE IMPORTANT LESSONS I LEARNED BY BEING IN MY TWENTIES AND MAKING A TON OF DUMB MISTAKES.
No!! I can't do that.
Sorryyyyy!
Finally learned nothing bad will happen if I say "no," sort of.
YOU CAN SAY NO.
YOU CAN SAY NO.
YOU CAN SAY NO.
YOU CAN SAY NO.
THESE COMICS AND DRAWINGS HELPED LAY THE FOUNDATION FOR ALL THE STUFF I'VE DONE SINCE. AND IT'S NOT LIKE I'VE CHANGED THAT MUCH — I STILL HAVE ALL THE SAME INTERESTS AND FIXATIONS.
INTERESTS
FASHION
PRINTS + PATTERNS
HATS (ON ANIMALS)
HUMOR
PUNS
SWEAR WORDS
BODIES
BUTTS
GENITALS
DISEASE
FLAWS
FLUIDS
BOOBS
ANIMALS
WEARING HATS
NATURE
REGULAR BUGS
SEX BUGS
MODES OF TRANSPORTATION
HELICOPTERS
AIRPLANES
TRAINS
CAR CRASHES
FOOD
CHIPS
SANDWICHES
SEXUALITY
BONERS
HORNINESS
ANXIETY
PANIC ATTACKS
SELF-DOUBT
LONELINESS

POTENTIAL MISSTEPS ON THE WAY TO BECOMING A WISE OLDER MENTOR-TYPE

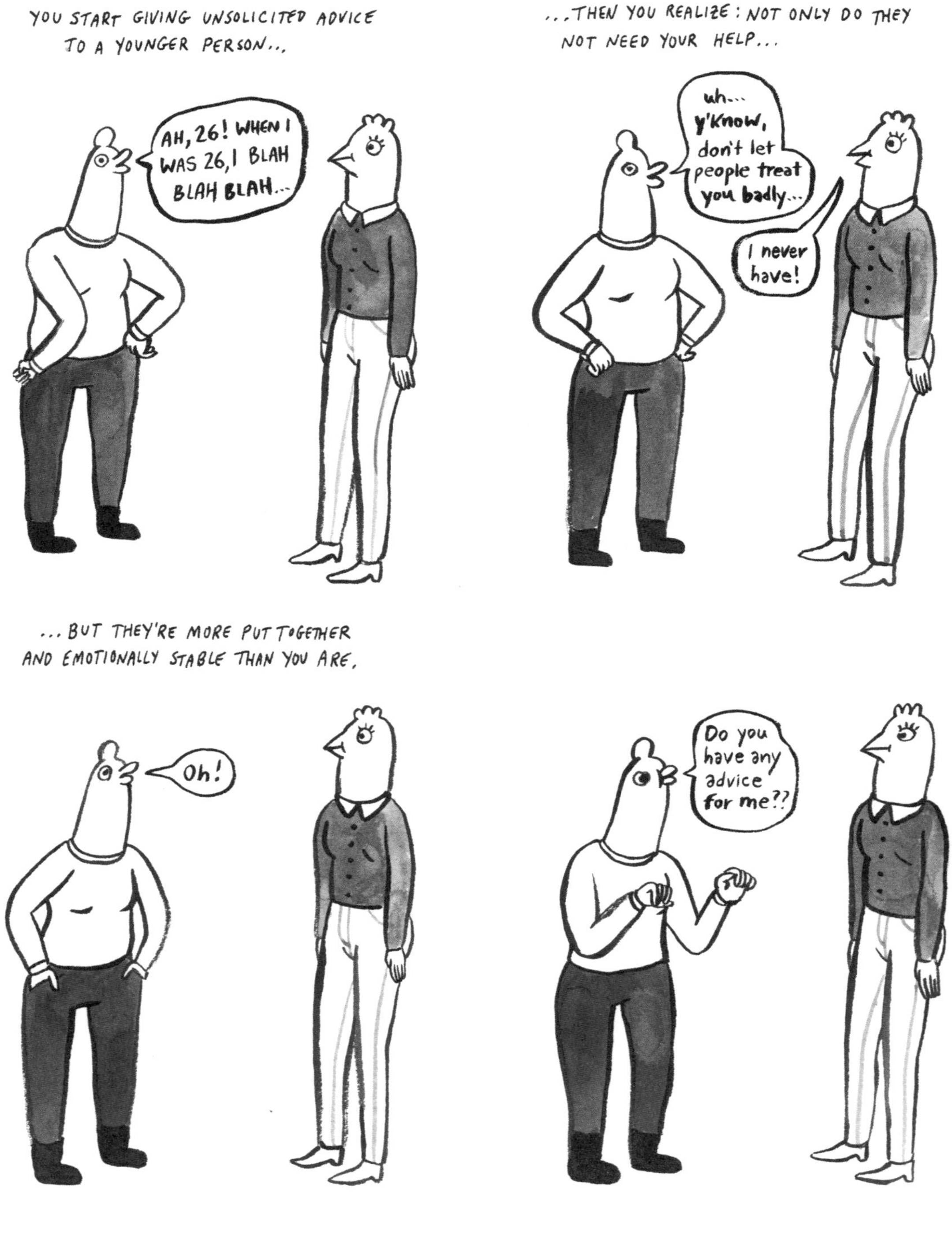
YOU START GIVING UNSOLICITED ADVICE TO A YOUNGER PERSON...
AH, 26! WHEN I WAS 26, I BLAH BLAH BLAH...
...THEN YOU REALIZE: NOT ONLY DO THEY NOT NEED YOUR HELP...
uh... y'know, don't let people treat you badly...
I never have!
...BUT THEY'RE MORE PUT TOGETHER AND EMOTIONALLY STABLE THAN YOU ARE.
Oh!
Do you have any advice for me??

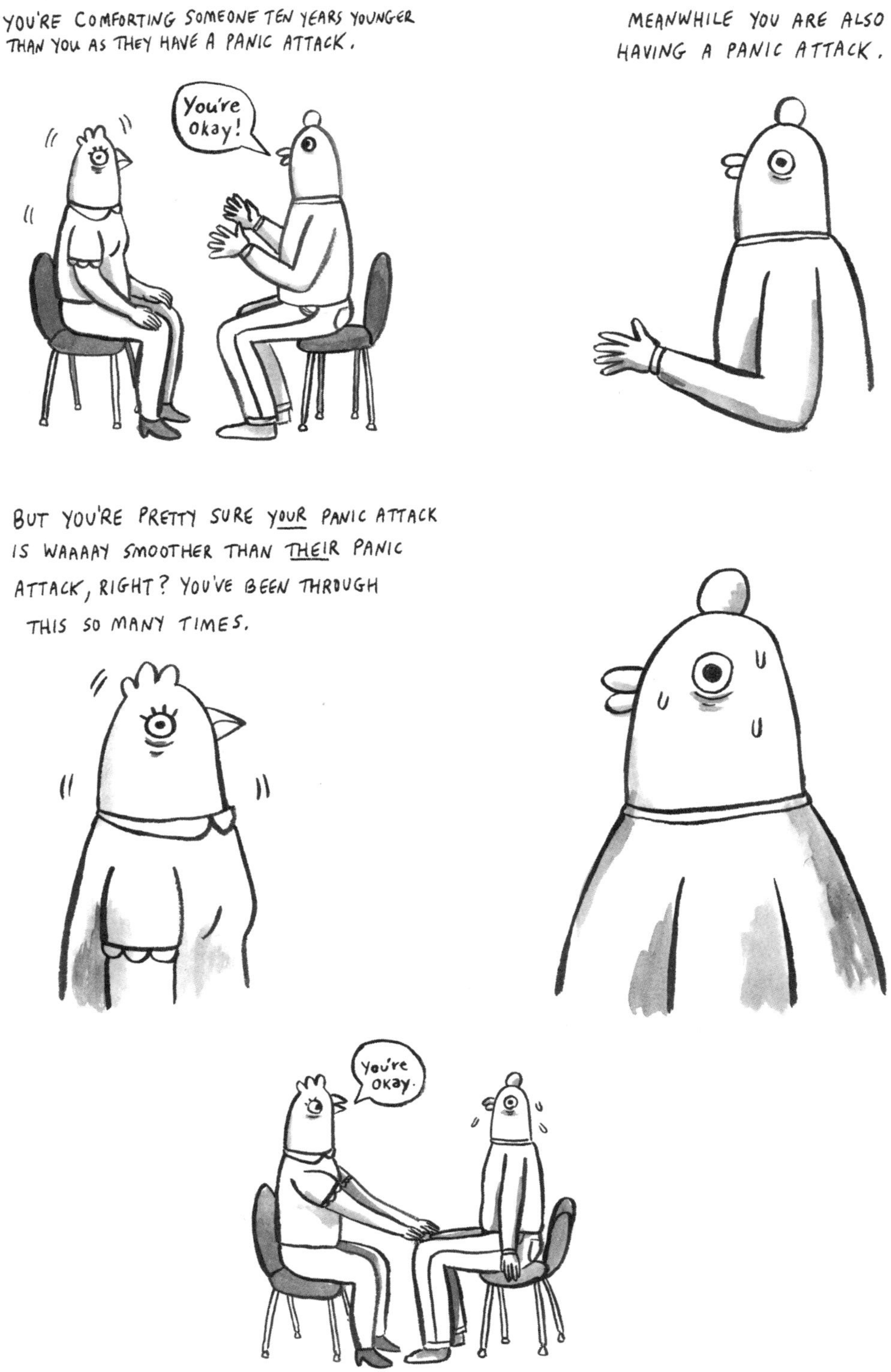
YOU'RE COMFORTING SOMEONE TEN YEARS YOUNGER THAN YOU AS THEY HAVE A PANIC ATTACK.
You're okay!
MEANWHILE YOU ARE ALSO HAVING A PANIC ATTACK.
BUT YOU'RE PRETTY SURE YOUR PANIC ATTACK IS WAAAAY SMOOTHER THAN THEIR PANIC ATTACK, RIGHT? YOU'VE BEEN THROUGH THIS SO MANY TIMES.
You're okay.

I DON'T FEEL MUCH SMARTER THAN I DID IN MY TWENTIES. SOMETIMES I FEEL DUMBER, LIKE I'M IN A FOG.

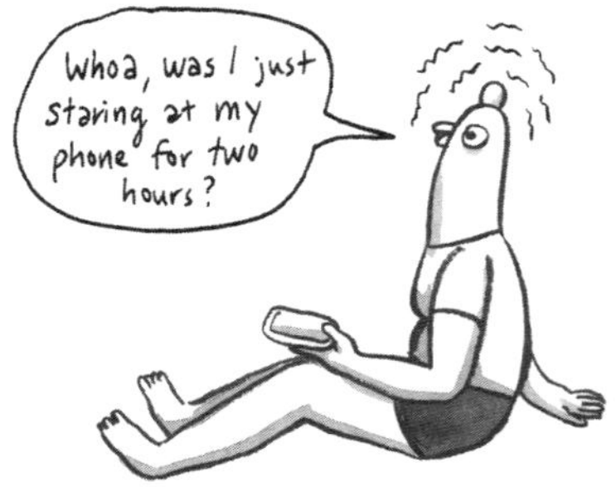
Whoa, was I just staring at my phone for two hours?

BUT OCCASIONALLY I'LL MEET A YOUNGER PERSON WHO'S HAVING A ROUGH TIME AND I'LL THINK:

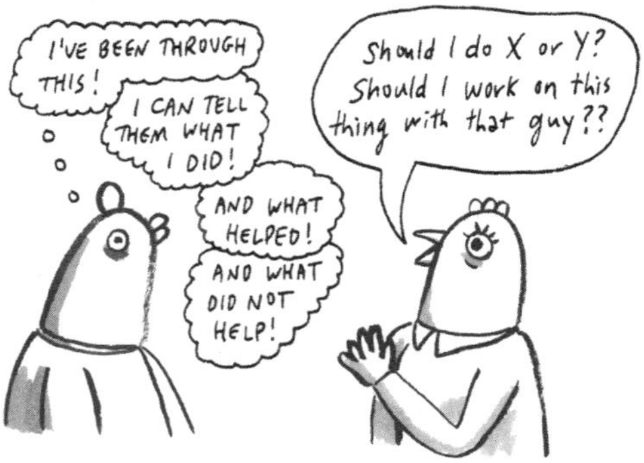
I'VE BEEN THROUGH THIS!
I CAN TELL THEM WHAT I DID!
AND WHAT HELPED!
AND WHAT DID NOT HELP!
Should I do X or Y? Should I work on this thing with that guy??

AND I'LL LEAVE OUT SOME BREADCRUMBS TO HELP THEM NAVIGATE THOSE BUMPY BITS, OR AT LEAST REASSURE THEM THAT THEY'RE ON THE RIGHT PATH.

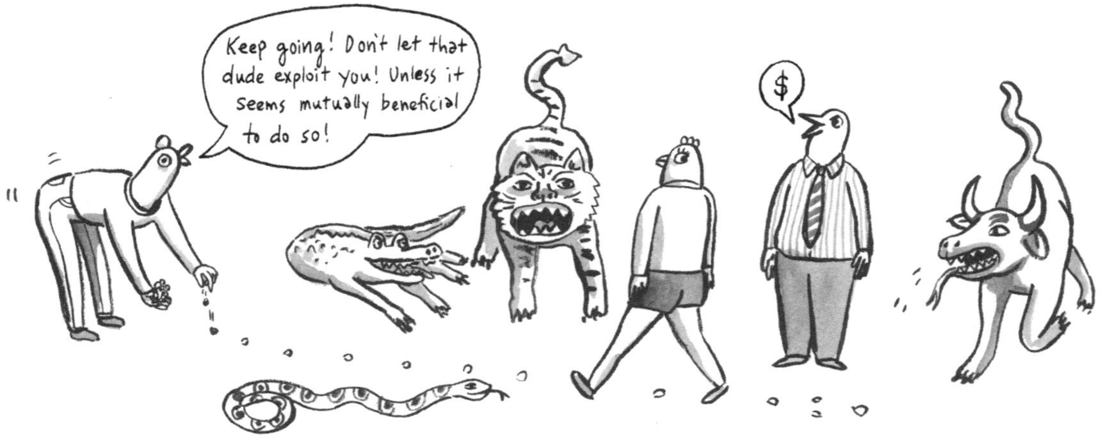
Keep going! Don't let that dude exploit you! Unless it seems mutually beneficial to do so!
$

MAYBE I DO HAVE SOME WISDOM AND MY OWN BATTLE SCARS CAN SERVE AS A WARNING?

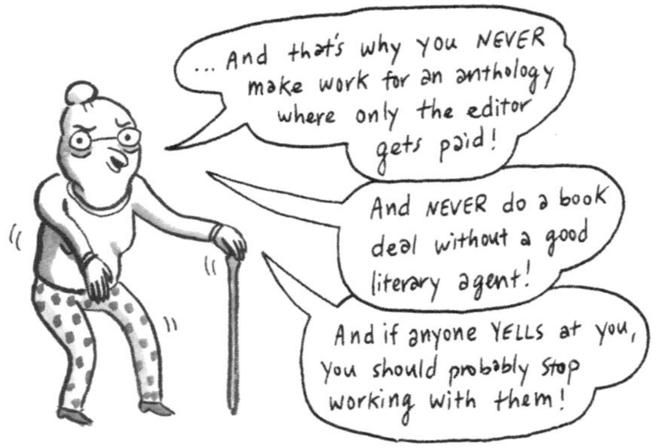
...And that's why you NEVER make work for an anthology where only the editor gets paid!
And NEVER do a book deal without a good literary agent!
And if anyone YELLS at you, you should probably stop working with them!

NOW... WOULD SOMEBODY TELL ME WHAT TO DO?? BECAUSE I HAVE NO FUCKING IDEA.

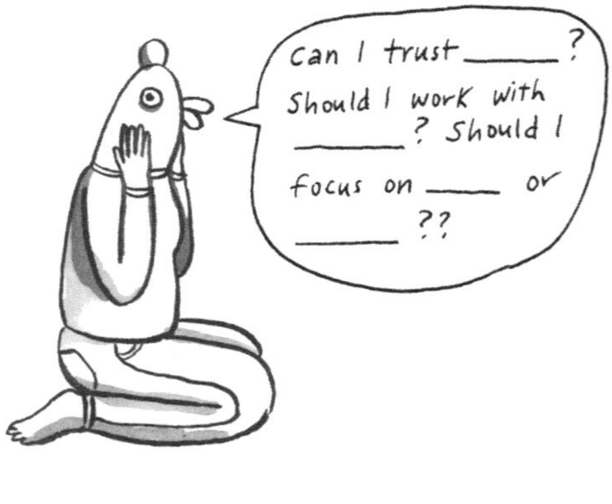
Can I trust _____? Should I work with _____? Should I focus on _____ or _____??

I
want
you

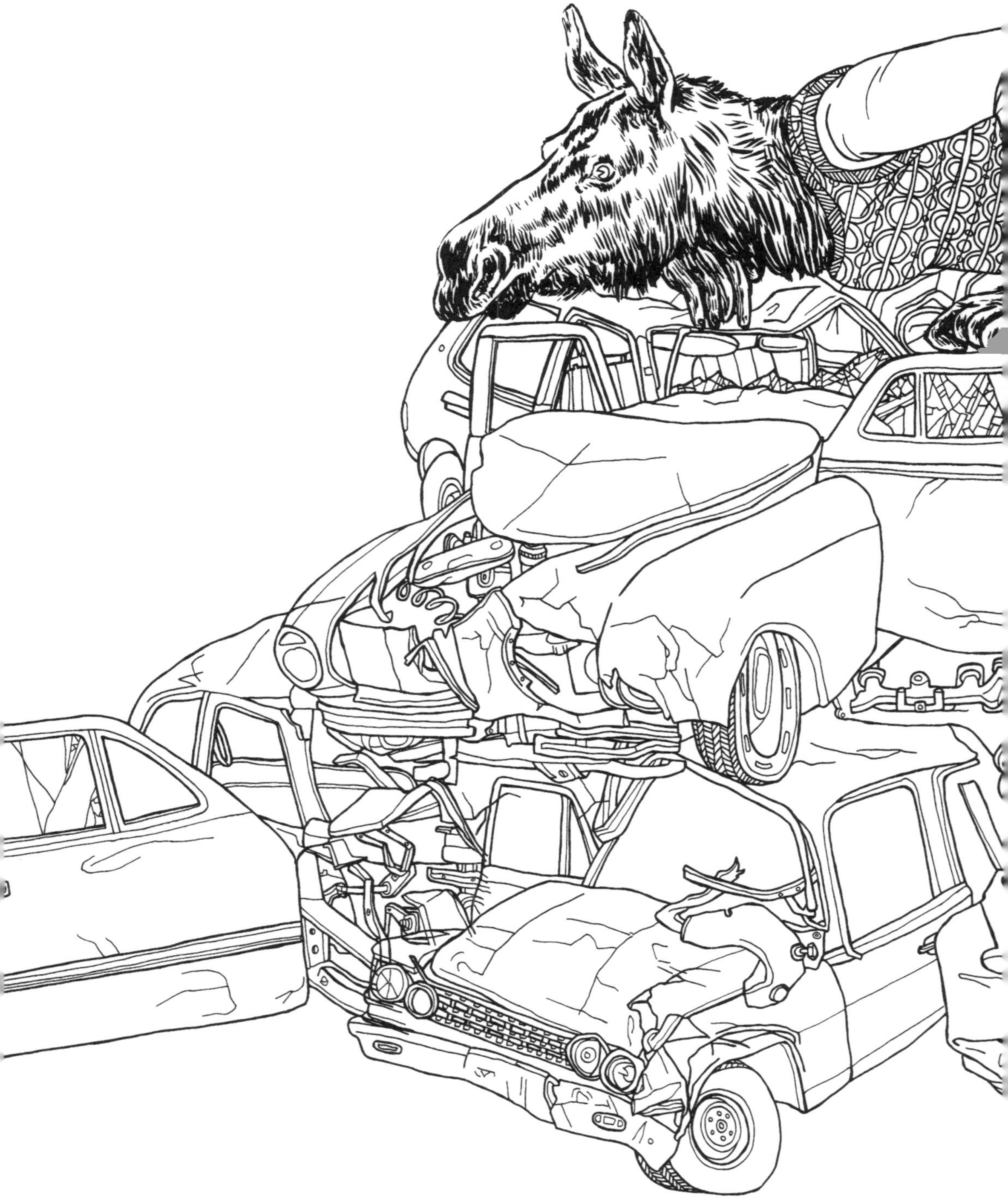

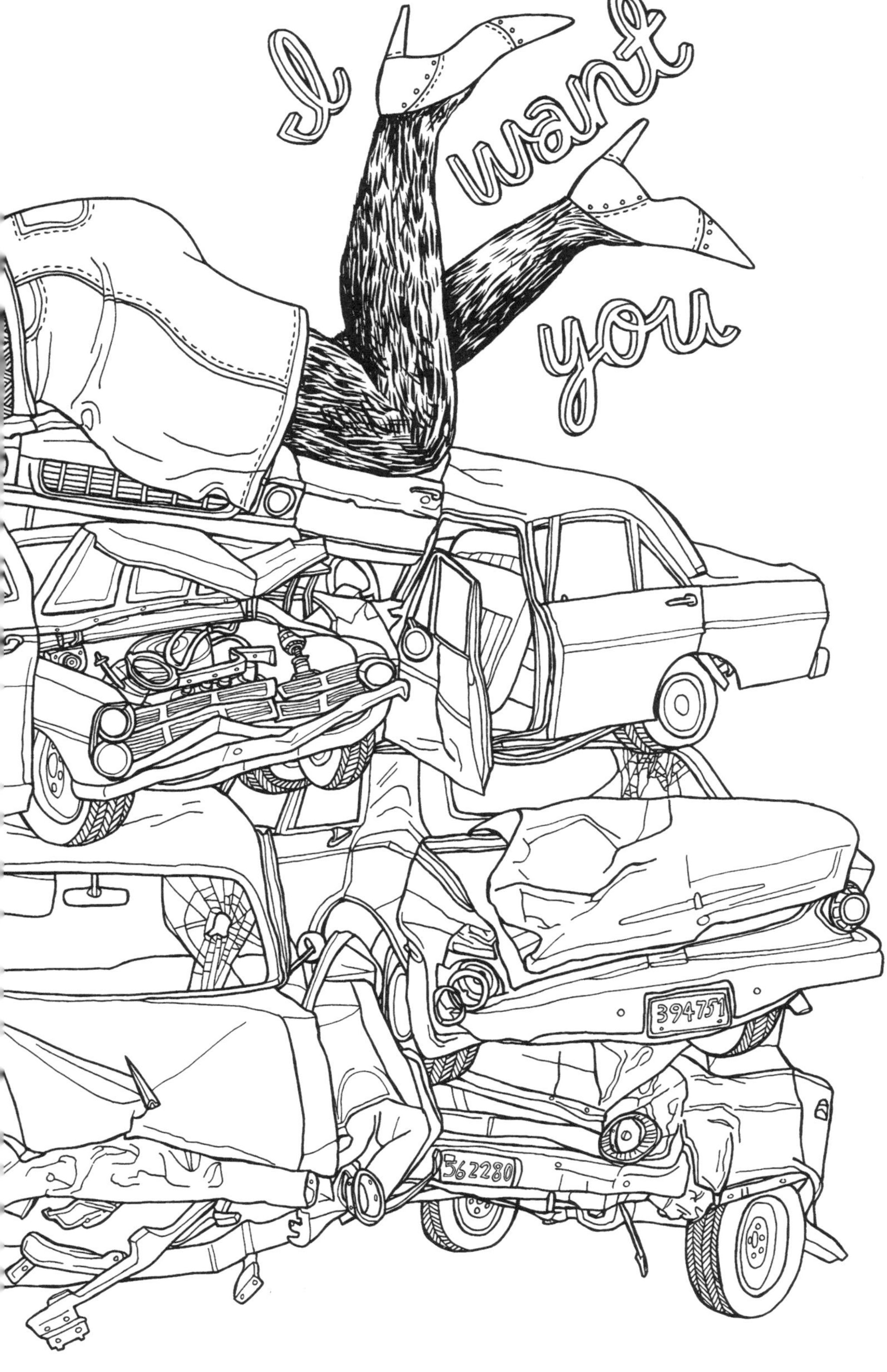
I want you
394751
562280

MISTAKES WE MADE AT THE GROCERY STORE

① WE SANG TOO LOUDLY IN THE PARKING LOT WITH THE WINDOWS DOWN

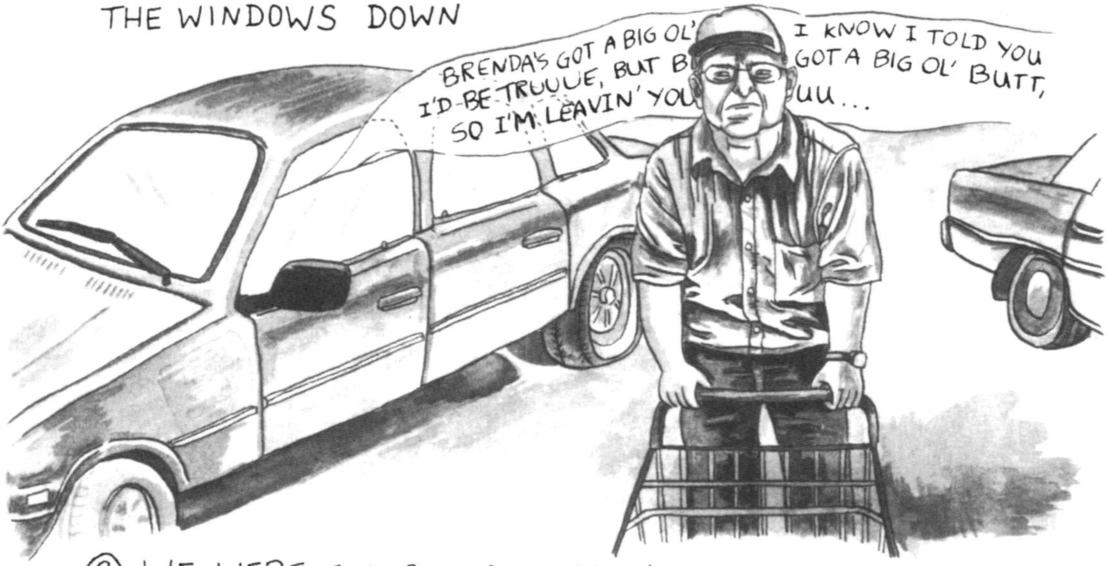
BRENDA'S GOT A BIG OL'
I'D BE TRUUUE, BUT B
SO I'M LEAVIN' YOU
I KNOW I TOLD YOU
GOT A BIG OL' BUTT,
UU...

② WE WERE TOO SEXUAL WHEN WE CHECKED OUR EGGS FOR CRACKS

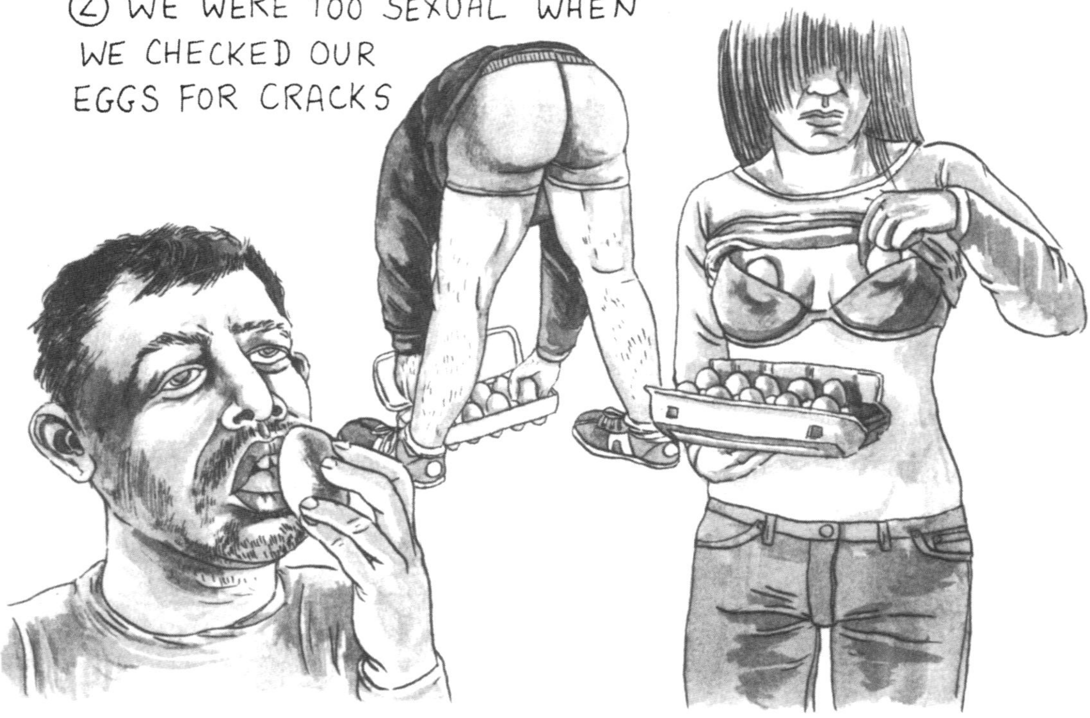

③ WE LET OUR FRUIT GET BRUISED

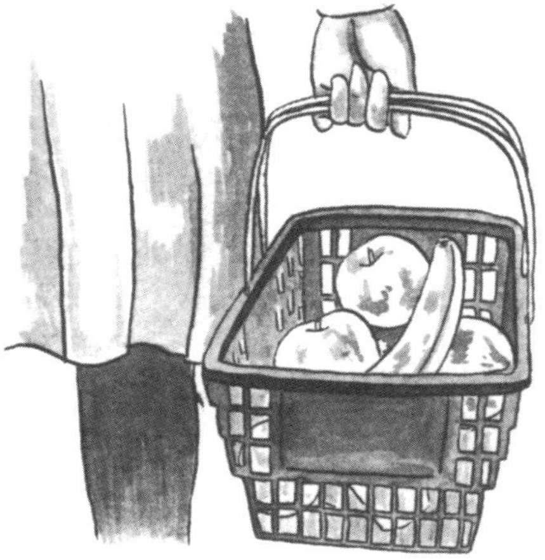

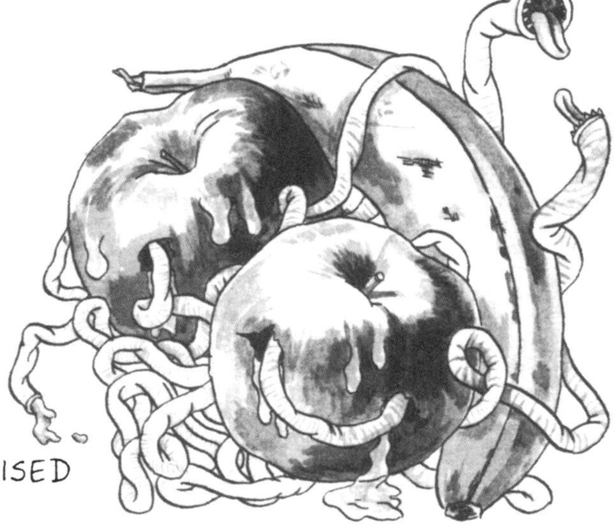

(AND OUR EGOS WERE BRUISED IN THE PROCESS)

④ WE ALSO MIGHT HAVE BEEN HALLUCINATING

⑤ AS IF POSSESSED, WE USED THE COFFEE GRINDER INCORRECTLY

⑥ WE FORGOT TO BRING A SWEATER

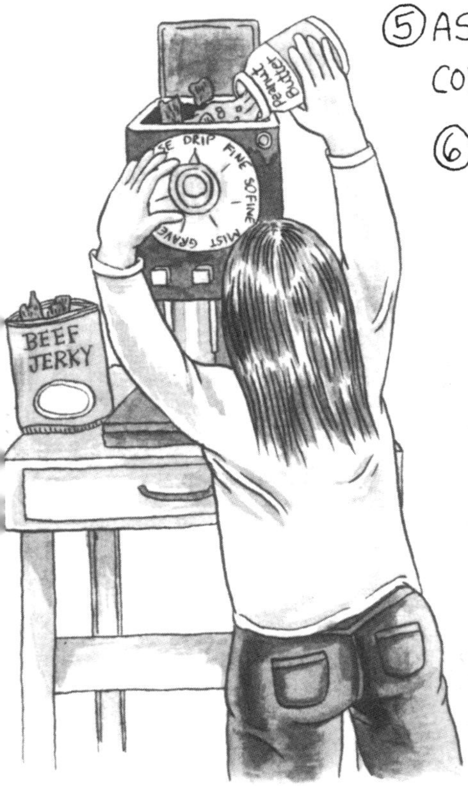
Peanut Butter
DRIP
FINE
SO FINE
MIST
BEEF JERKY

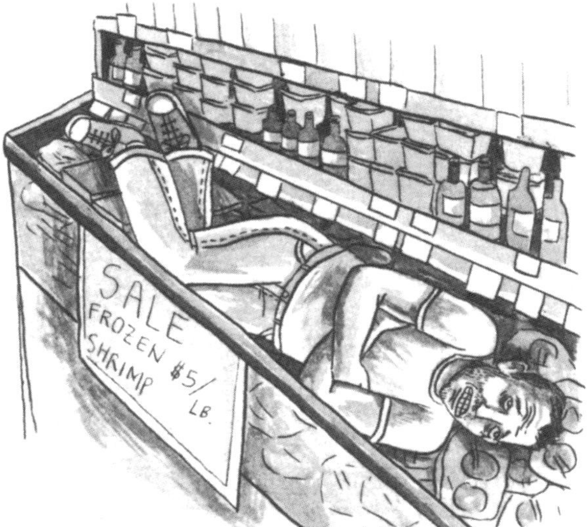
SALE
FROZEN SHRIMP $5/ LB.

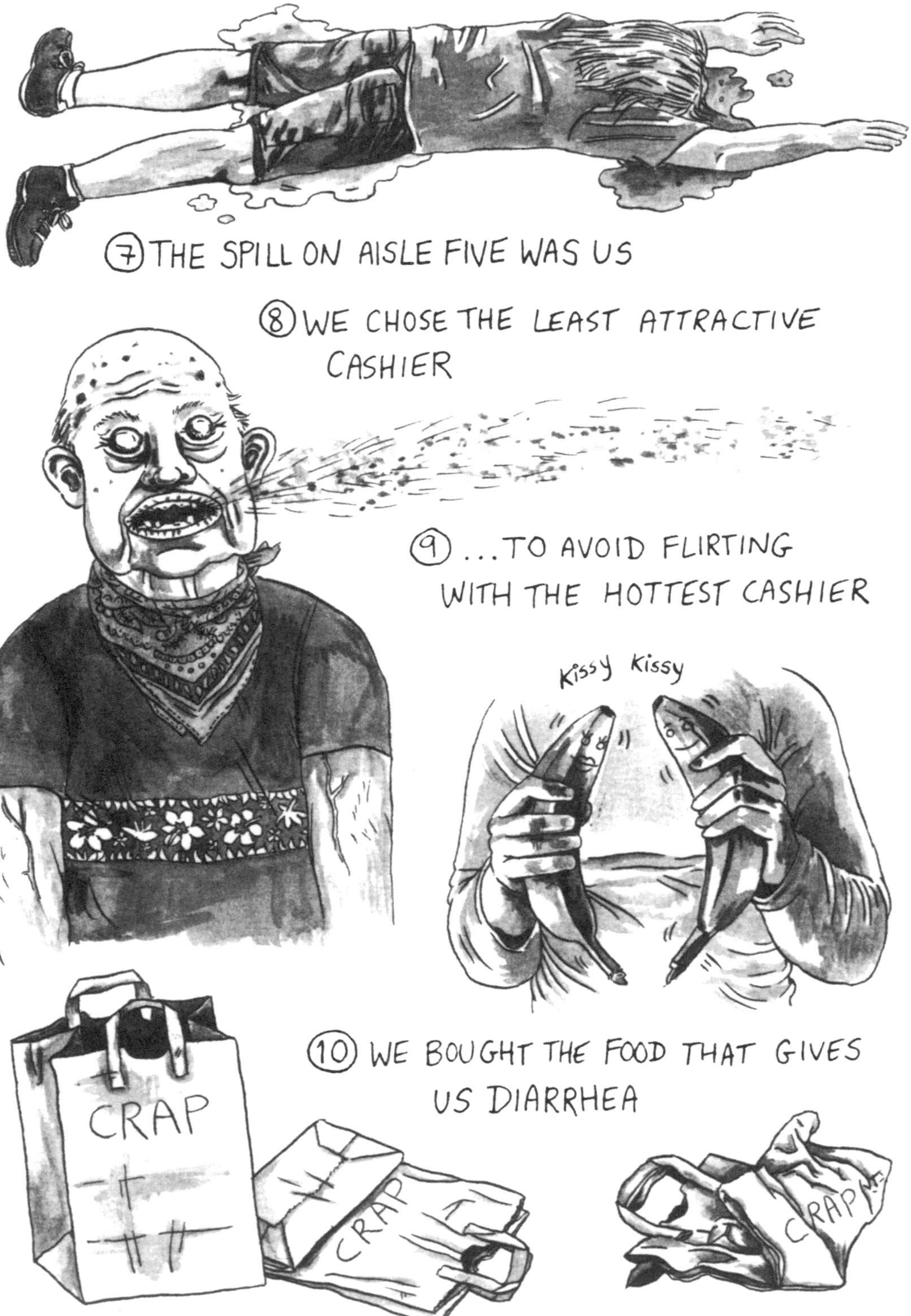
(7) THE SPILL ON AISLE FIVE WAS US
(8) WE CHOSE THE LEAST ATTRACTIVE CASHIER
(9) ...TO AVOID FLIRTING WITH THE HOTTEST CASHIER
Kissy Kissy
(10) WE BOUGHT THE FOOD THAT GIVES US DIARRHEA
CRAP
CRAP
CRAP

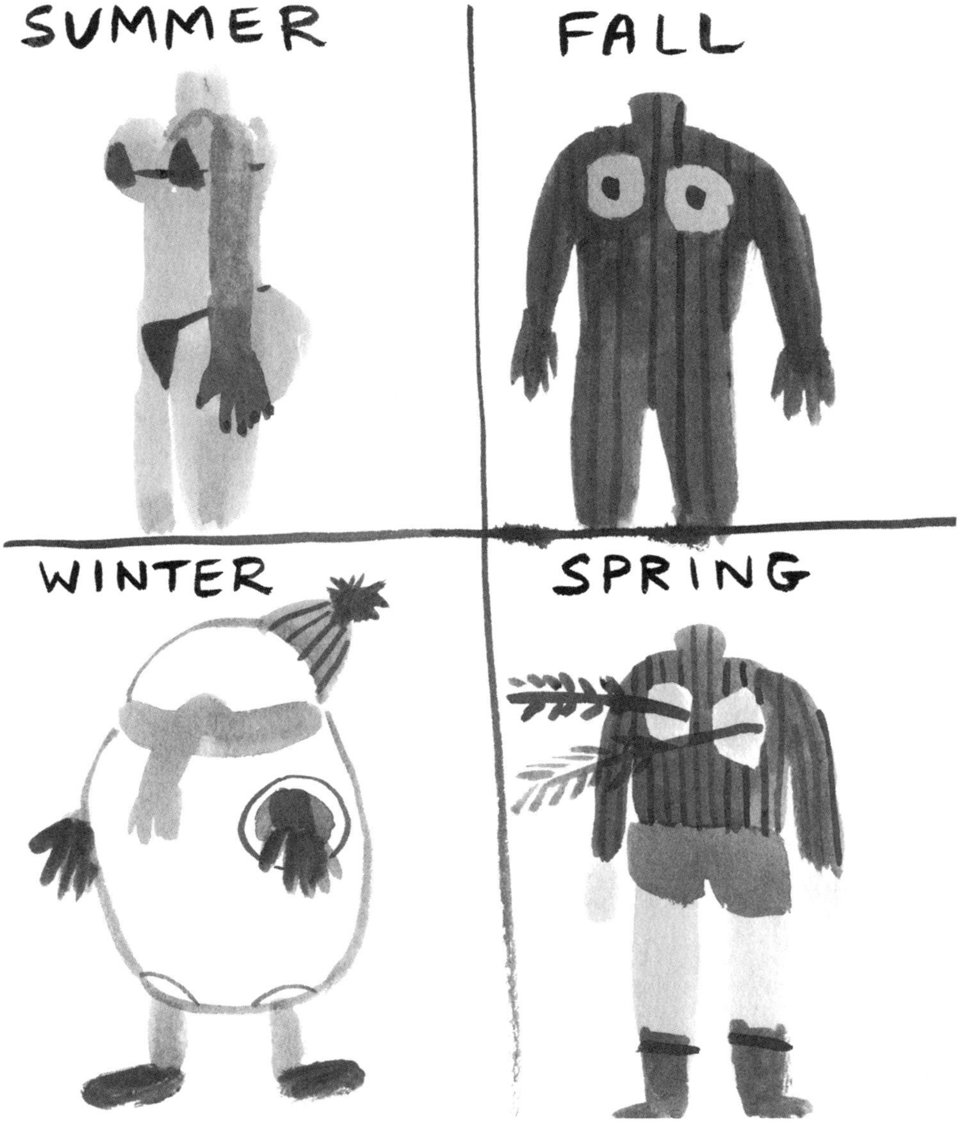
SUMMER
FALL
WINTER
SPRING

ONE DAY AT WORK

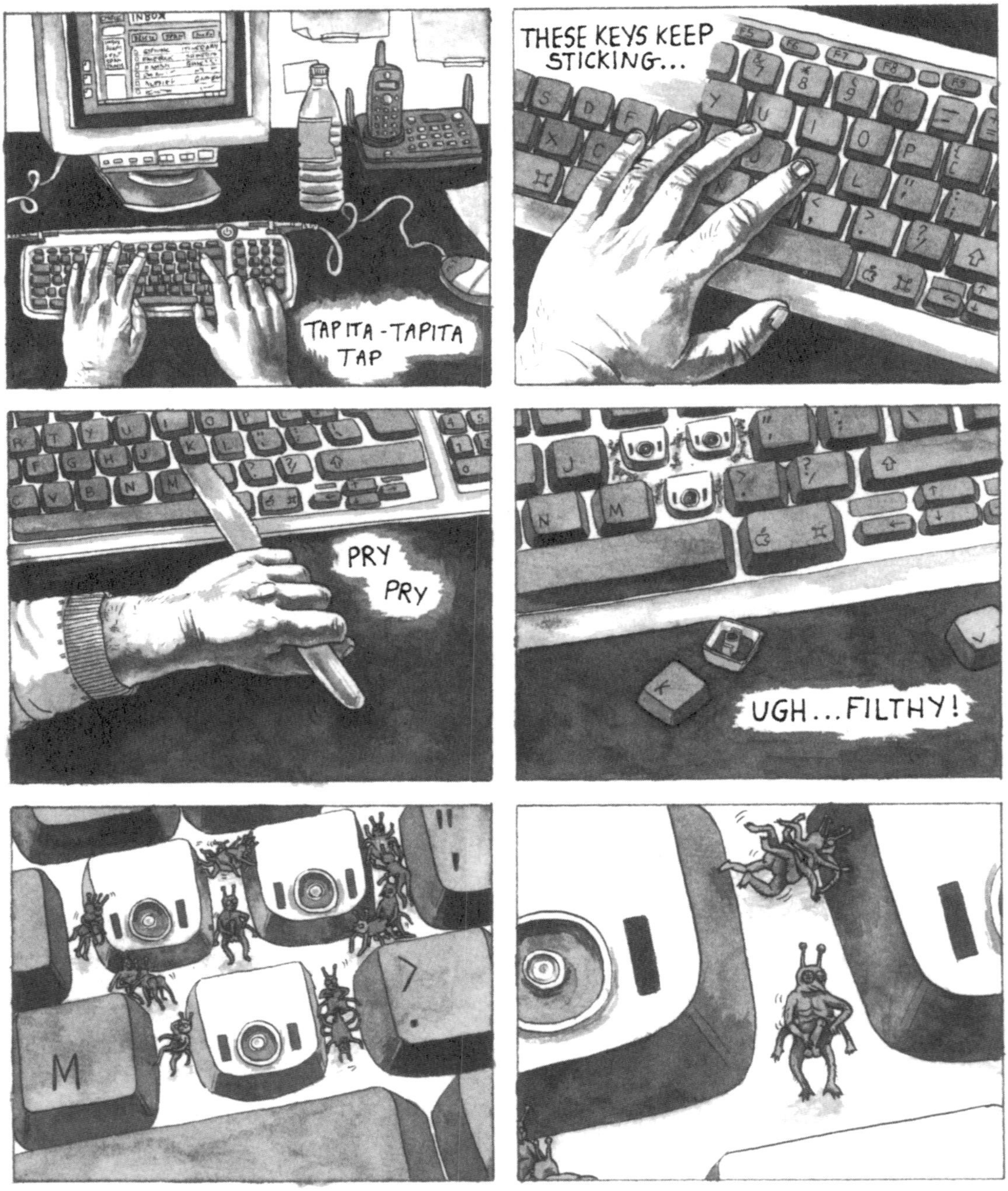
TAPITA - TAPITA TAP
THESE KEYS KEEP STICKING...
PRY PRY
UGH... FILTHY!

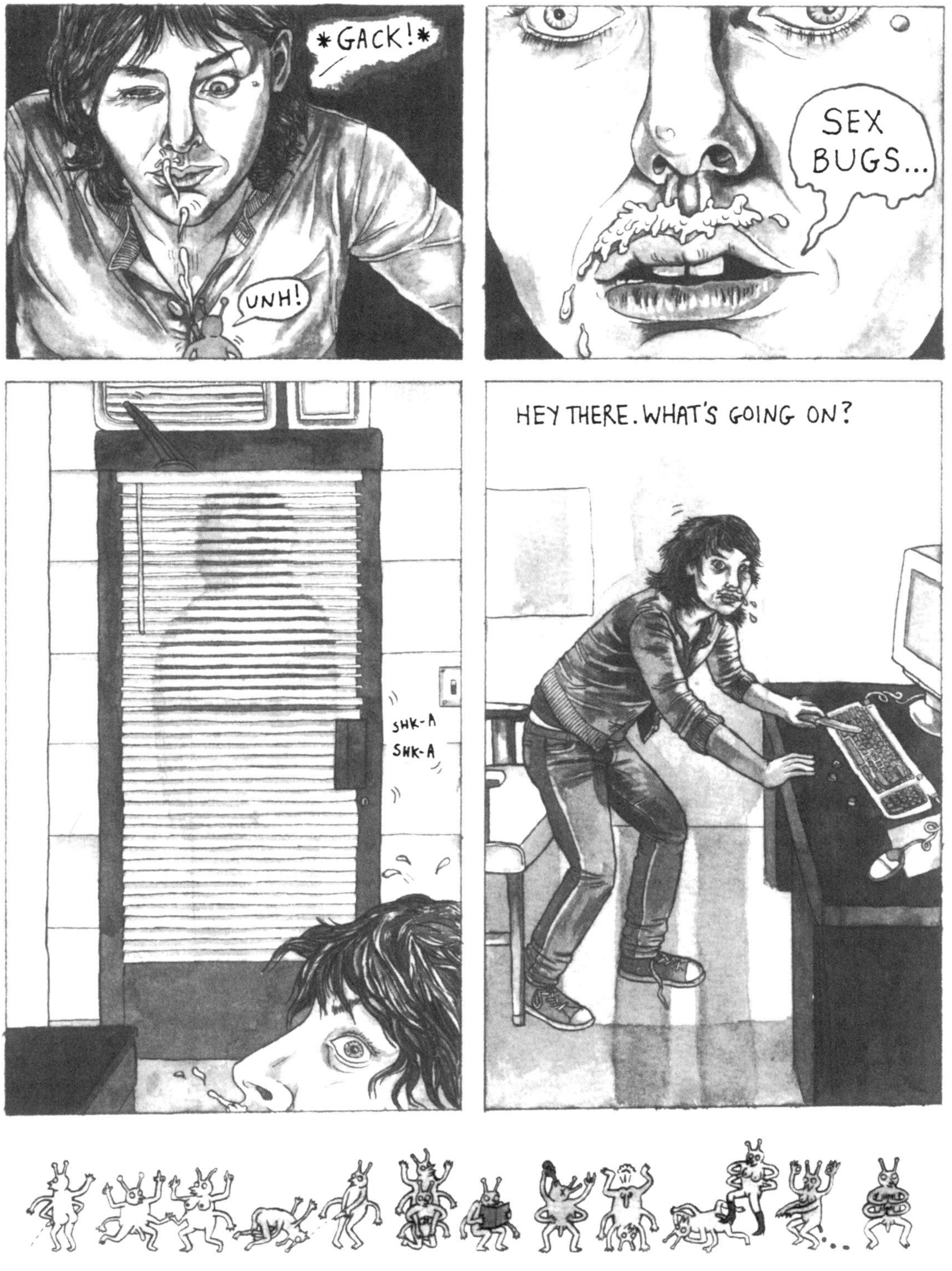
GACK!
UNH!
SEX BUGS...
SHK-A
SHK-A
HEY THERE. WHAT'S GOING ON?

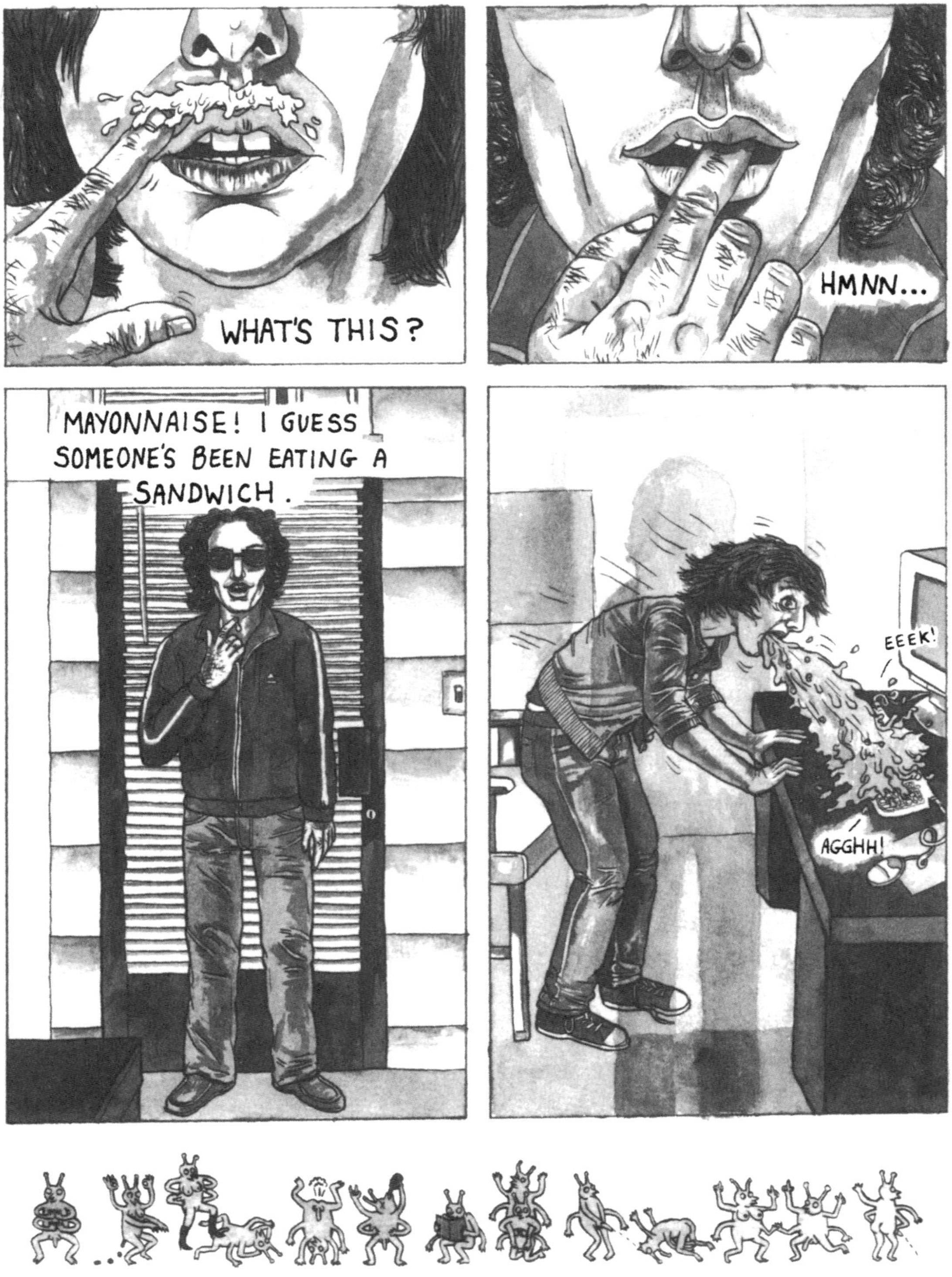
WHAT'S THIS?
HMNN...
MAYONNAISE! I GUESS SOMEONE'S BEEN EATING A SANDWICH.
EEEK!
AGGHH!

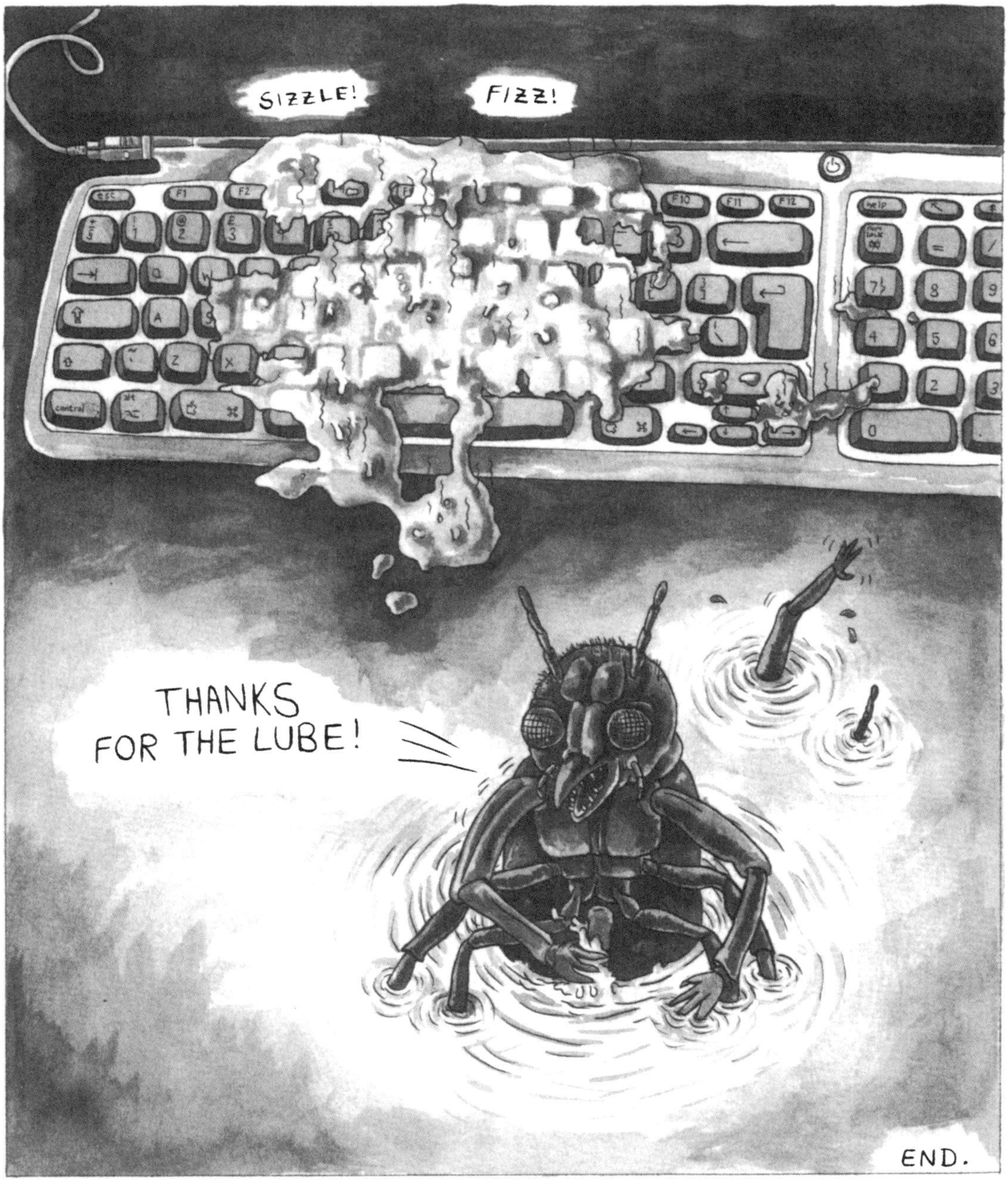
SIZZLE!
FIZZ!
THANKS FOR THE LUBE!
END.

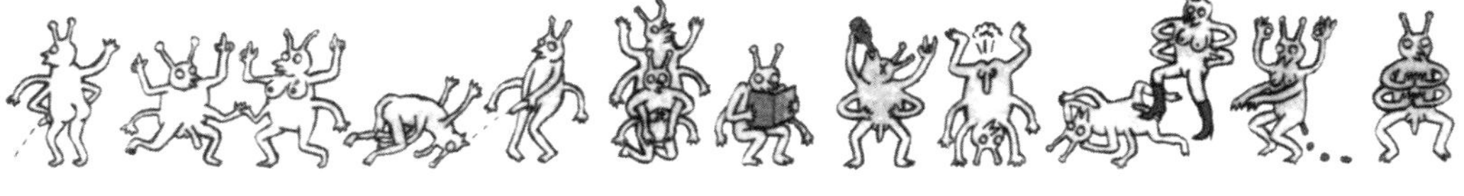

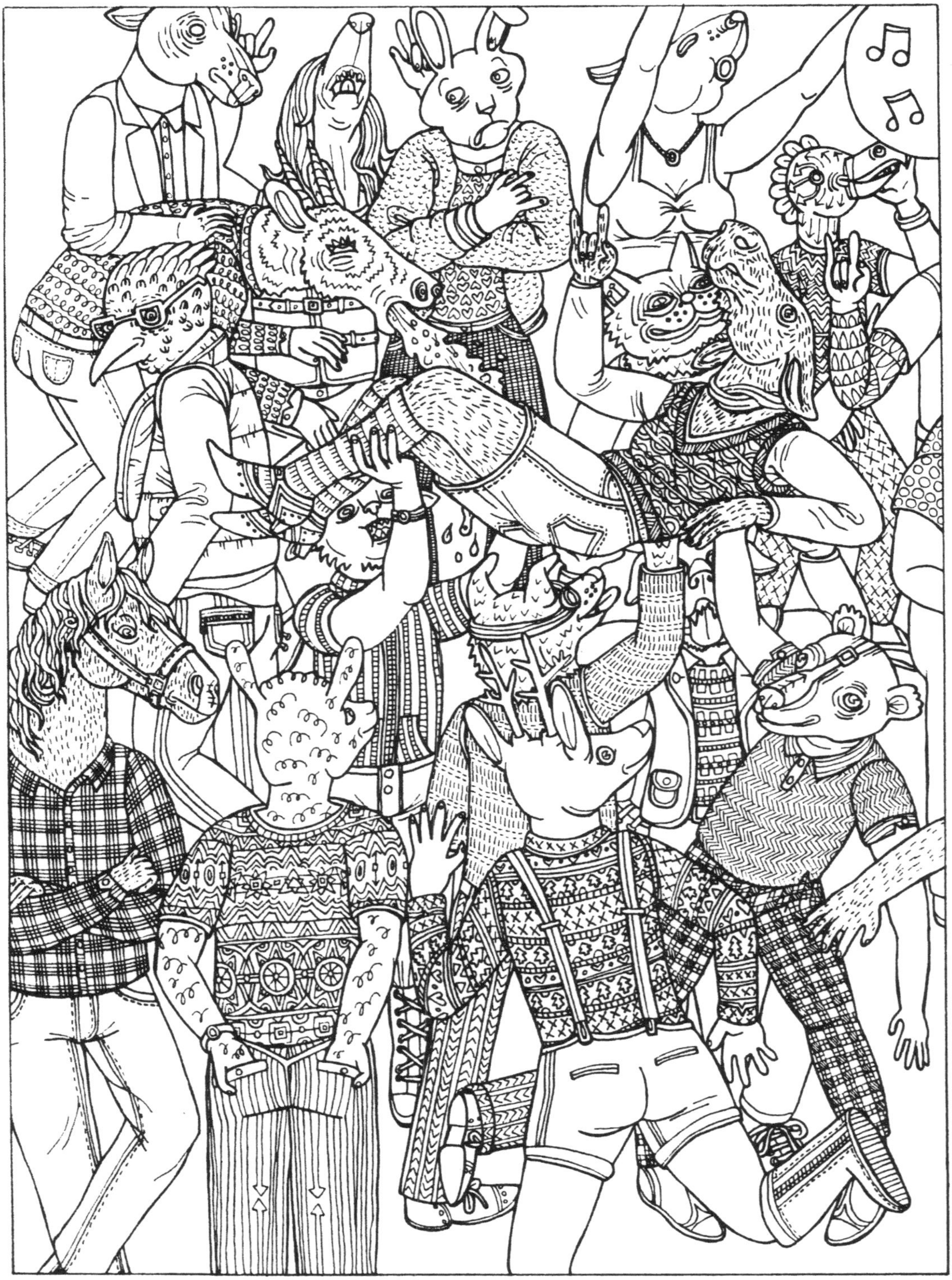

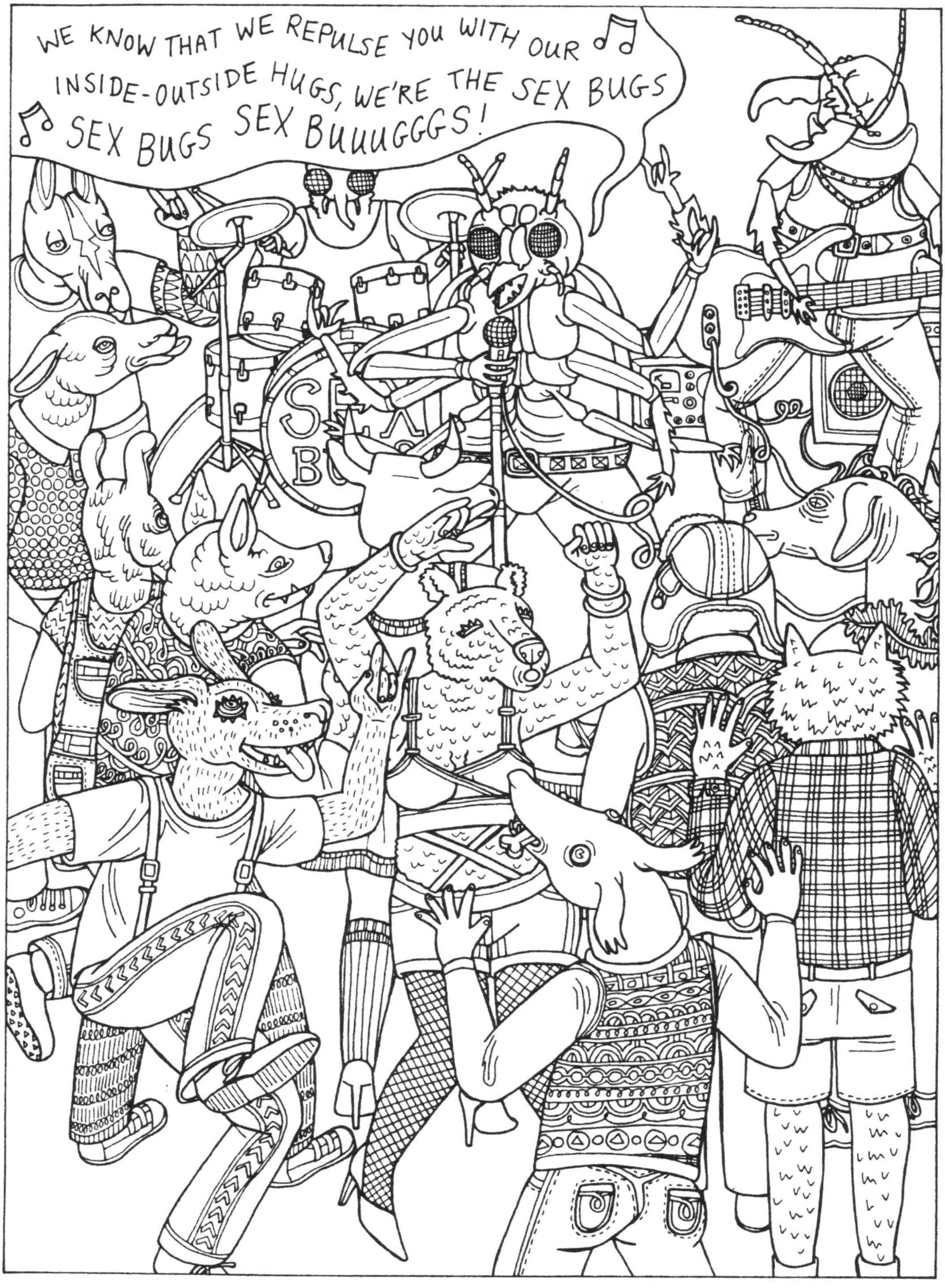
WE KNOW THAT WE REPULSE YOU WITH OUR INSIDE-OUTSIDE HUGS, WE'RE THE SEX BUGS SEX BUGS SEX BUUUGGGS!
SEX BUGS

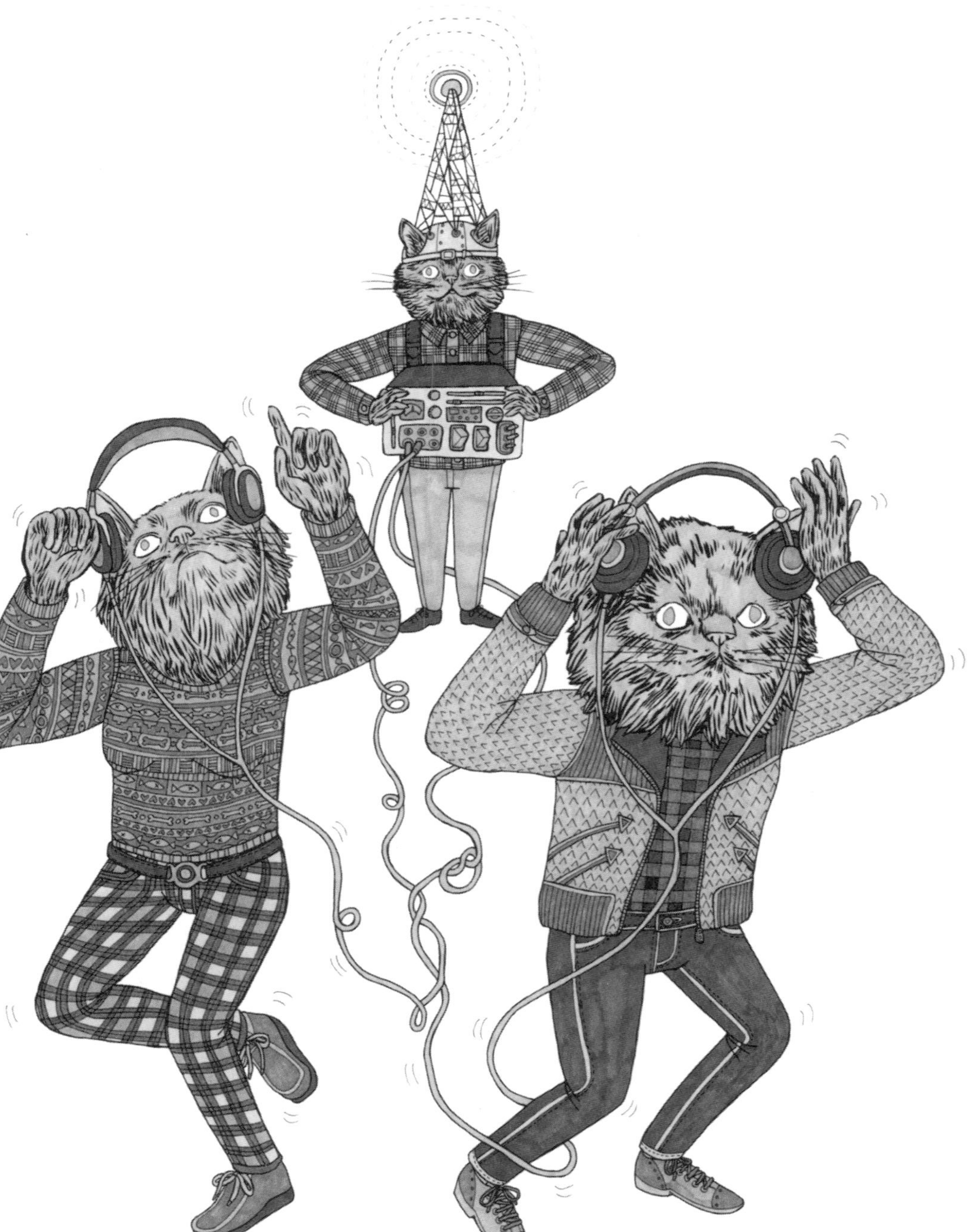

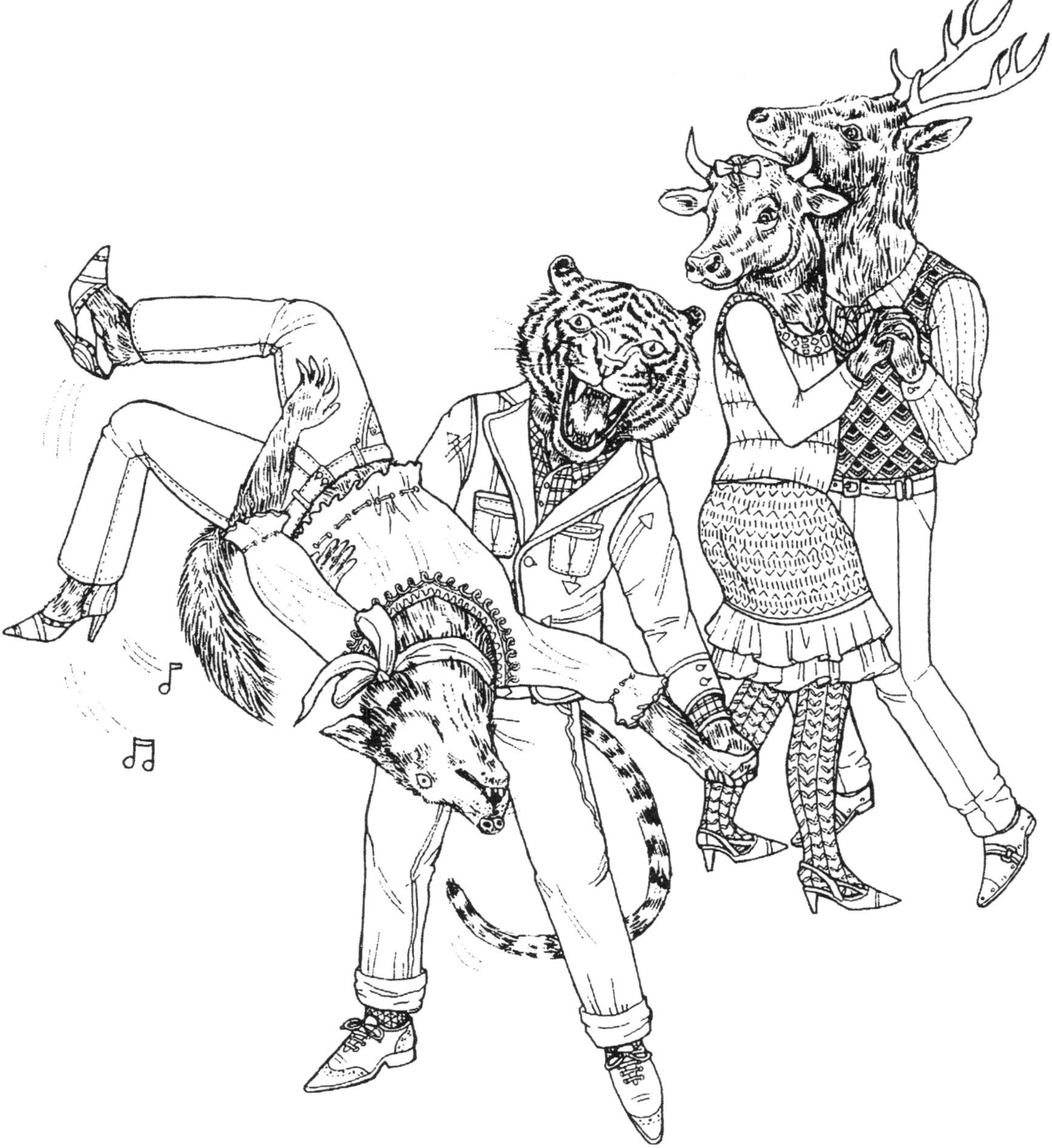

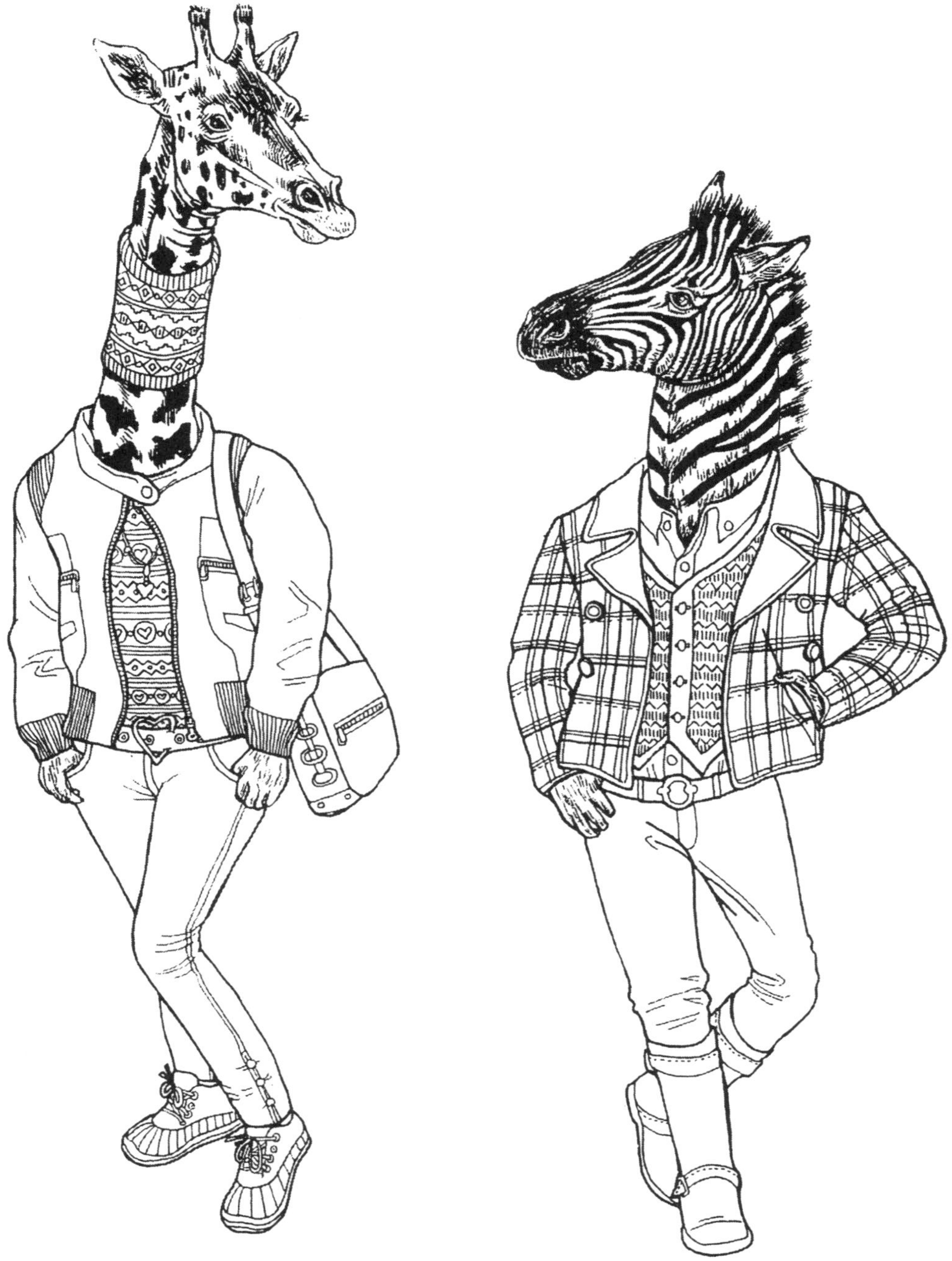

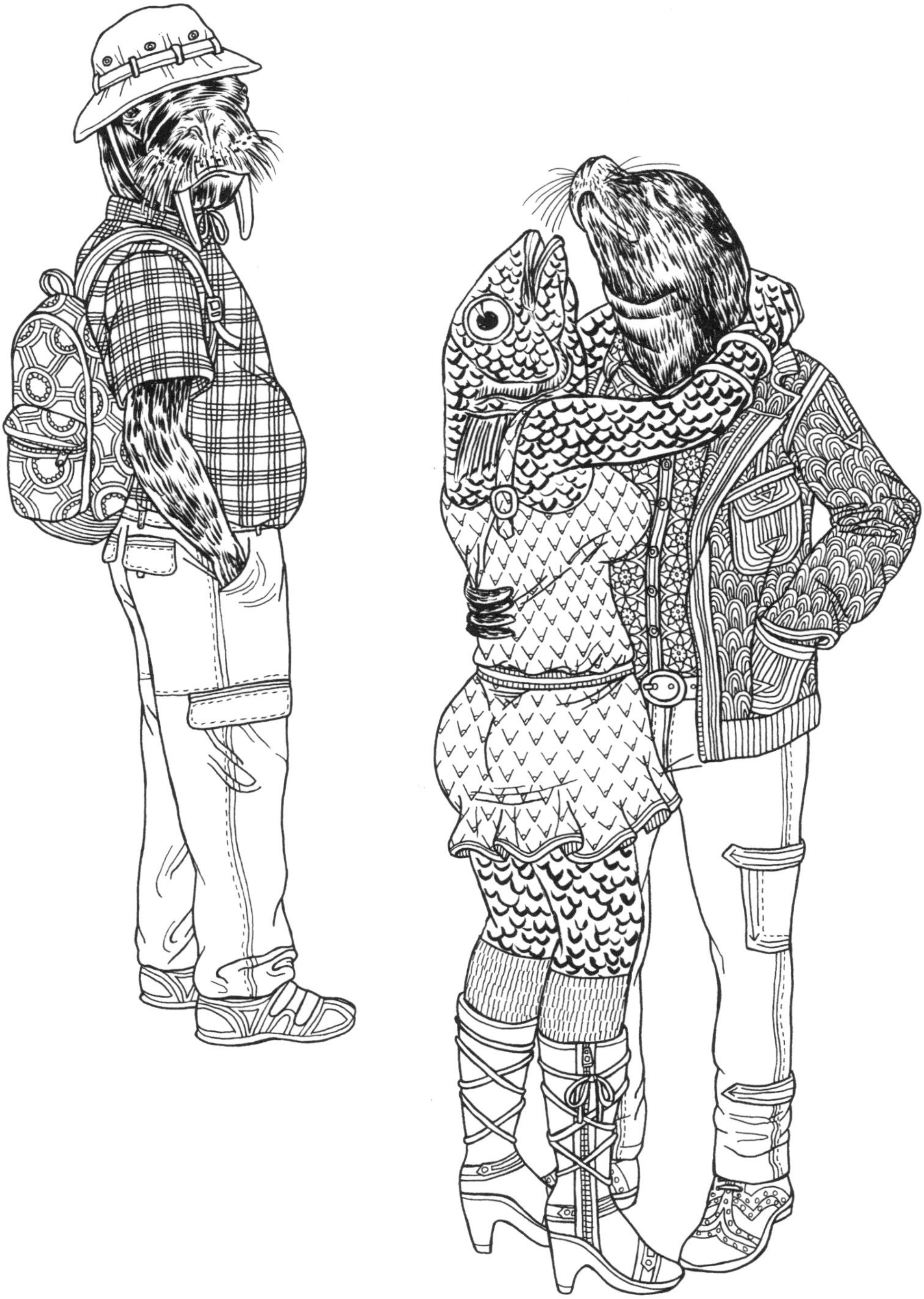

INDIANA JONES

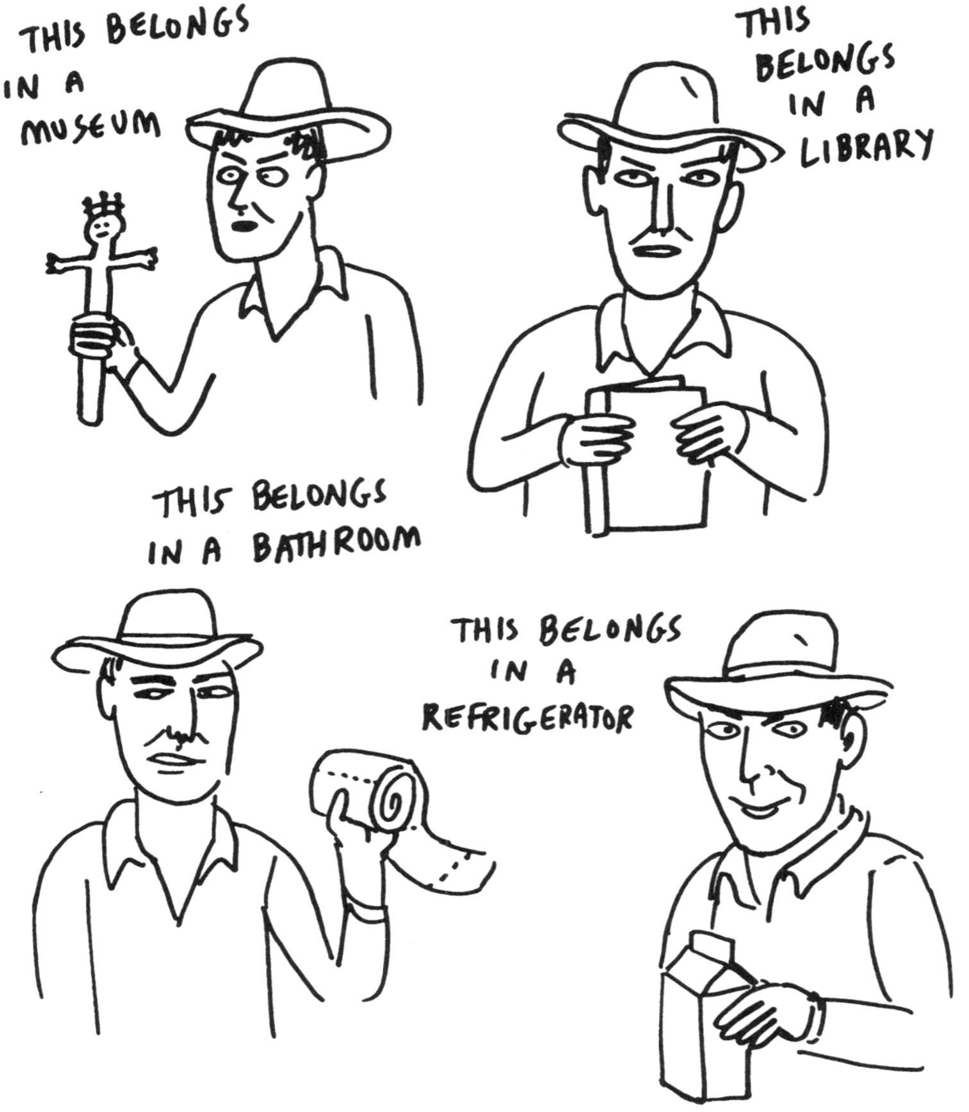
THIS BELONGS IN A MUSEUM
THIS BELONGS IN A LIBRARY
THIS BELONGS IN A BATHROOM
THIS BELONGS IN A REFRIGERATOR

MOVIES I'D LIKE TO SEE

- A MAN CHUGS LAXATIVES AND THEN DANCES FOR 100 MINUTES
- ROMANTIC COMEDY WHERE AN EROTIC CAKE BAKER FALLS IN LOVE WITH AN EROTIC HAT [redacted] OWNER
- AN EVIL HORSE THAT KILLS PEOPLE (BUT IS REALLY PRETTY AND FAST AND MAYBE HE BELONGS TO A WITCH)

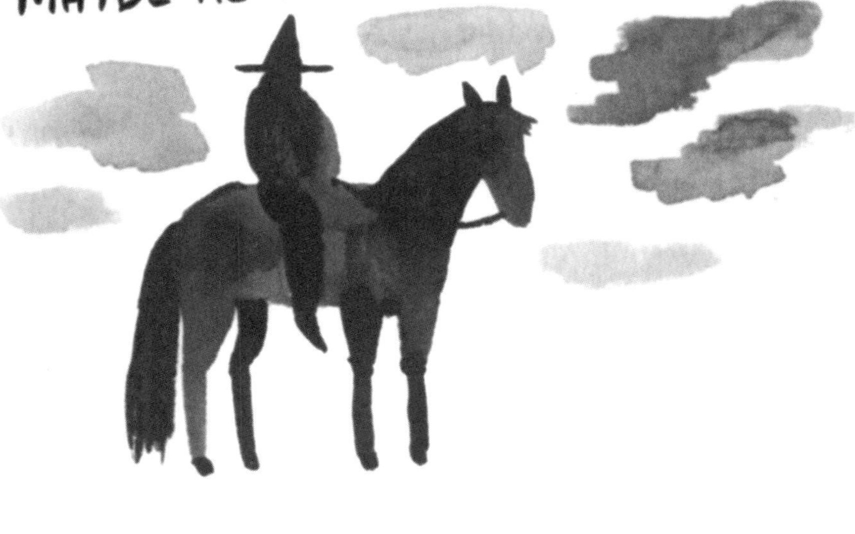

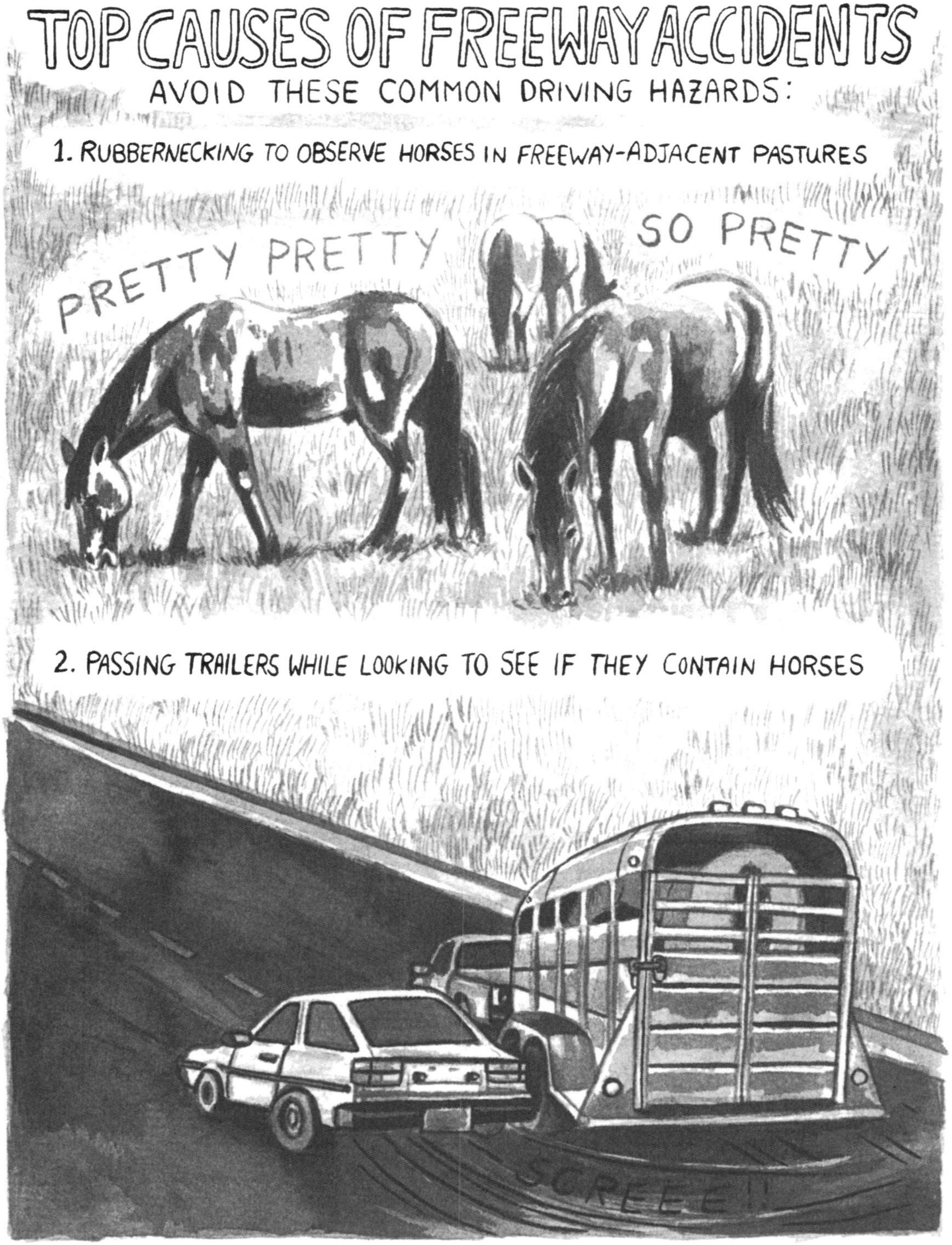
TOP CAUSES OF FREEWAY ACCIDENTS
AVOID THESE COMMON DRIVING HAZARDS:
1. RUBBERNECKING TO OBSERVE HORSES IN FREEWAY-ADJACENT PASTURES
PRETTY PRETTY PRETTY
SO PRETTY
2. PASSING TRAILERS WHILE LOOKING TO SEE IF THEY CONTAIN HORSES
SCREEE!!

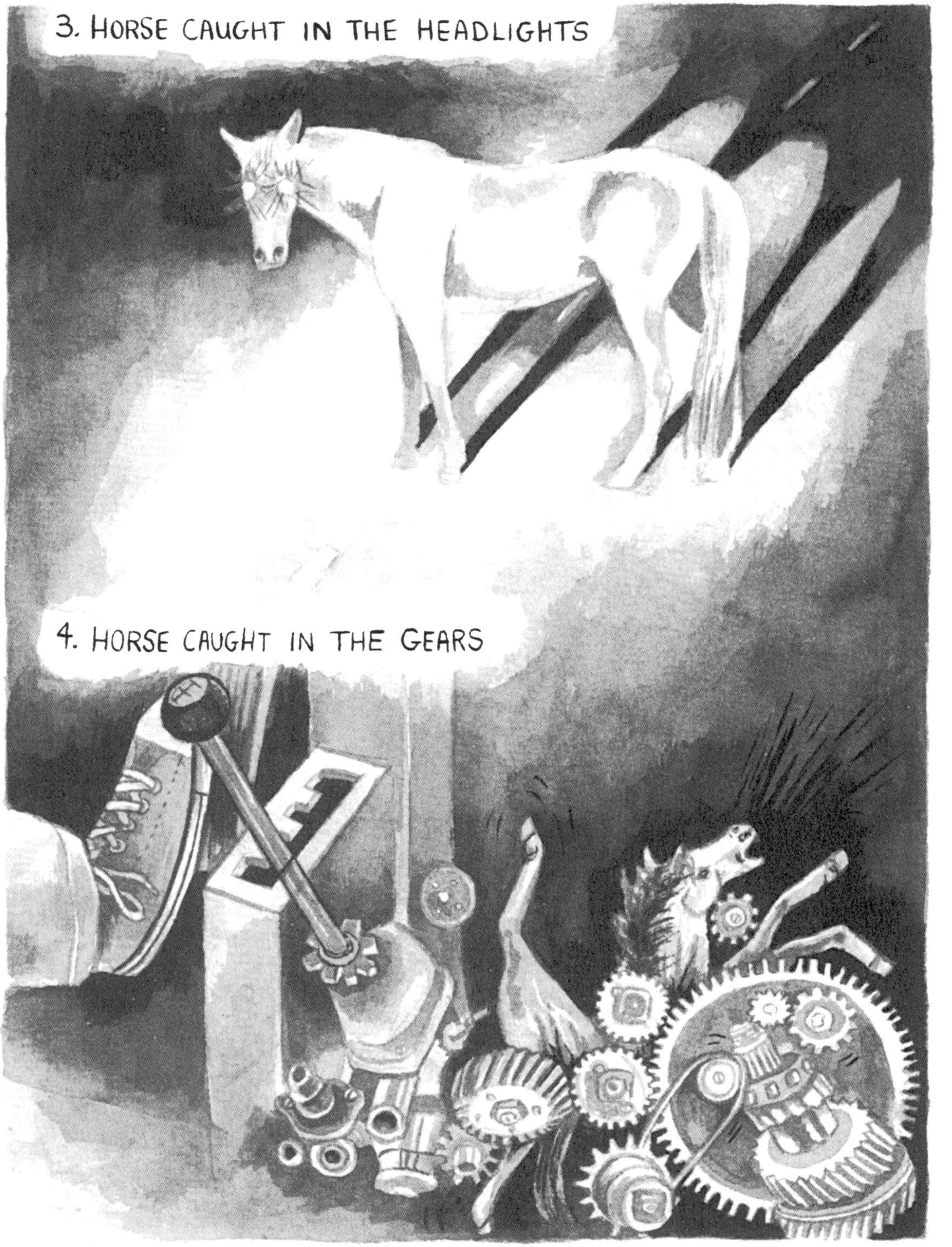
3. HORSE CAUGHT IN THE HEADLIGHTS
4. HORSE CAUGHT IN THE GEARS

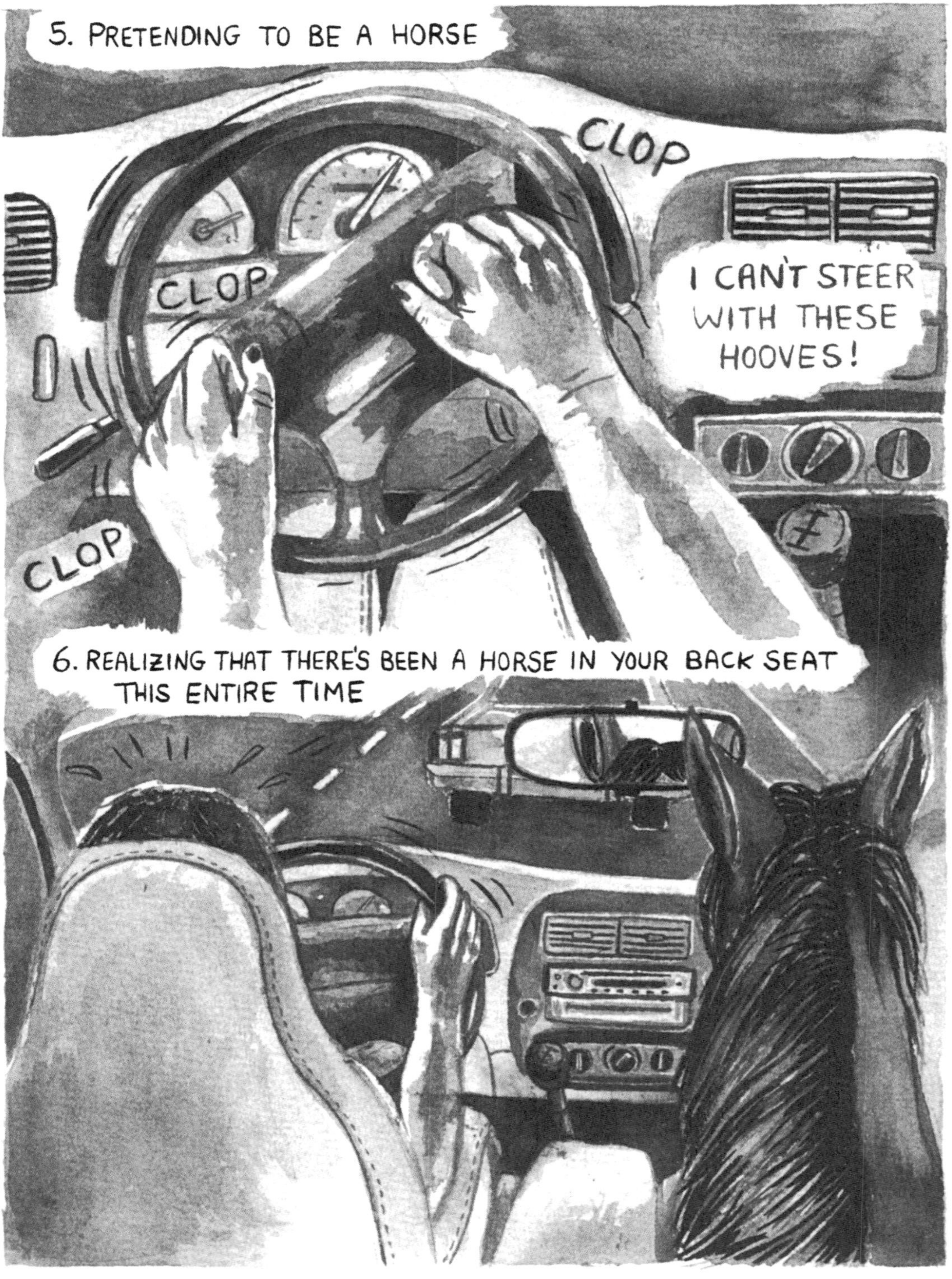
5. PRETENDING TO BE A HORSE
CLOP
CLOP
I CAN'T STEER WITH THESE HOOVES!
CLOP
6. REALIZING THAT THERE'S BEEN A HORSE IN YOUR BACK SEAT THIS ENTIRE TIME

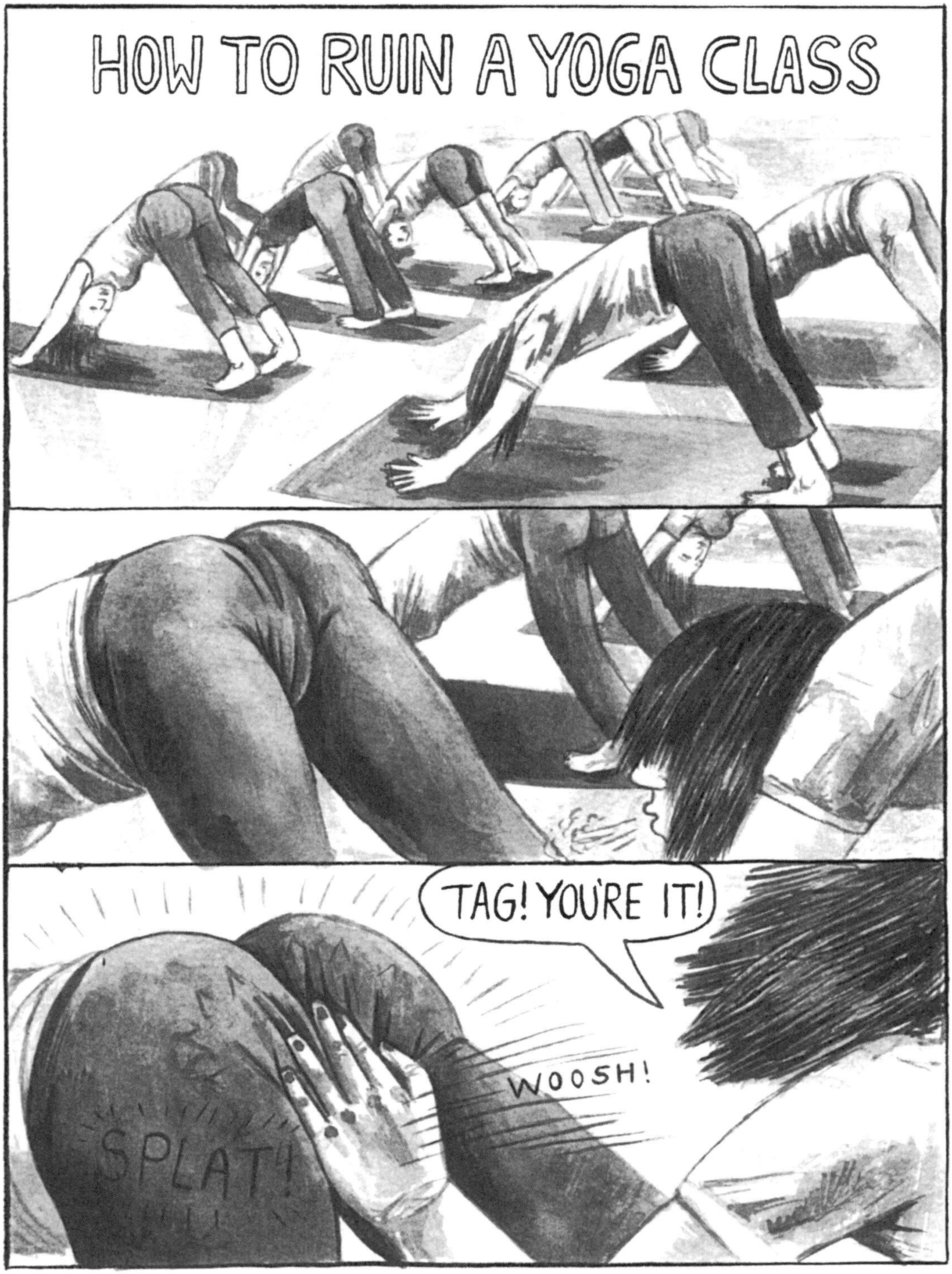
HOW TO RUIN A YOGA CLASS
TAG! YOU'RE IT!
WOOSH!
SPLAT!

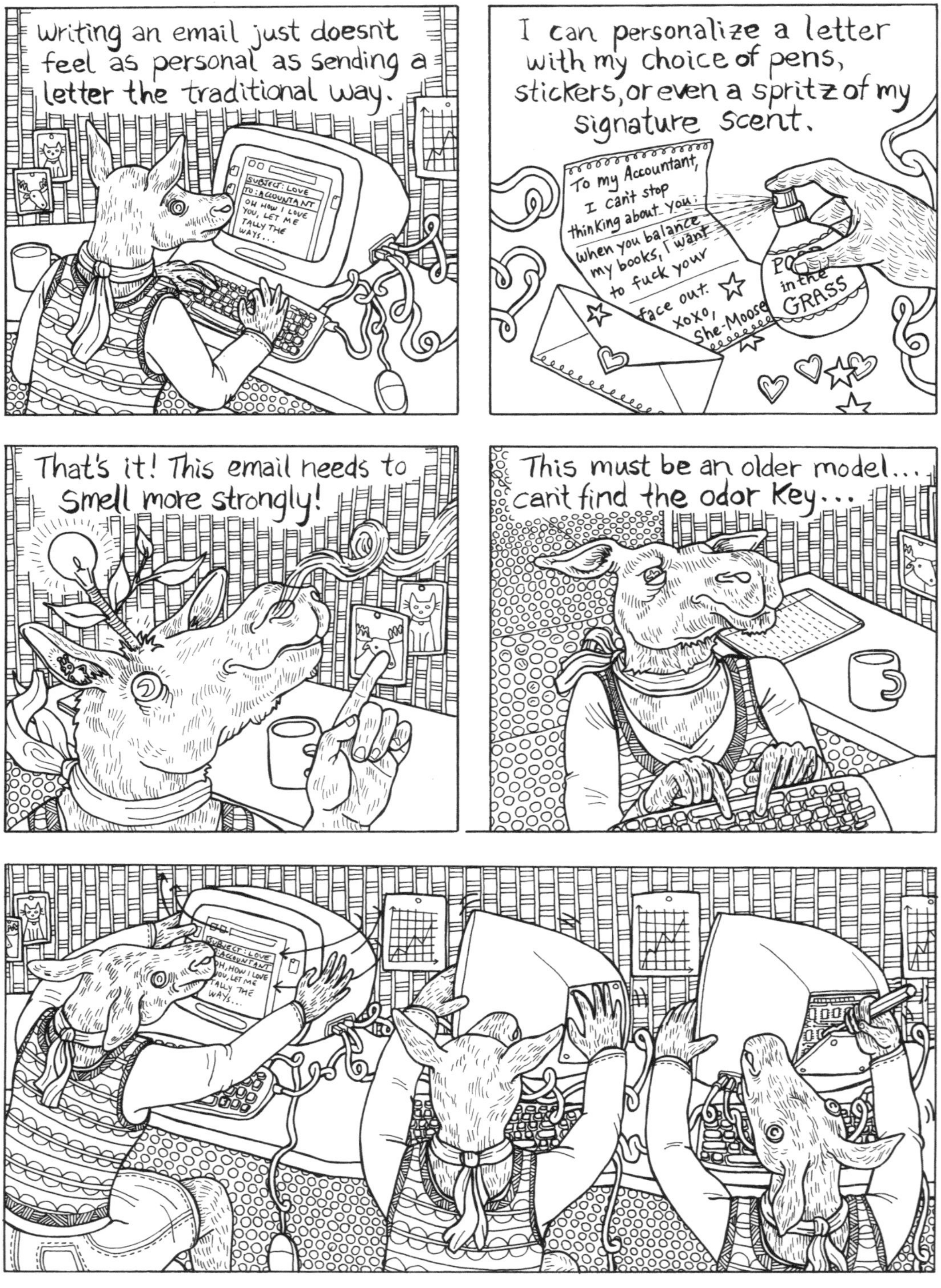
Writing an email just doesn't feel as personal as sending a letter the traditional way.
SUBJECT: LOVE
TO: ACCOUNTANT
OH HOW I LOVE YOU, LET ME TALLY THE WAYS...
I can personalize a letter with my choice of pens, stickers, or even a spritz of my signature scent.
To my Accountant, I can't stop thinking about you. When you balance my books, I want to fuck your face out. xoxo, She-Moose
in the GRASS
That's it! This email needs to smell more strongly!
This must be an older model... can't find the odor key...
SUBJECT: LOVE
ACCOUNTANT
OH, HOW I LOVE YOU, LET ME TALLY THE WAYS...

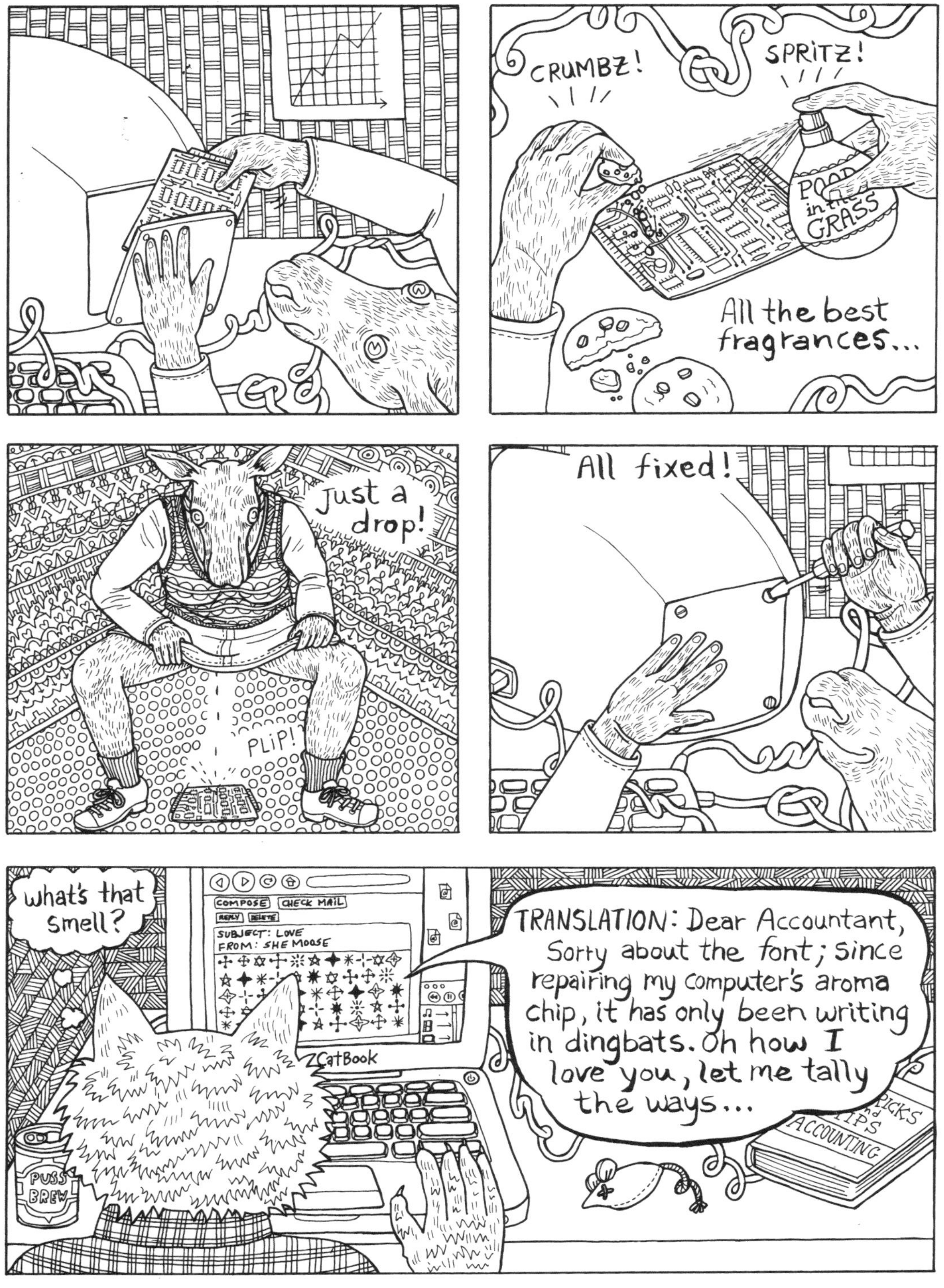
CRUMBZ!
SPRITZ!
POOP in the GRASS
All the best fragrances...
Just a drop!
PLIP!
All fixed!
what's that smell?
COMPOSE
CHECK MAIL
REPLY
DELETE
SUBJECT: LOVE
FROM: SHE MOOSE
CatBook
TRANSLATION: Dear Accountant, Sorry about the font; since repairing my computer's aroma chip, it has only been writing in dingbats. Oh how I love you, let me tally the ways...
PUSS BREW
ACCOUNTING

COMMON DIRTY TALK and the QUESTIONS IT RAISES

1. I'VE GOT A RASH AND I'D LIKE YOU TO HELP ME IDENTIFY IT
   Q: WHAT IS THE LOCATION OF THE PRIMARY LESION?

"SHOW ME YOUR GLUTEAL CLEFT, BABY"

  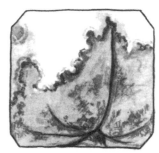

PSORIASIS VULGARIS · ECZEMA PUSTULOSA · ITCHY FUCKER

2. FUCK ME LIKE AN OCTOGENARIAN
   Q: ONE THAT HAS HYPOTHETICALLY LED A HEALTHY LIFESTYLE?

3. I WANT YOU TO CHOP MY BOOBS OFF, MOLD THEM INTO A
   PENIS, THEN FUCK ME WITH MY OWN BOOBS
   Q: WHAT IS THE BEST WAY TO ADHERE BREASTS TOGETHER
      AND GET THEM TO STAY IN A SOLID CYLINDRICAL SHAPE,
   ALSO Q: WHAT IS WRONG WITH YOU?

"THE SOUTH-SIDER" · "THE MEAT LOVER" · "A CHILD IS IN THE KITCHEN"

4. YOU ARE MY SECOND-FAVORITE TYPE OF SANDWICH
   Q: (OBVIOUS)

5. I WANT TO HAVE SEX ON TOP OF SOME BUBBLEWRAP
   A: OKAY

AVAILABLE SIZES:

SMALL

MID-RACKET

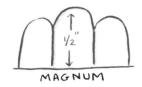

MAGNUM

ALTERNATIVE: MOON JUMP

6. YOU ARE FILTHY AND YOUR MAN MEAT IS SALTIER THAN ANYTHING
   Q: IS THIS REALLY THE BEST TIME TO BE CRITICIZING MY RESTAURANT?

7. I WOULD LIKE FOR US TO BE A FUCK FACTORY AND FIND THE MOST EFFICIENT WAY TO HARNESS THAT ENERGY AND SELL IT WHILE ALSO SAVING ON COMMERCIAL PROPERTY RENTAL COSTS
   Q: DO YOU ENVISION A MOM AND POP-TYPE BUSINESS, OR A LARGER CORPORATION OR CHAIN? SHOULD WE HIRE EMPLOYEES OR RELY ON CONTRACTORS WHO CAN FUCK FROM HOME?

8. I WANT TO BE YOUR LITTLE SLUT
   Q: HOW LITTLE?

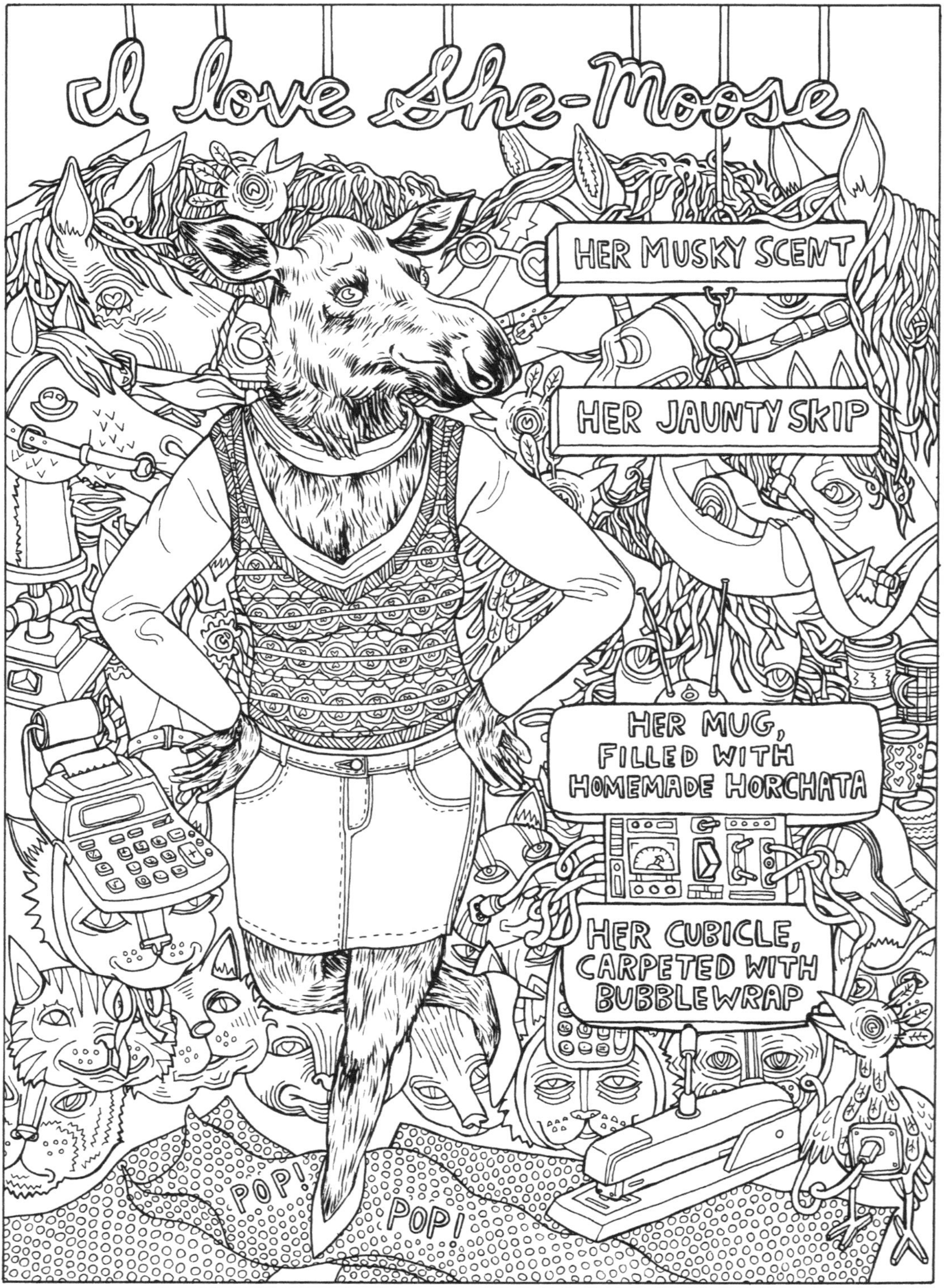
I love She-Moose
HER MUSKY SCENT
HER JAUNTY SKIP
HER MUG, FILLED WITH HOMEMADE HORCHATA
HER CUBICLE, CARPETED WITH BUBBLEWRAP
POP!
POP!

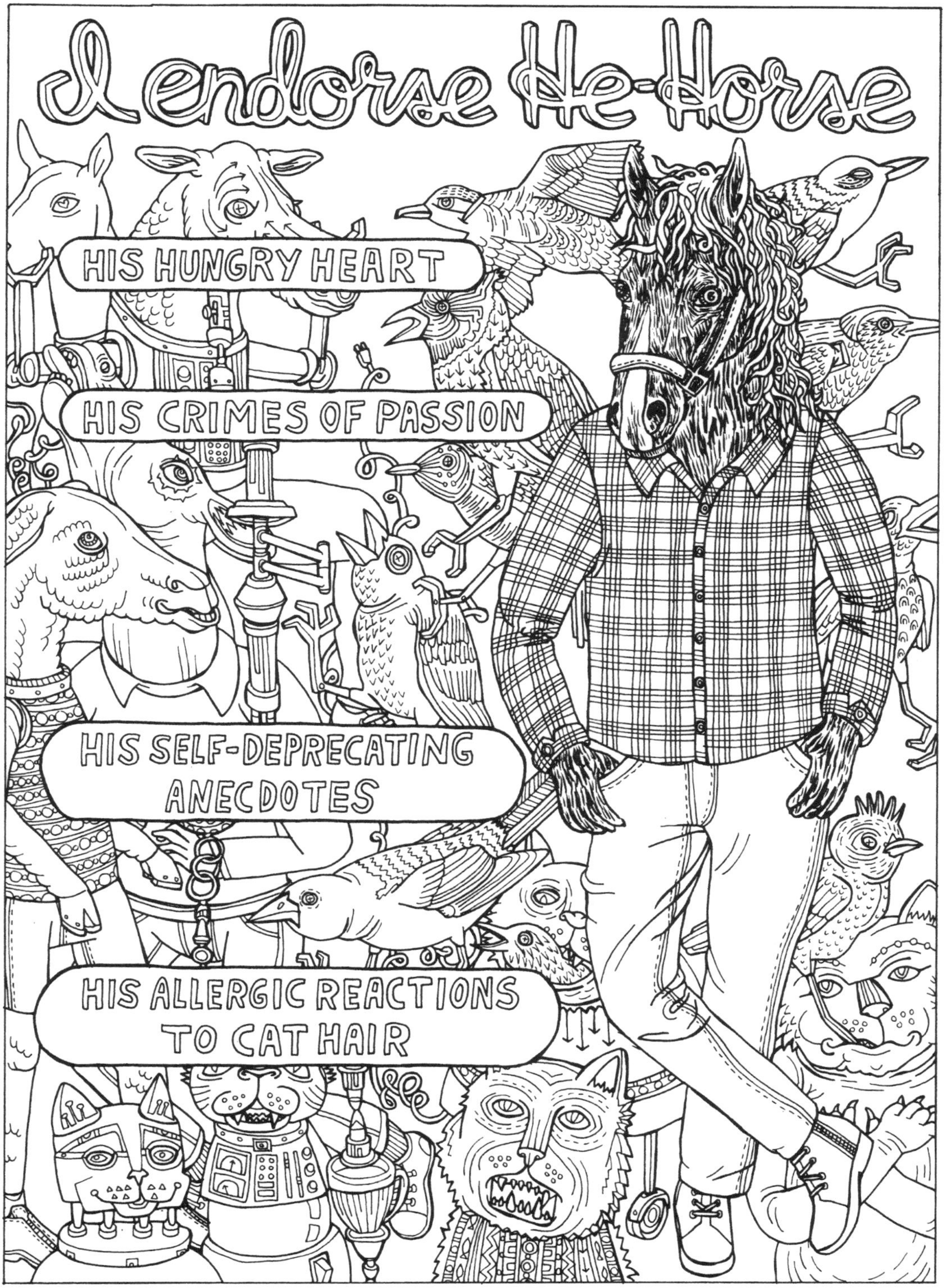
I endorse He-Horse
HIS HUNGRY HEART
HIS CRIMES OF PASSION
HIS SELF-DEPRECATING ANECDOTES
HIS ALLERGIC REACTIONS TO CAT HAIR

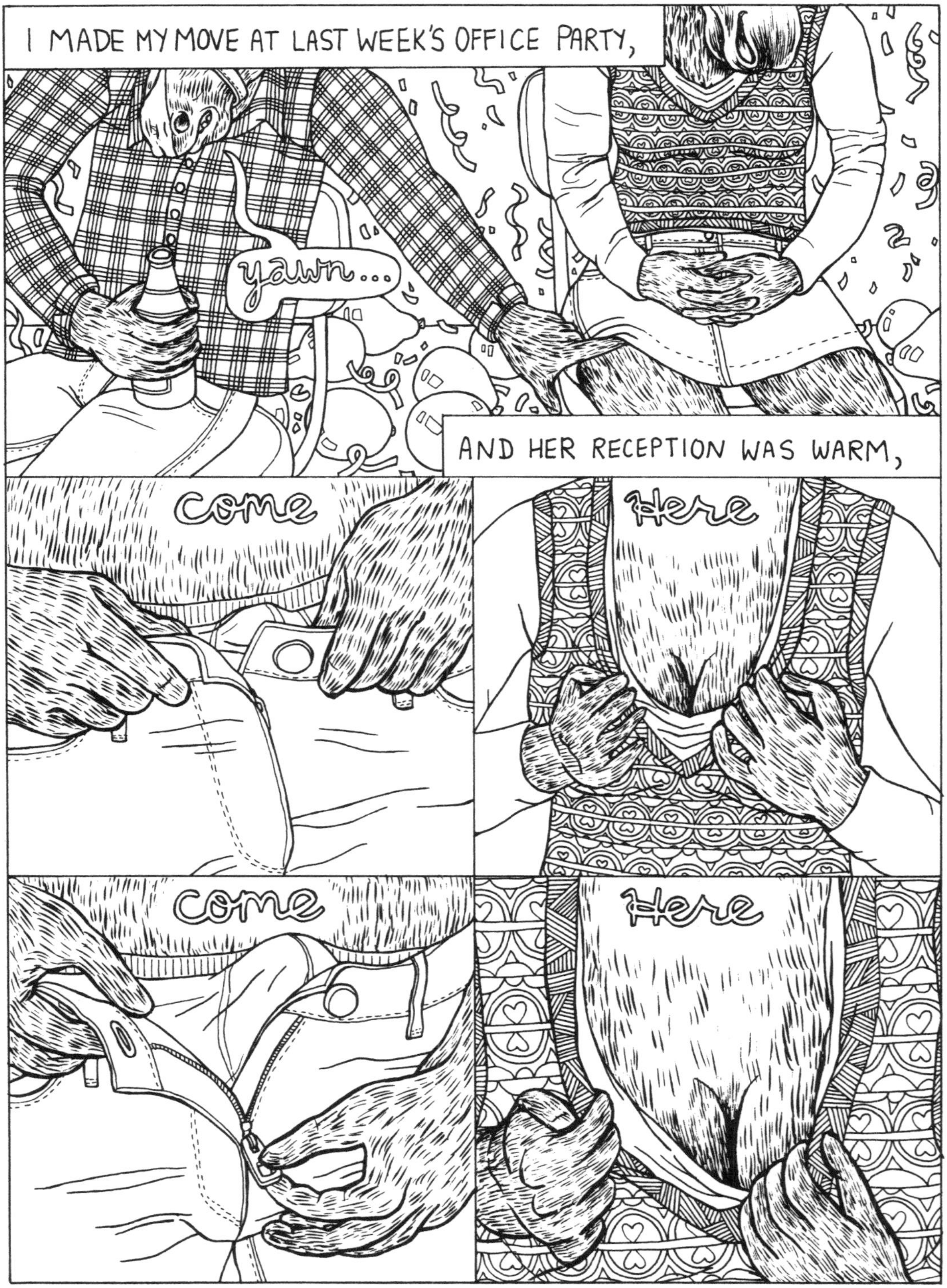
I MADE MY MOVE AT LAST WEEK'S OFFICE PARTY,
yawn...
AND HER RECEPTION WAS WARM,
come
Here
come
Here

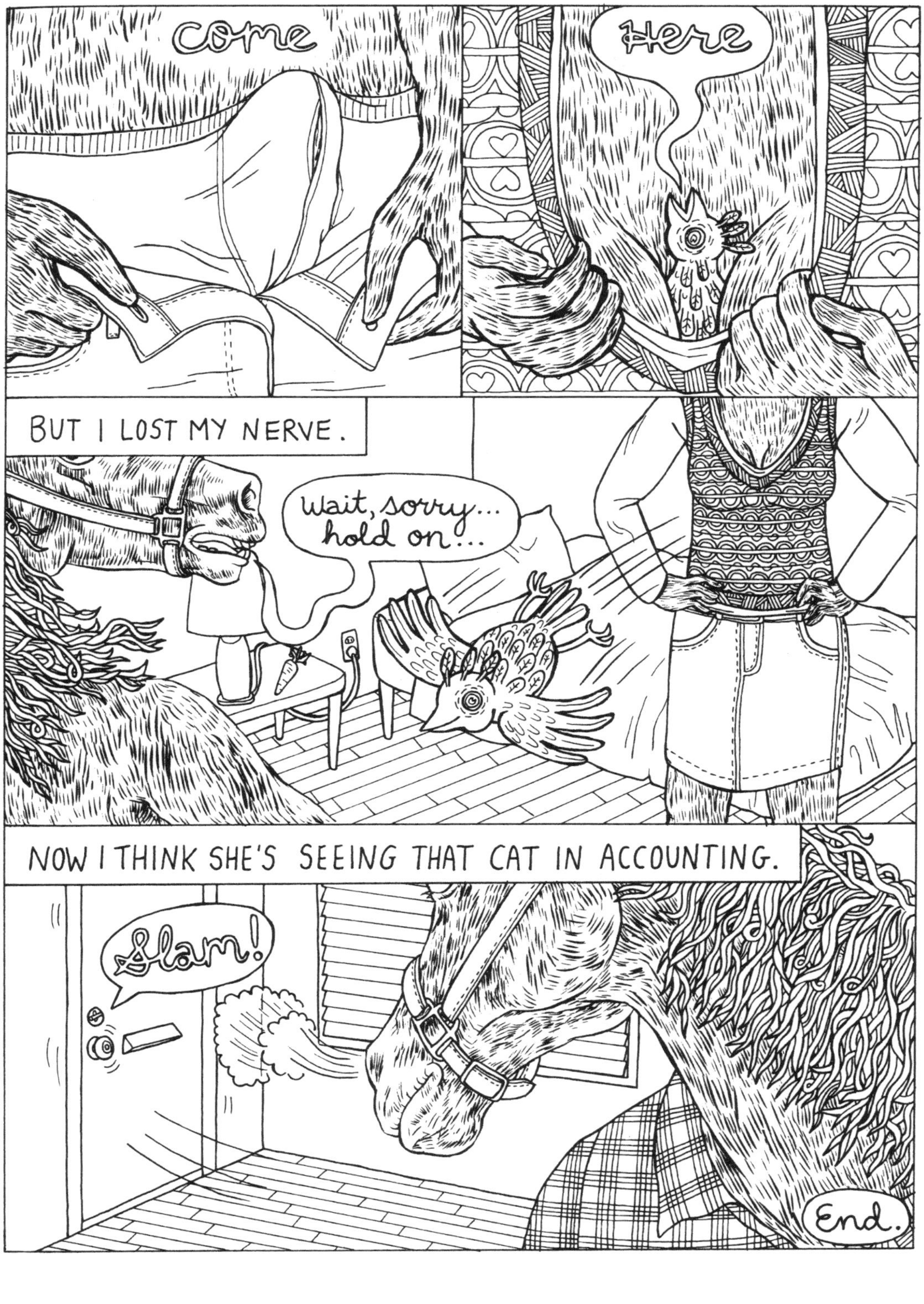
Come
Here
BUT I LOST MY NERVE.
Wait, sorry... hold on...
NOW I THINK SHE'S SEEING THAT CAT IN ACCOUNTING.
Slam!
End.

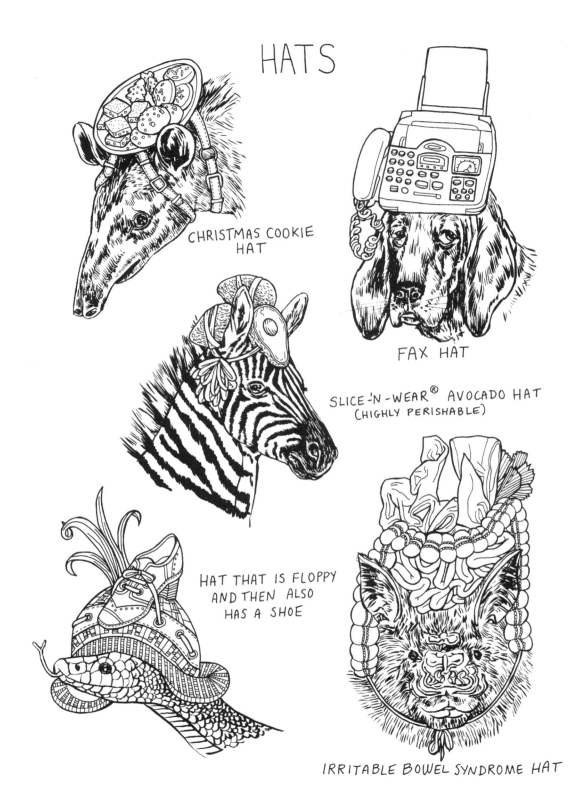

HATS

CHRISTMAS COOKIE
HAT

FAX HAT

SLICE-'N-WEAR® AVOCADO HAT
(HIGHLY PERISHABLE)

HAT THAT IS FLOPPY
AND THEN ALSO
HAS A SHOE

IRRITABLE BOWEL SYNDROME HAT

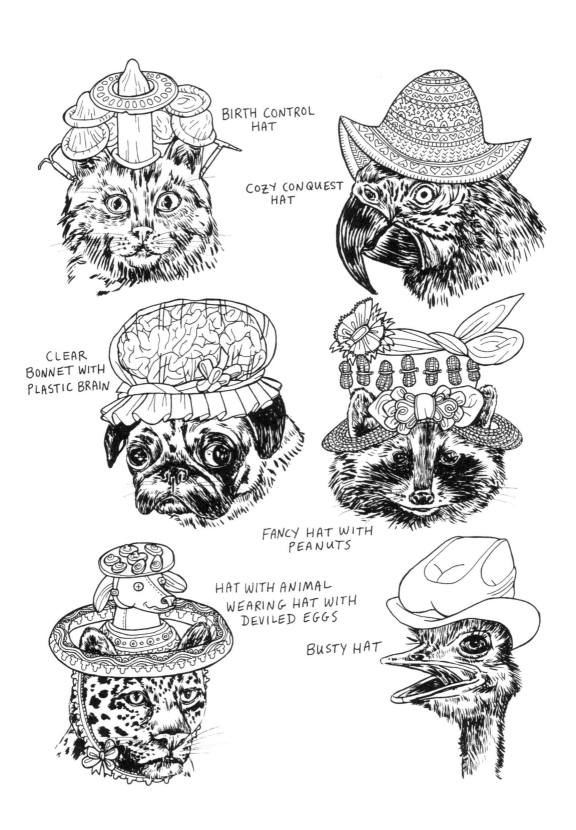

BIRTH CONTROL HAT

COZY CONQUEST HAT

CLEAR BONNET WITH PLASTIC BRAIN

FANCY HAT WITH PEANUTS

HAT WITH ANIMAL WEARING HAT WITH DEVILED EGGS

BUSTY HAT

Things We Are Sorry We Did Last Night

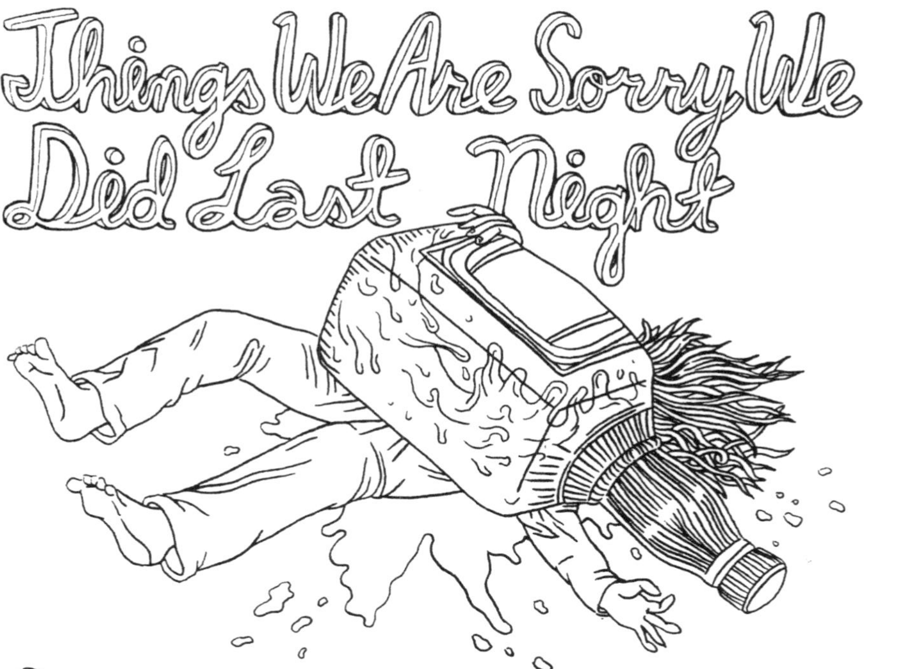

① WE SHOULDN'T HAVE GONE HOME WITH THAT GUY

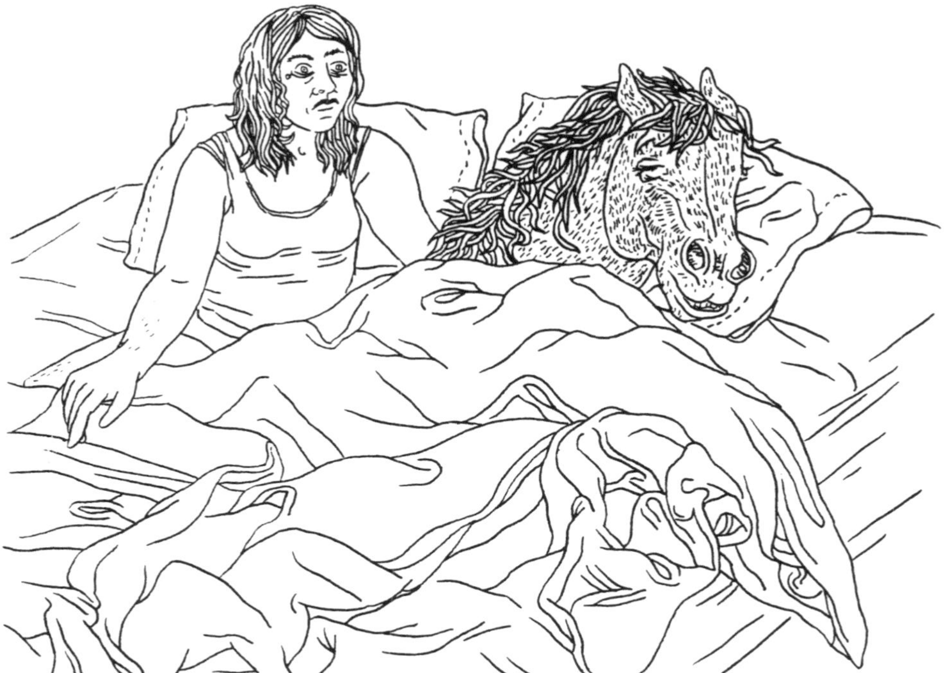

② OUR DECISION TO COOK WAS RECKLESS

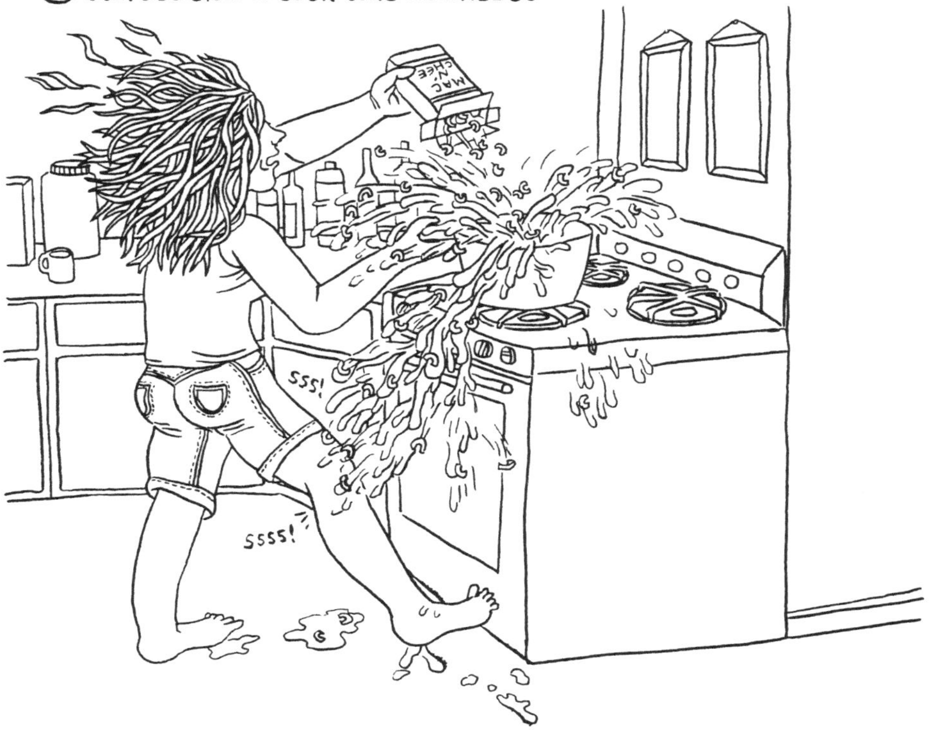
MAC N' CHEE
SSS!
SSSS!

③ WE DON'T REMEMBER HOW WE GOT ALL OF THESE WELTS

TO THE BEST OF OUR KNOWLEDGE:

① MACARONI BURNS
② VARIOLA-LIKE VIRUS
③ MIXED GRILL
④ PUSSY STAMP
⑤ CAT FACE
⑥ FINGER POKINGS (SELF-INFLICTED?)
⑦ SHARK BITE
⑧ TRILOBITE
⑨ TINY GLASSES

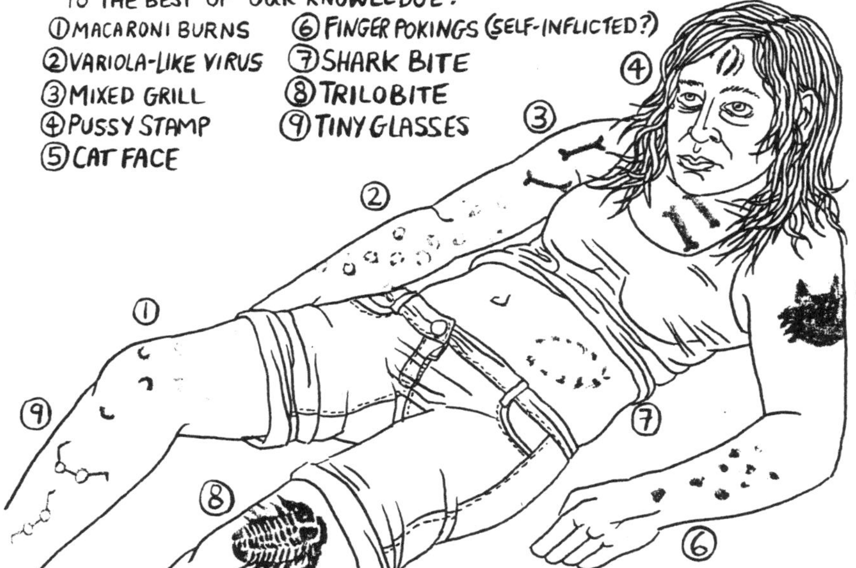
④
③
②
⑤
①
⑦
⑨
⑧
⑥

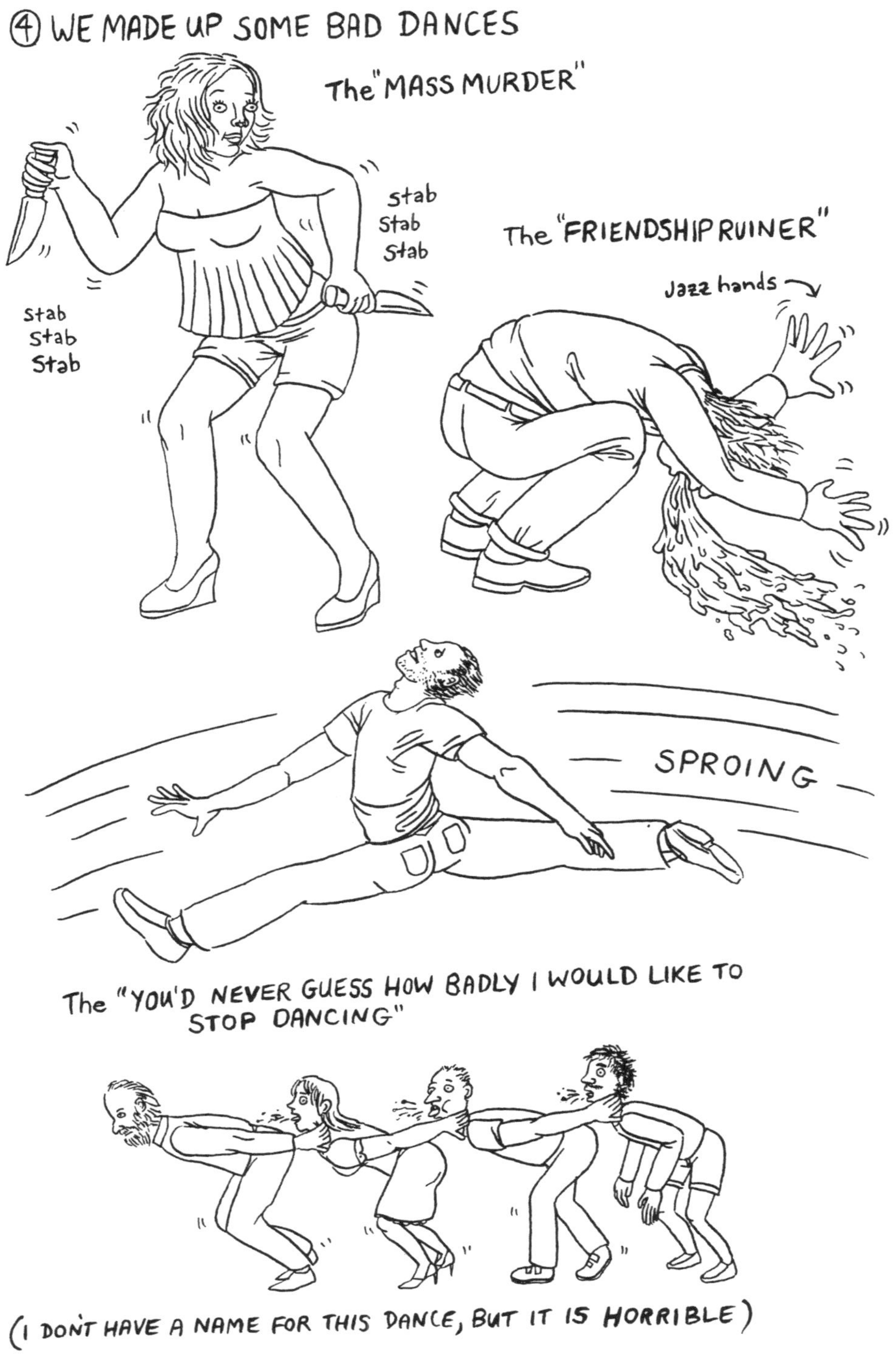
④ WE MADE UP SOME BAD DANCES
The "MASS MURDER"
stab
stab
stab
stab
stab
stab
The "FRIENDSHIP RUINER"
Jazz hands
SPROING
The "YOU'D NEVER GUESS HOW BADLY I WOULD LIKE TO STOP DANCING"
(I DON'T HAVE A NAME FOR THIS DANCE, BUT IT IS HORRIBLE)

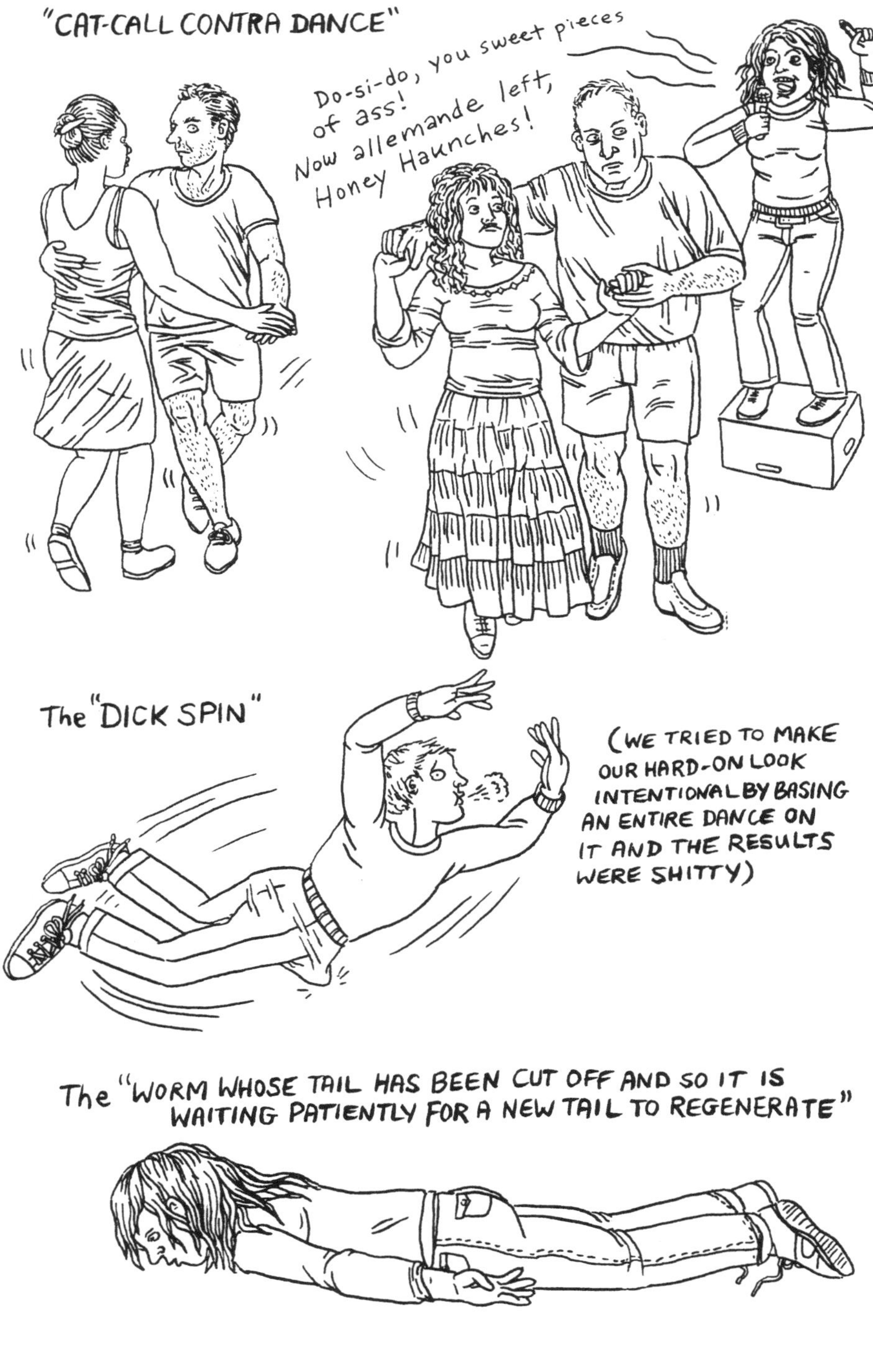
"CAT-CALL CONTRA DANCE"
Do-si-do, you sweet pieces of ass! Now allemande left, Honey Haunches!
The "DICK SPIN"
(WE TRIED TO MAKE OUR HARD-ON LOOK INTENTIONAL BY BASING AN ENTIRE DANCE ON IT AND THE RESULTS WERE SHITTY)
The "WORM WHOSE TAIL HAS BEEN CUT OFF AND SO IT IS WAITING PATIENTLY FOR A NEW TAIL TO REGENERATE"

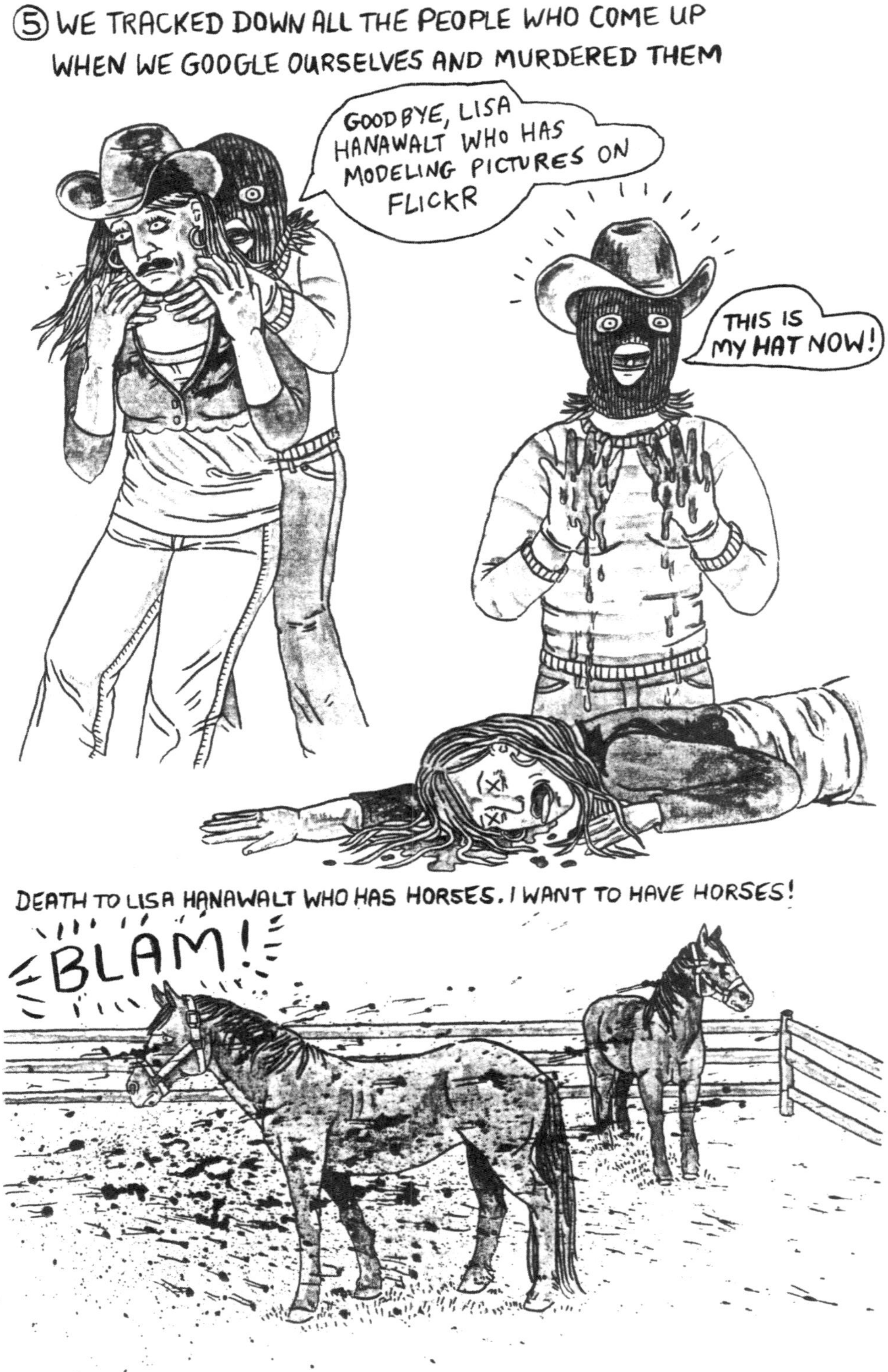
⑤ WE TRACKED DOWN ALL THE PEOPLE WHO COME UP WHEN WE GOOGLE OURSELVES AND MURDERED THEM
GOODBYE, LISA HANAWALT WHO HAS MODELING PICTURES ON FLICKR
THIS IS MY HAT NOW!
DEATH TO LISA HANAWALT WHO HAS HORSES. I WANT TO HAVE HORSES!
BLAM!

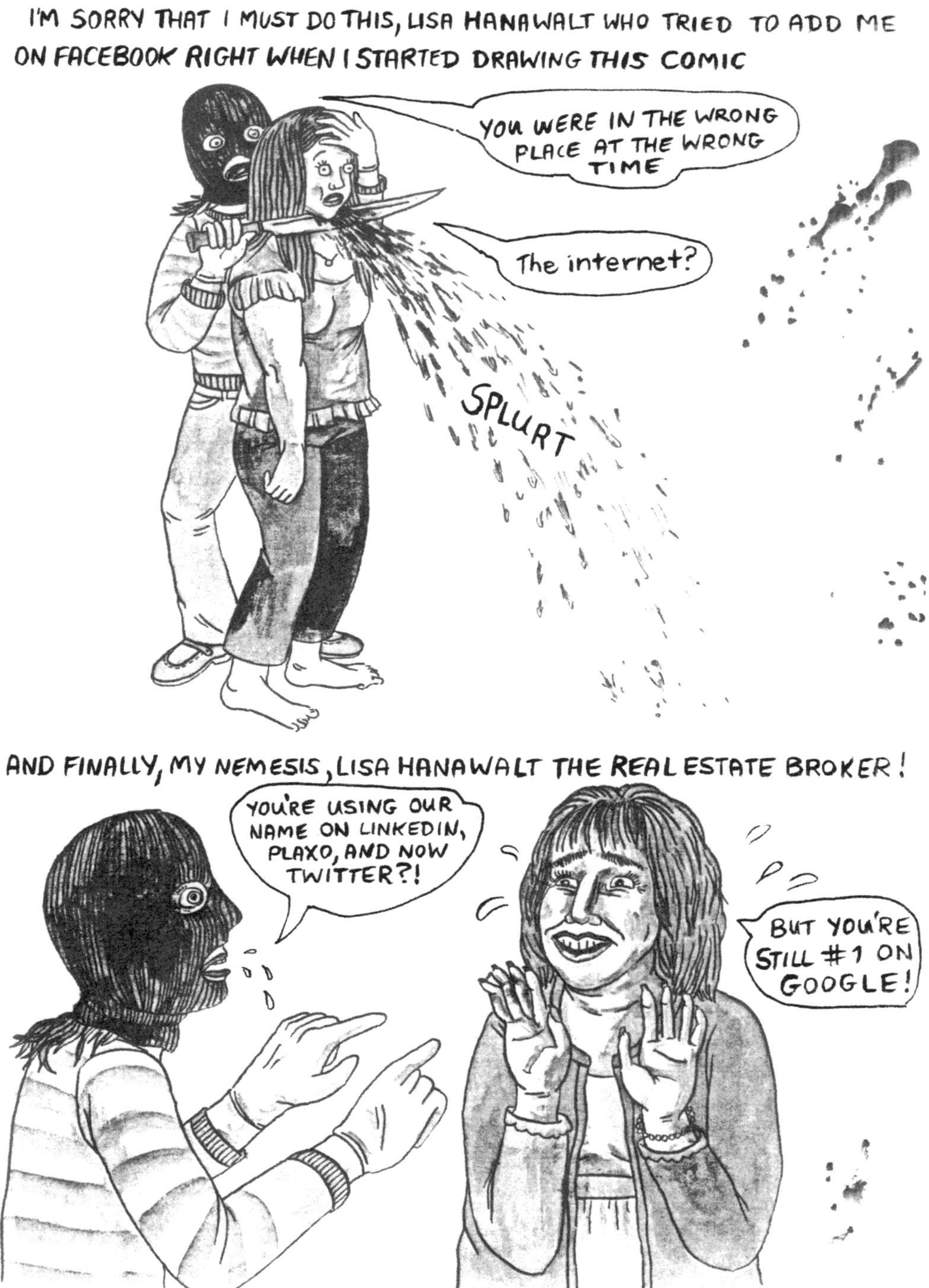
I'M SORRY THAT I MUST DO THIS, LISA HANAWALT WHO TRIED TO ADD ME ON FACEBOOK RIGHT WHEN I STARTED DRAWING THIS COMIC
YOU WERE IN THE WRONG PLACE AT THE WRONG TIME
The internet?
SPLURT
AND FINALLY, MY NEMESIS, LISA HANAWALT THE REAL ESTATE BROKER!
YOU'RE USING OUR NAME ON LINKEDIN, PLAXO, AND NOW TWITTER?!
BUT YOU'RE STILL #1 ON GOOGLE!

LATER:

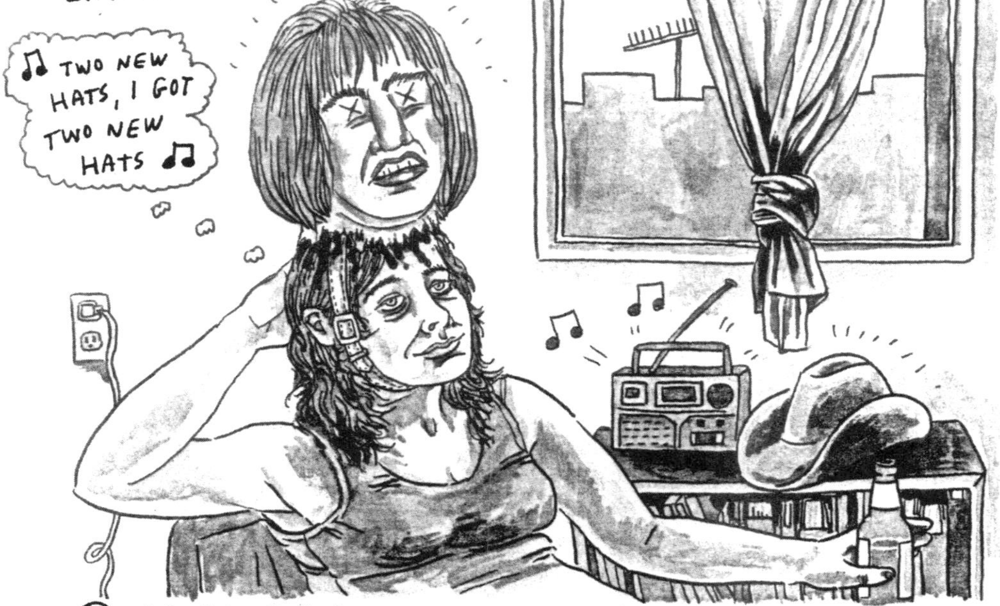
♫ TWO NEW HATS, I GOT TWO NEW HATS ♫

⑥ WE GAVE A MONSTER OUR DIGITS

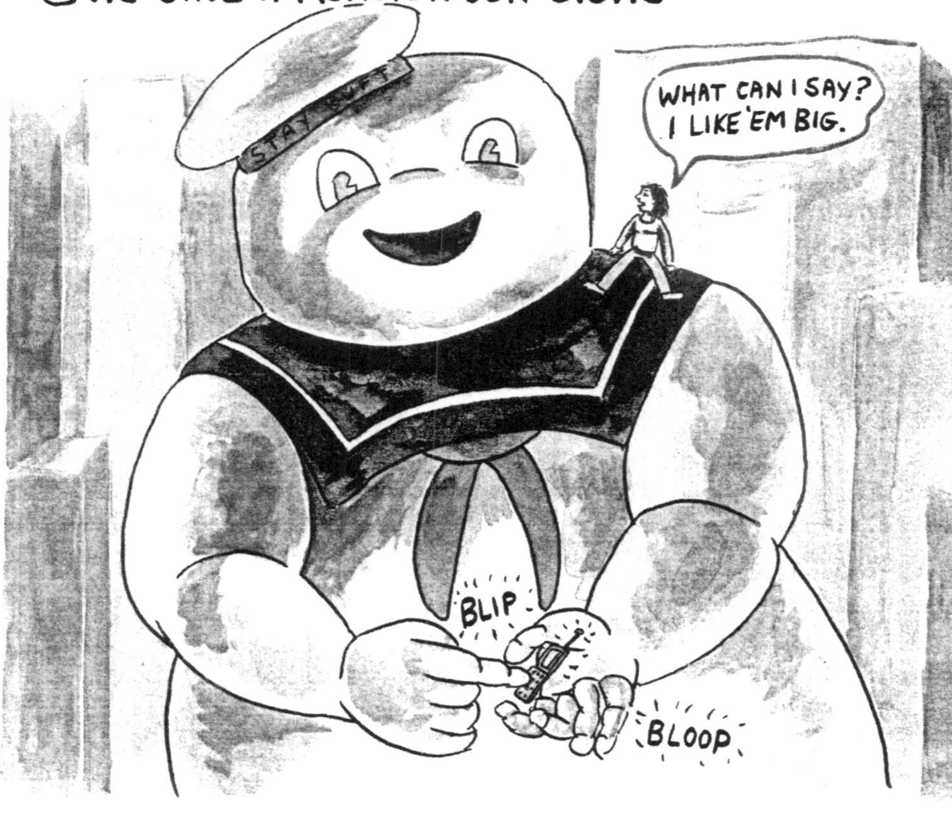
STAY PUFT
WHAT CAN I SAY? I LIKE 'EM BIG.
BLIP
BLOOP

7 WHEN THE TIME CAME TO TRANSFORM, WE PANICKED AND CHOSE POORLY

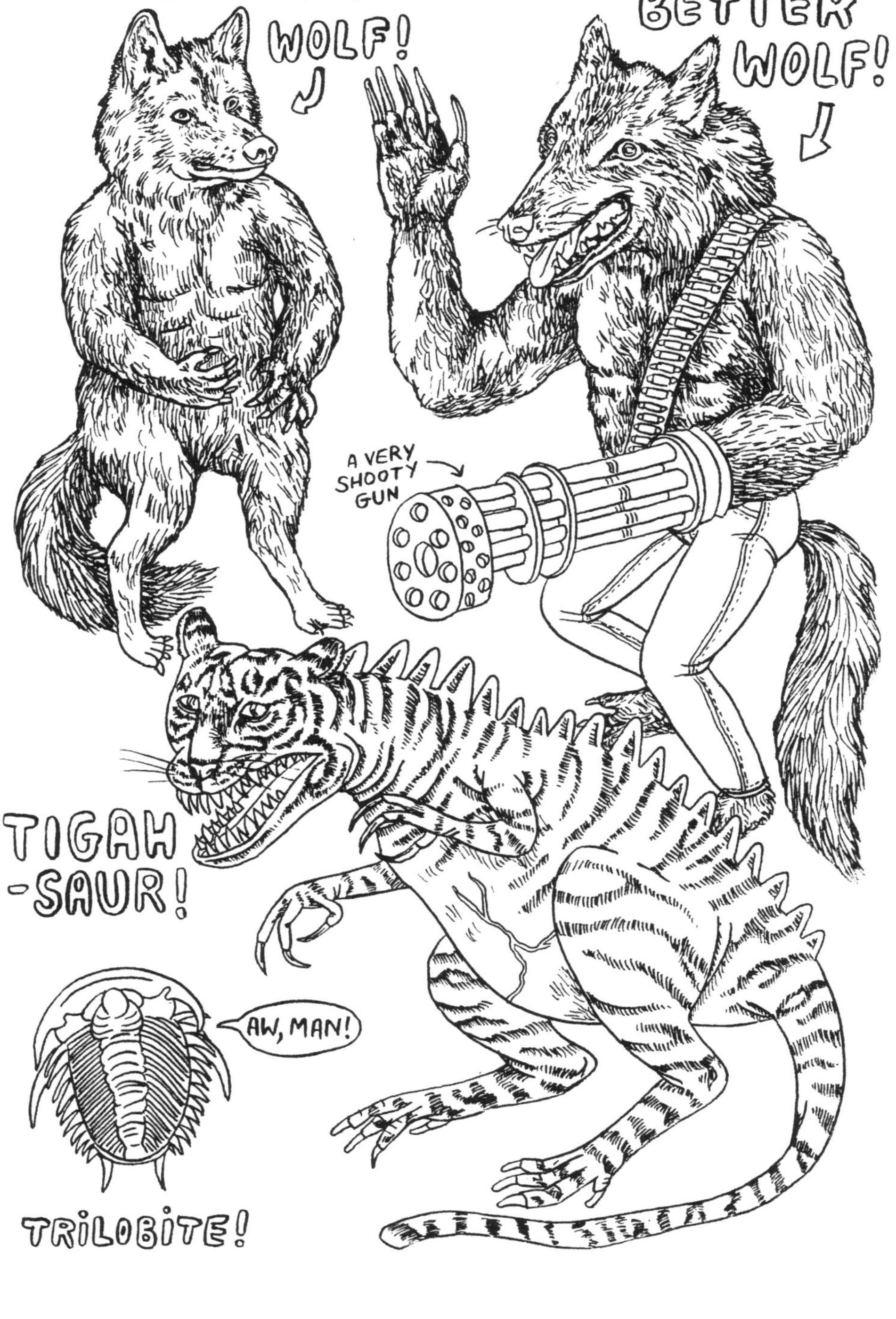
WOLF!
BETTER WOLF!
A VERY SHOOTY GUN
TIGAH-SAUR!
AW, MAN!
TRILOBITE!

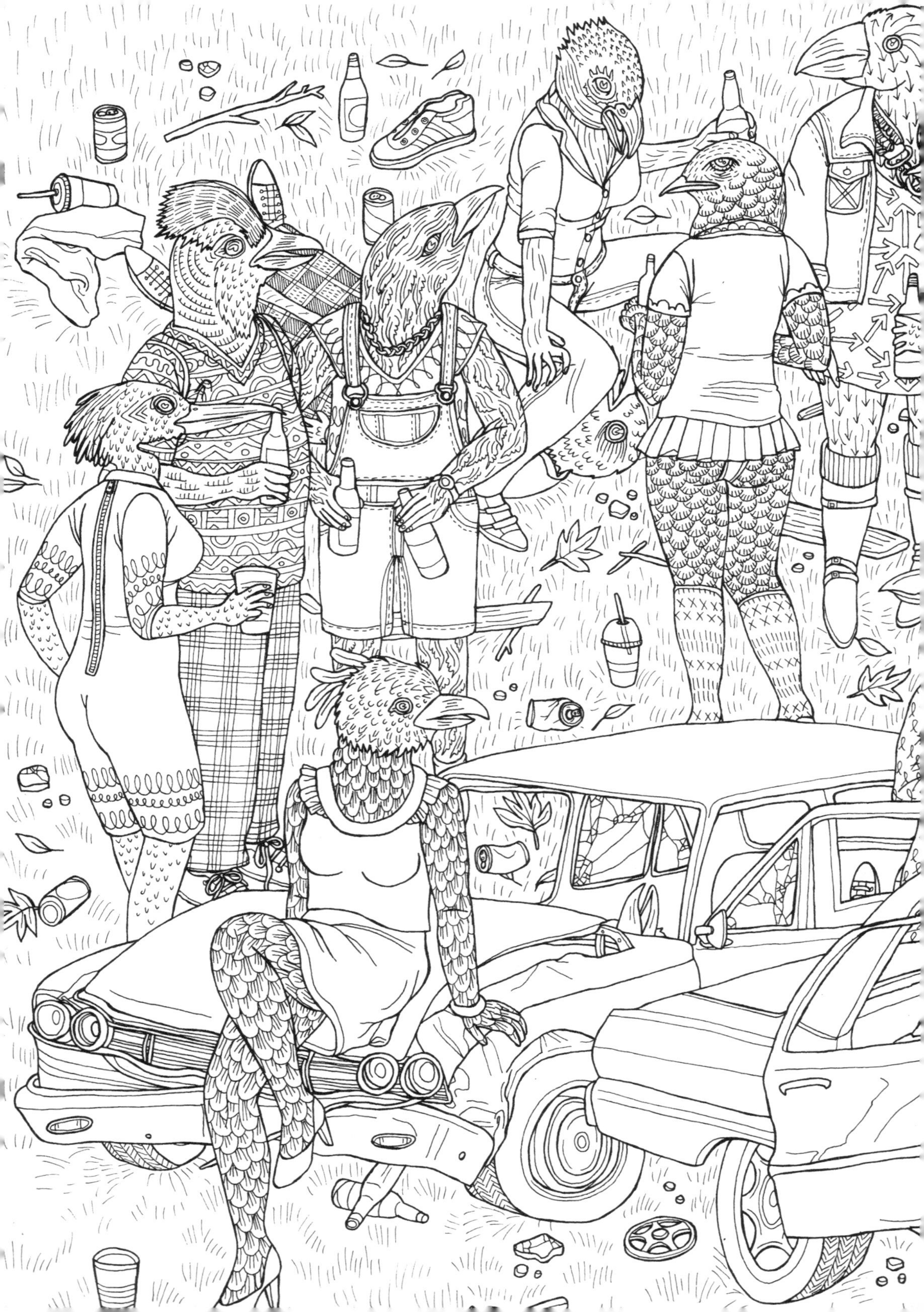

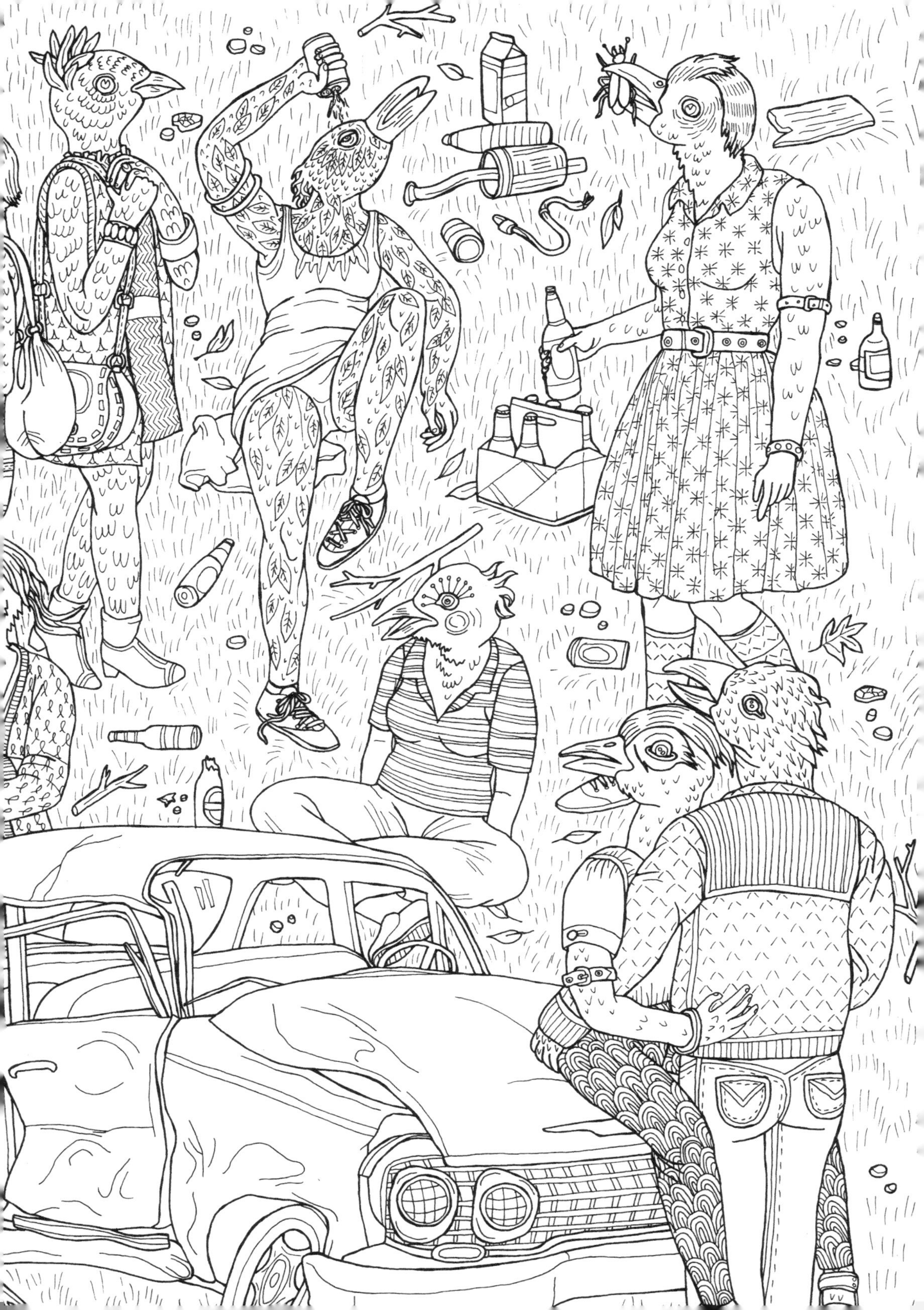

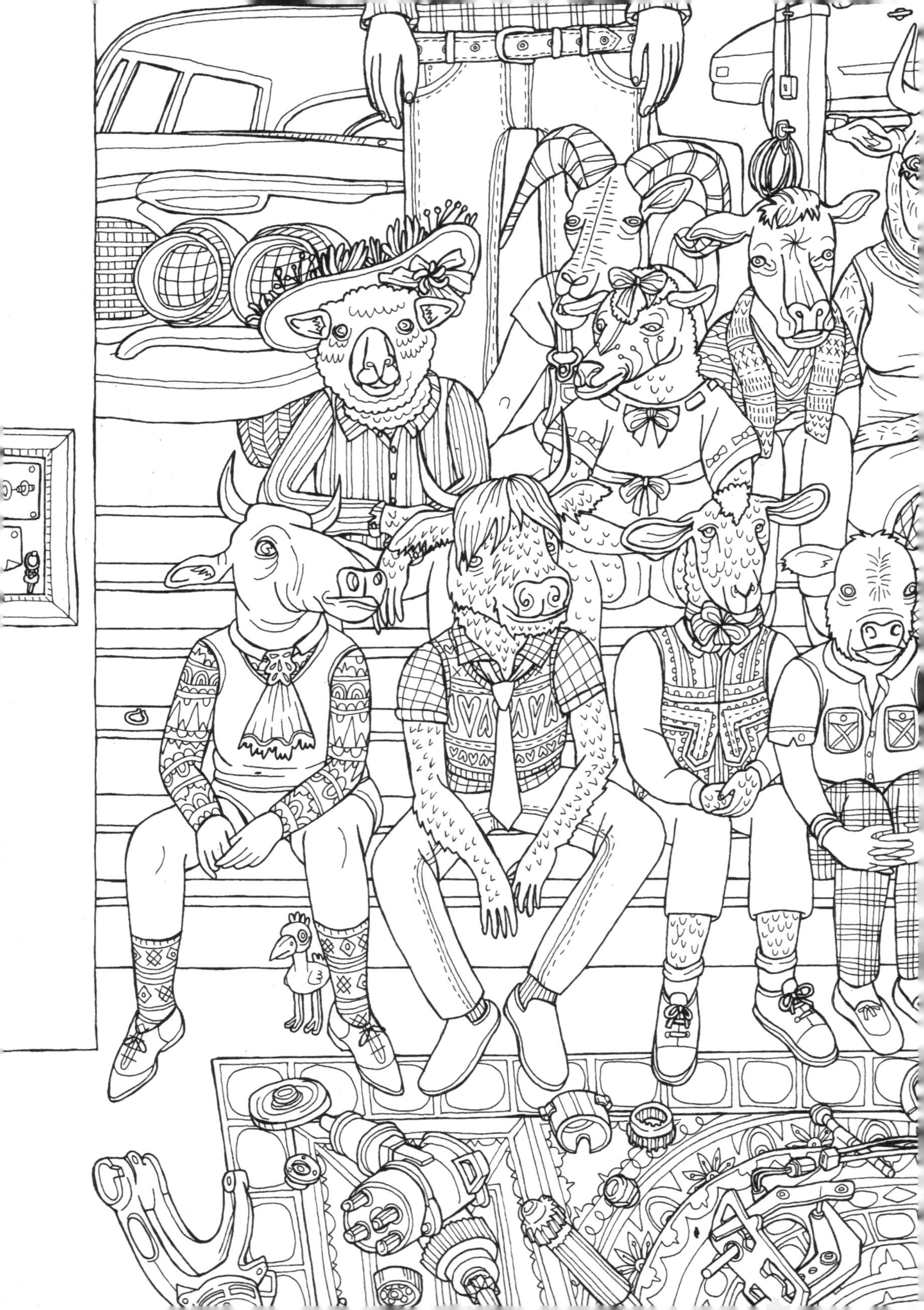

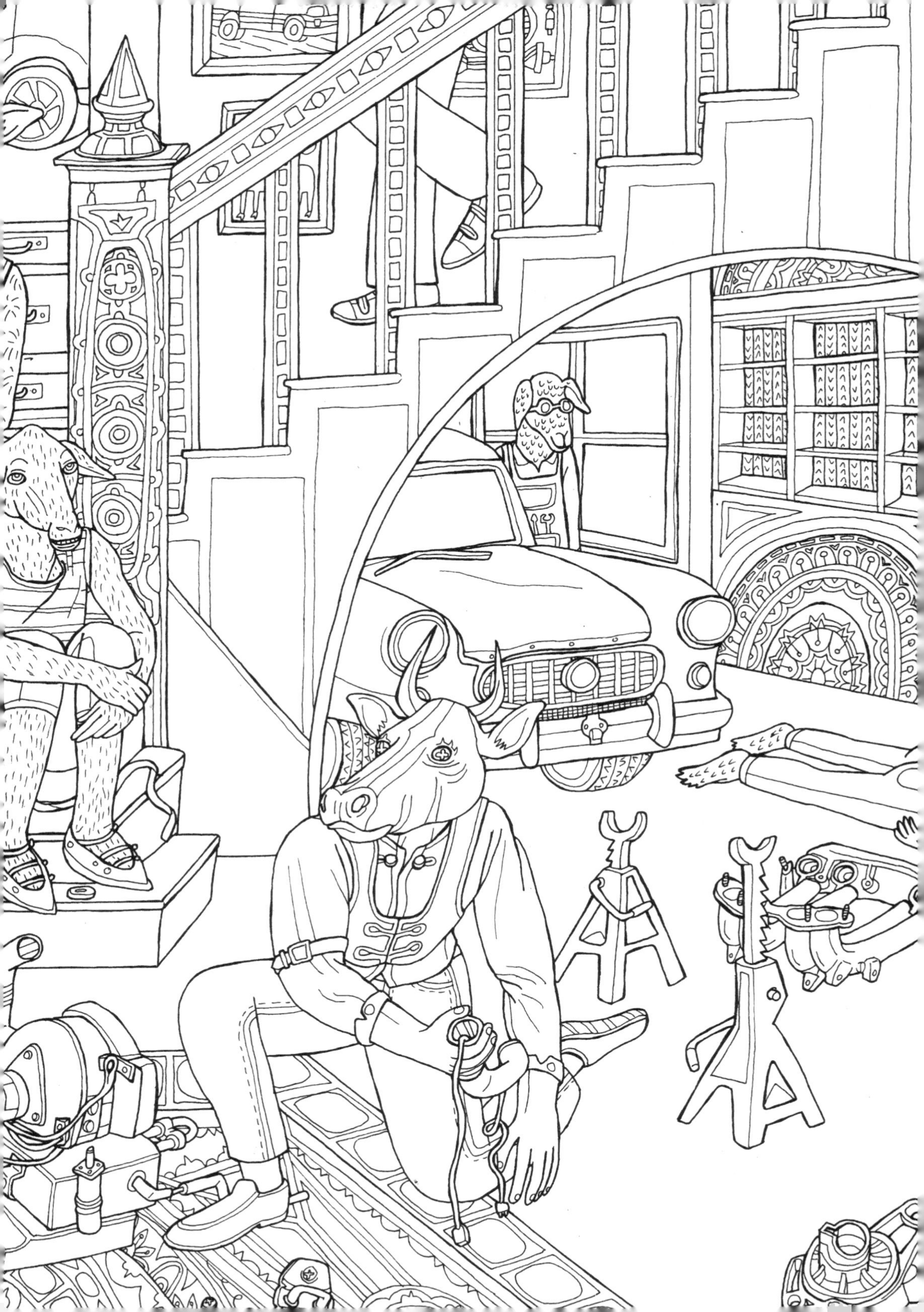

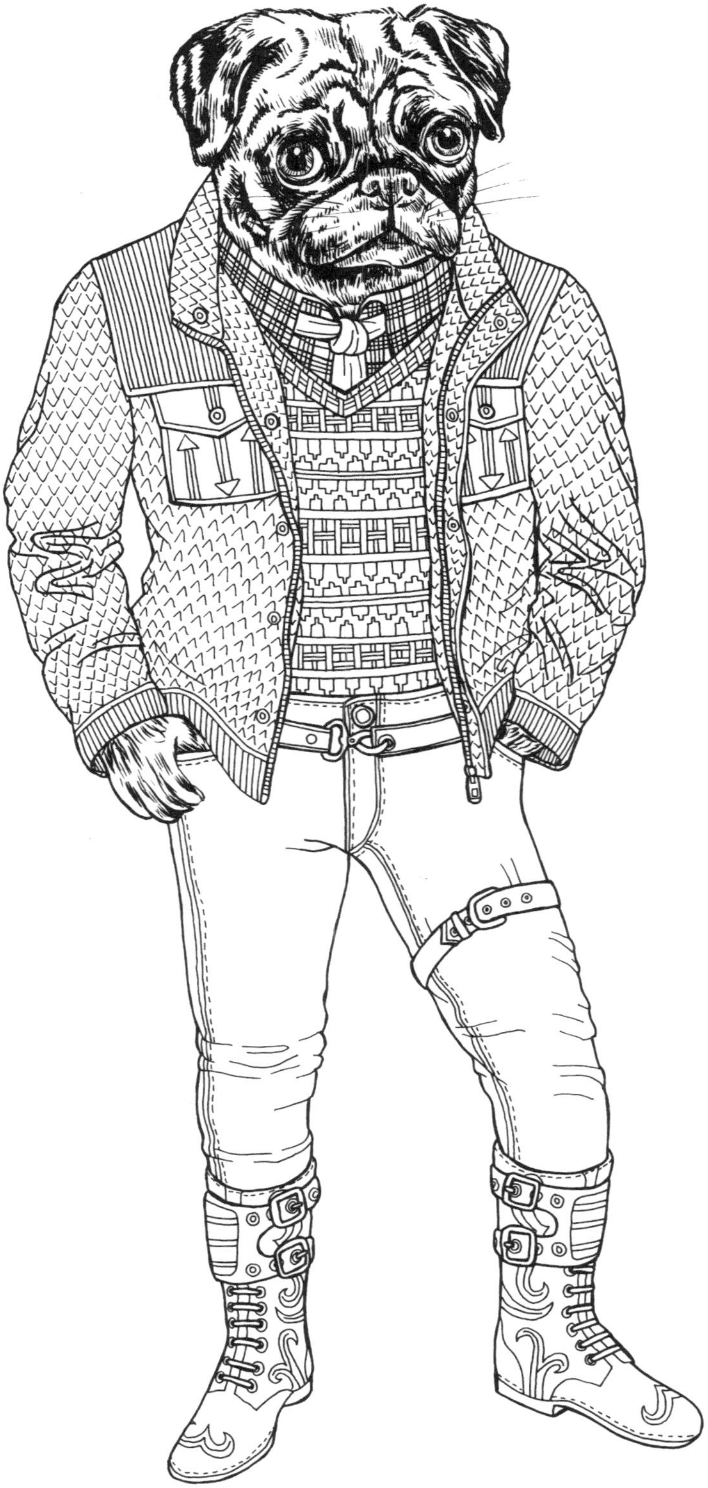

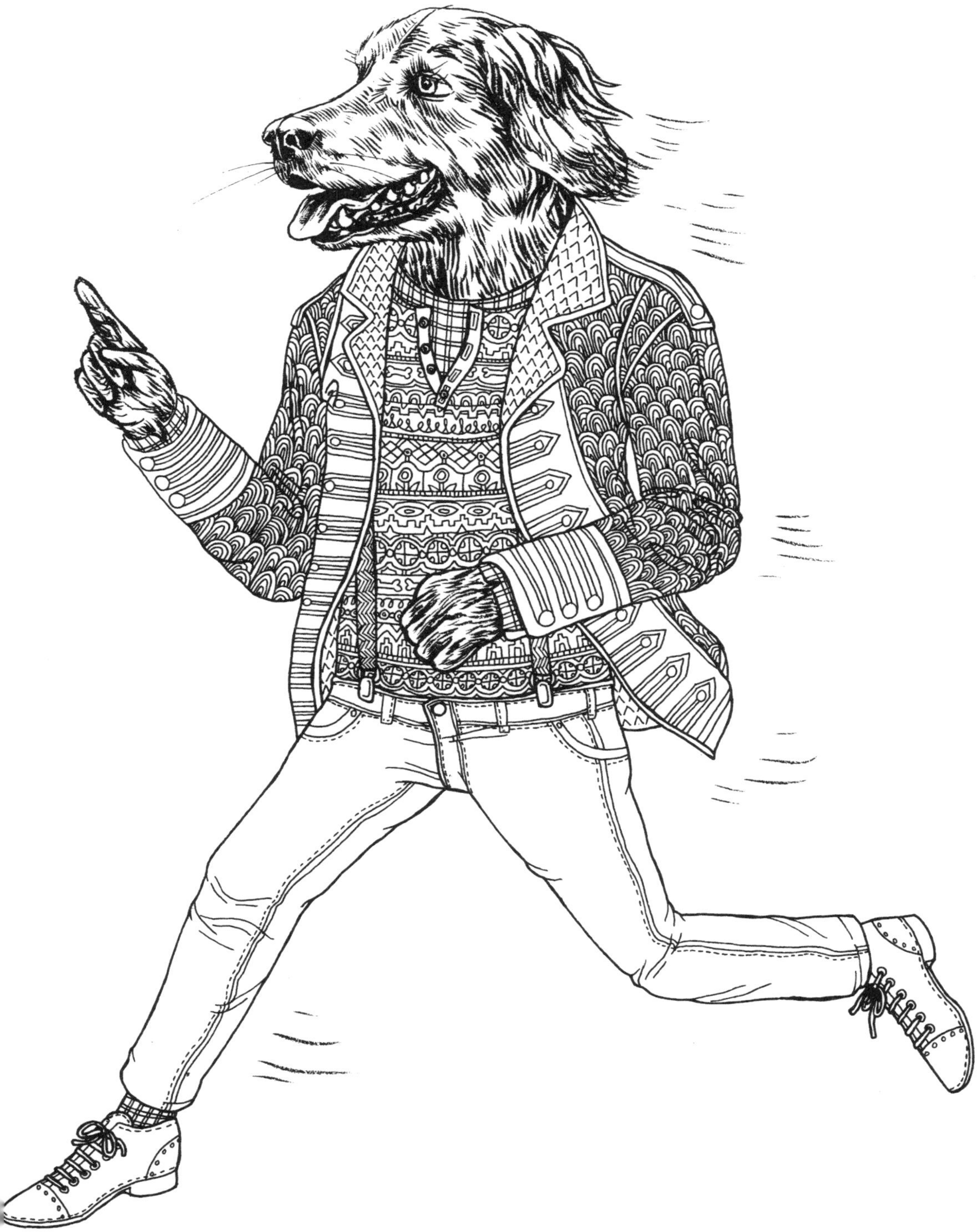

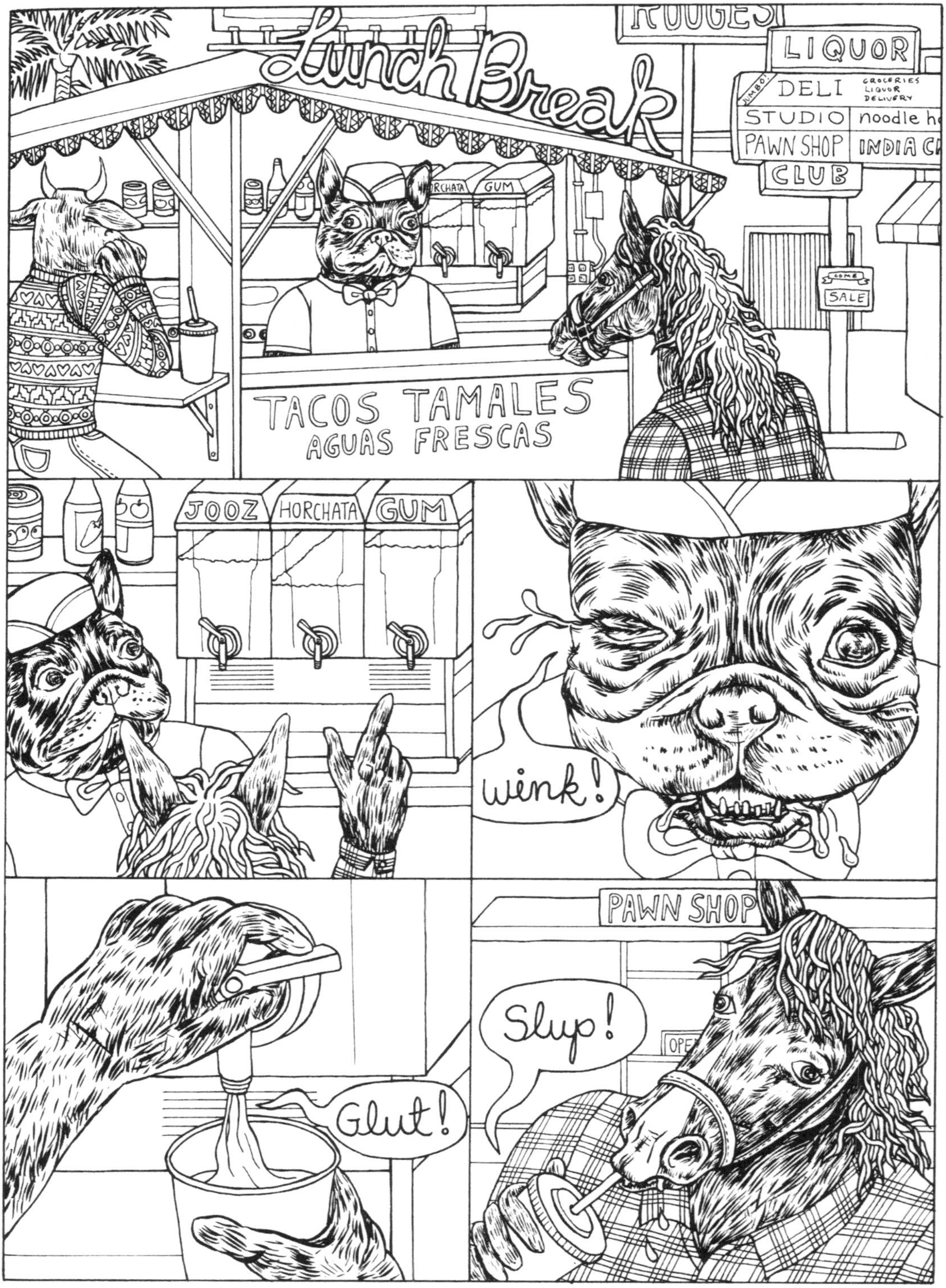
Lunch Break
LIQUOR
JUMBO
DELI
GROCERIES LIQUOR DELIVERY
STUDIO
noodle
PAWN SHOP
CLUB
SALE
HORCHATA
GUM
TACOS TAMALES
AGUAS FRESCAS
JOOZ
HORCHATA
GUM
wink!
Glut!
PAWN SHOP
Slup!

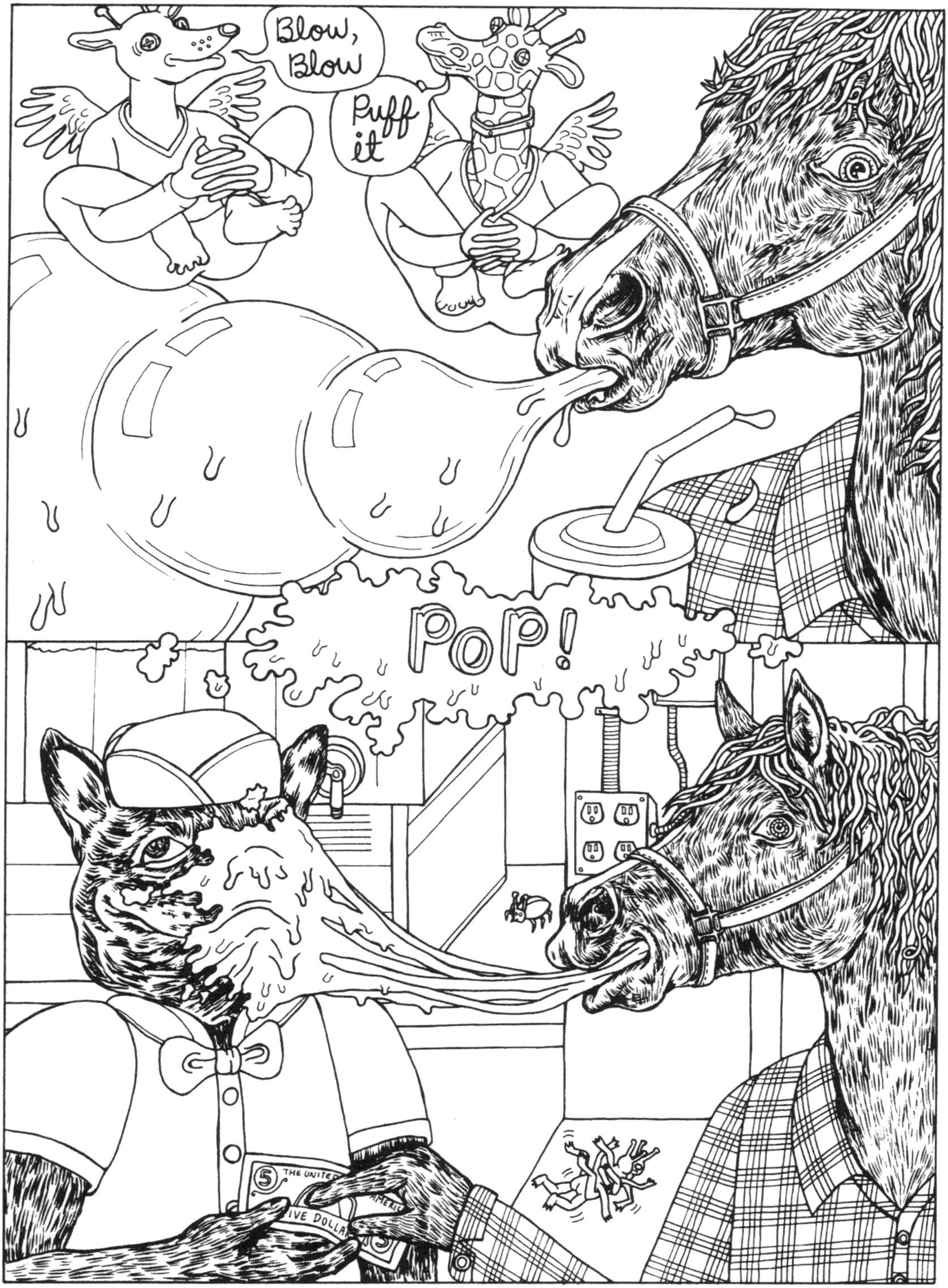

Blow, Blow
Puff it
POP!

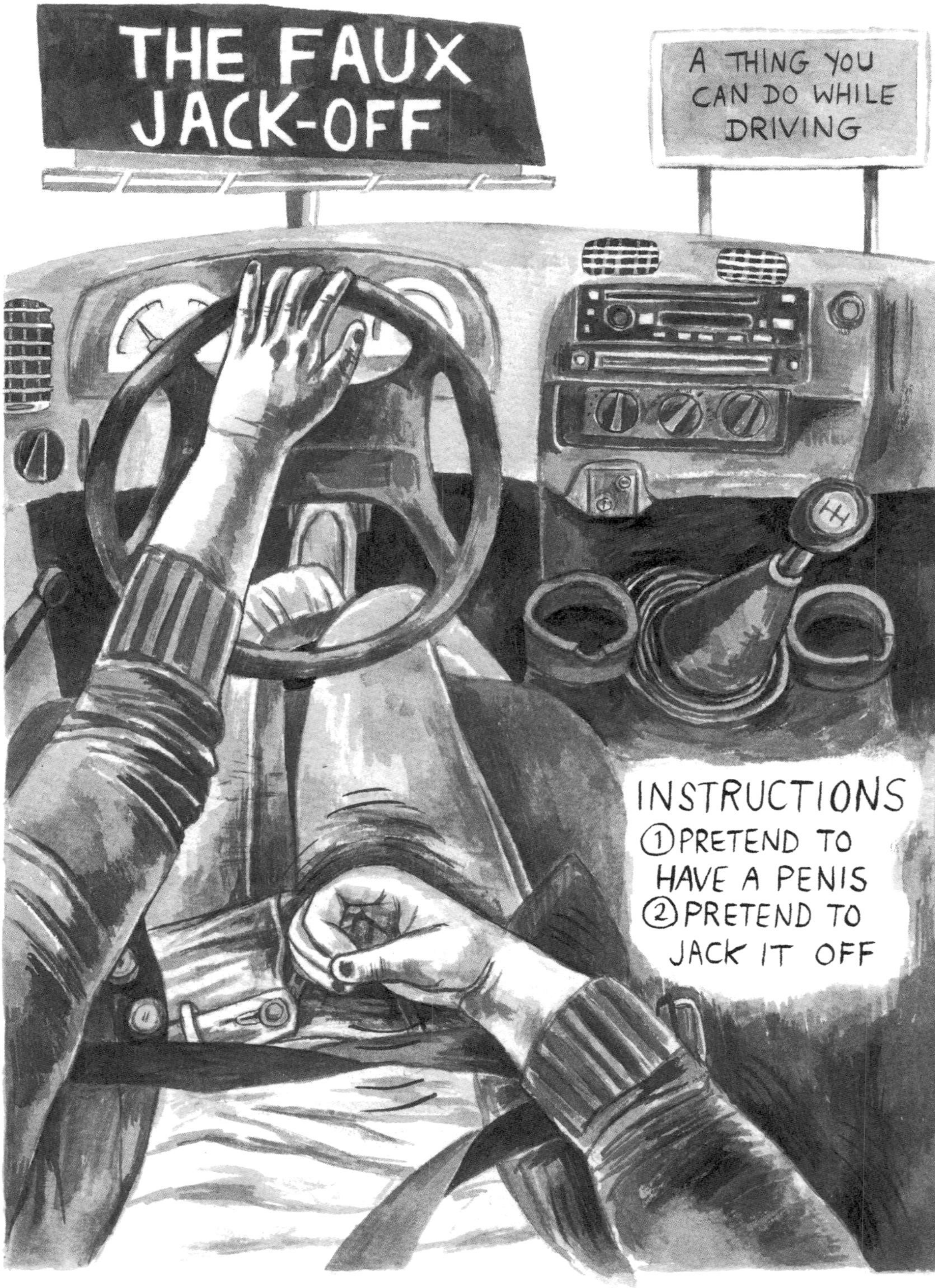
THE FAUX JACK-OFF
A THING YOU CAN DO WHILE DRIVING
INSTRUCTIONS
① PRETEND TO HAVE A PENIS
② PRETEND TO JACK IT OFF

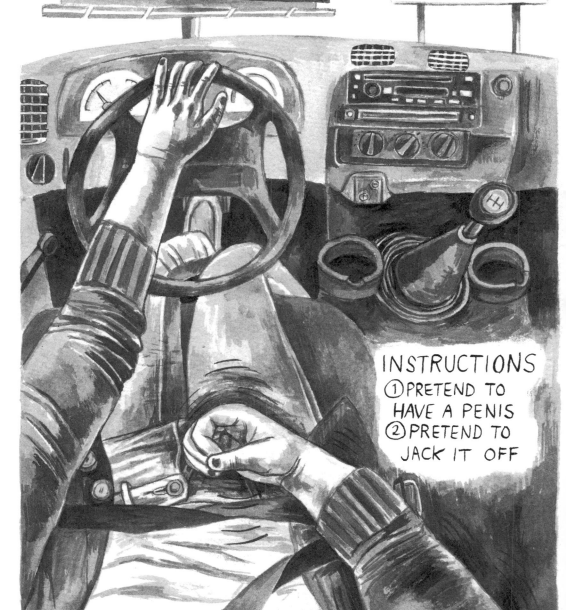

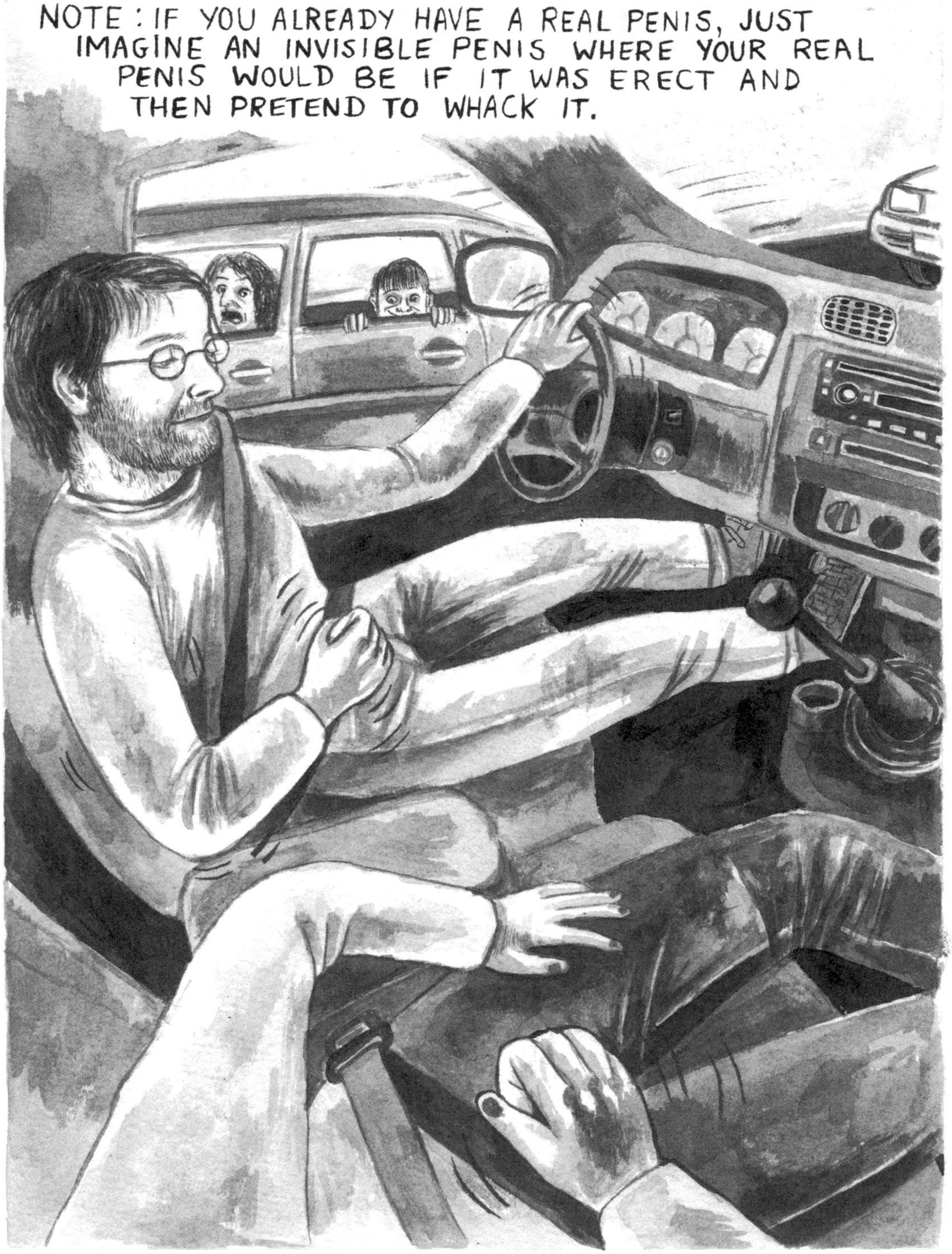
NOTE: IF YOU ALREADY HAVE A REAL PENIS, JUST IMAGINE AN INVISIBLE PENIS WHERE YOUR REAL PENIS WOULD BE IF IT WAS ERECT AND THEN PRETEND TO WHACK IT.

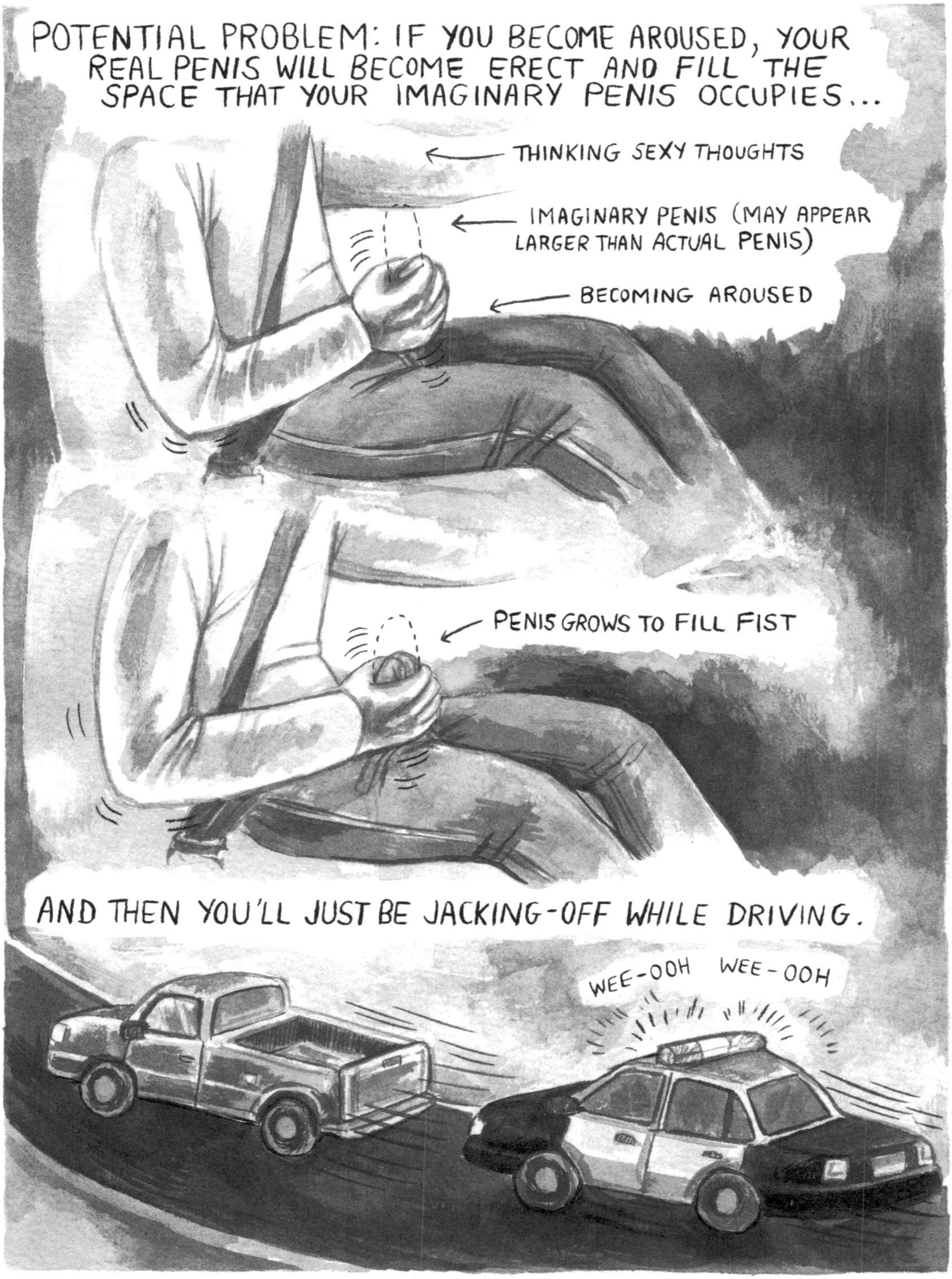
POTENTIAL PROBLEM: IF YOU BECOME AROUSED, YOUR REAL PENIS WILL BECOME ERECT AND FILL THE SPACE THAT YOUR IMAGINARY PENIS OCCUPIES...
THINKING SEXY THOUGHTS
IMAGINARY PENIS (MAY APPEAR LARGER THAN ACTUAL PENIS)
BECOMING AROUSED
PENIS GROWS TO FILL FIST
AND THEN YOU'LL JUST BE JACKING-OFF WHILE DRIVING.
WEE-OOH WEE-OOH

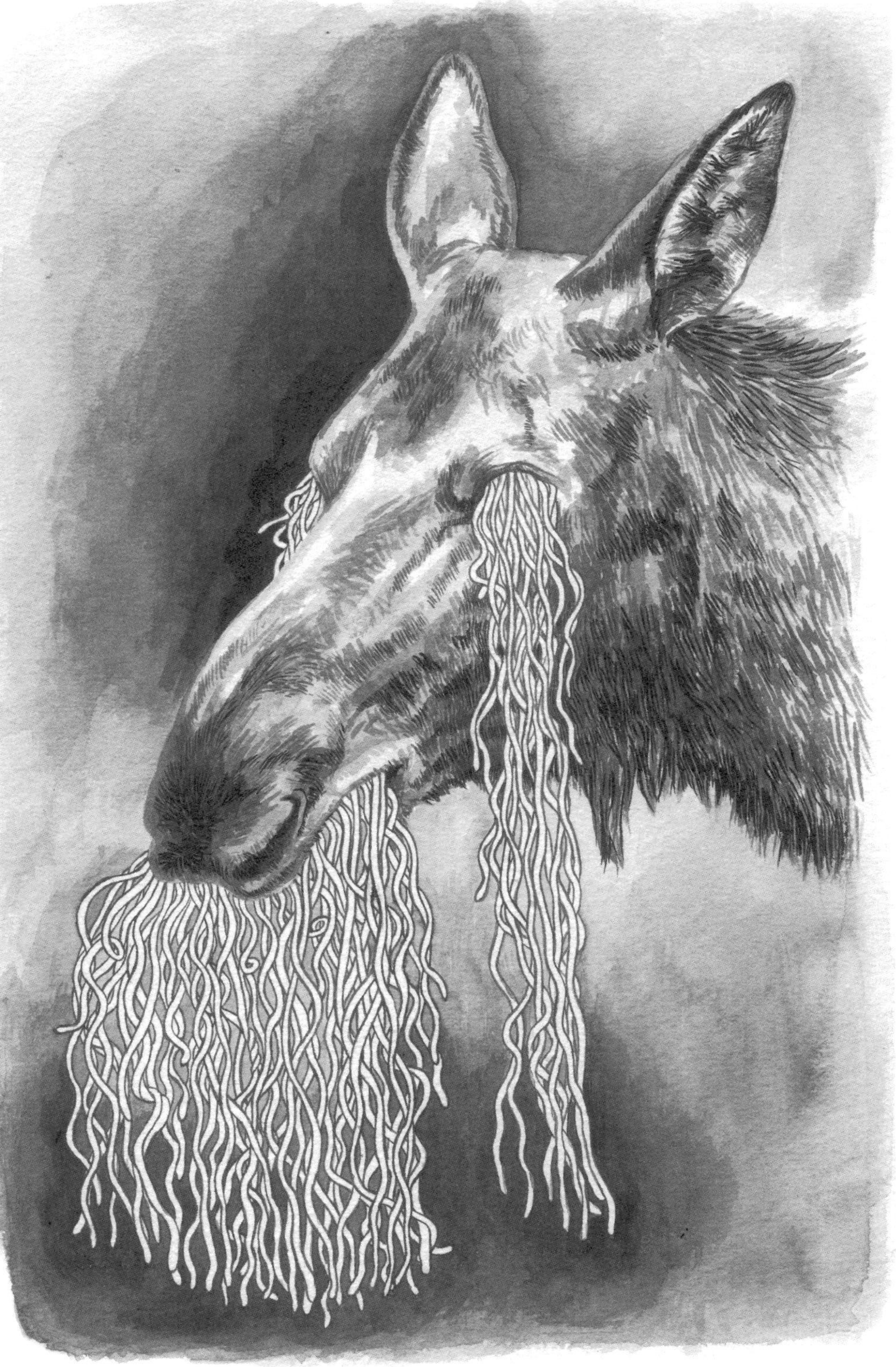

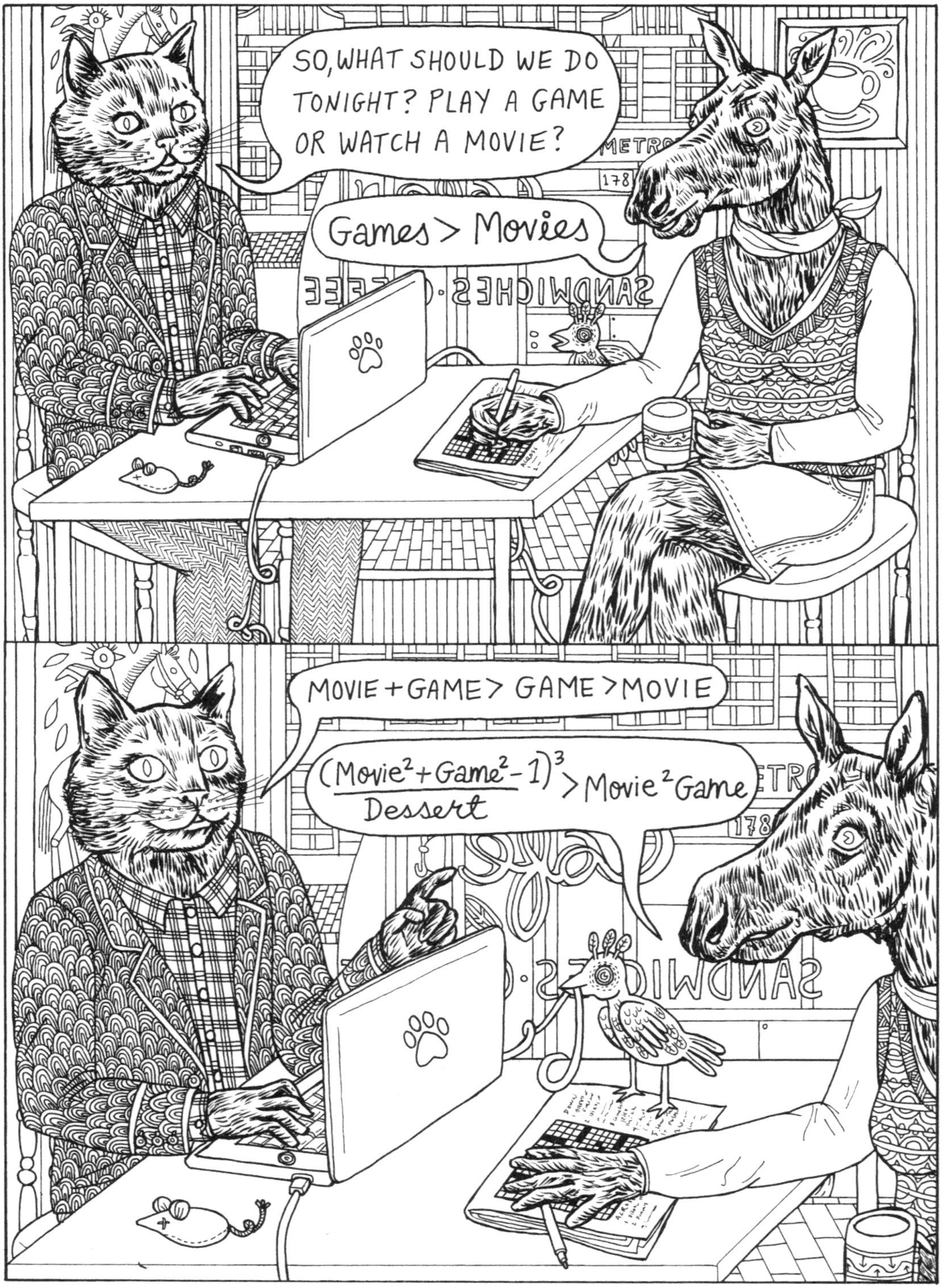
SO, WHAT SHOULD WE DO TONIGHT? PLAY A GAME OR WATCH A MOVIE?
Games > Movies
METRO
178
MOVIE + GAME > GAME > MOVIE
$\frac{(Movie^2+Game^2-1)^3}{Dessert} > Movie^2 Game$

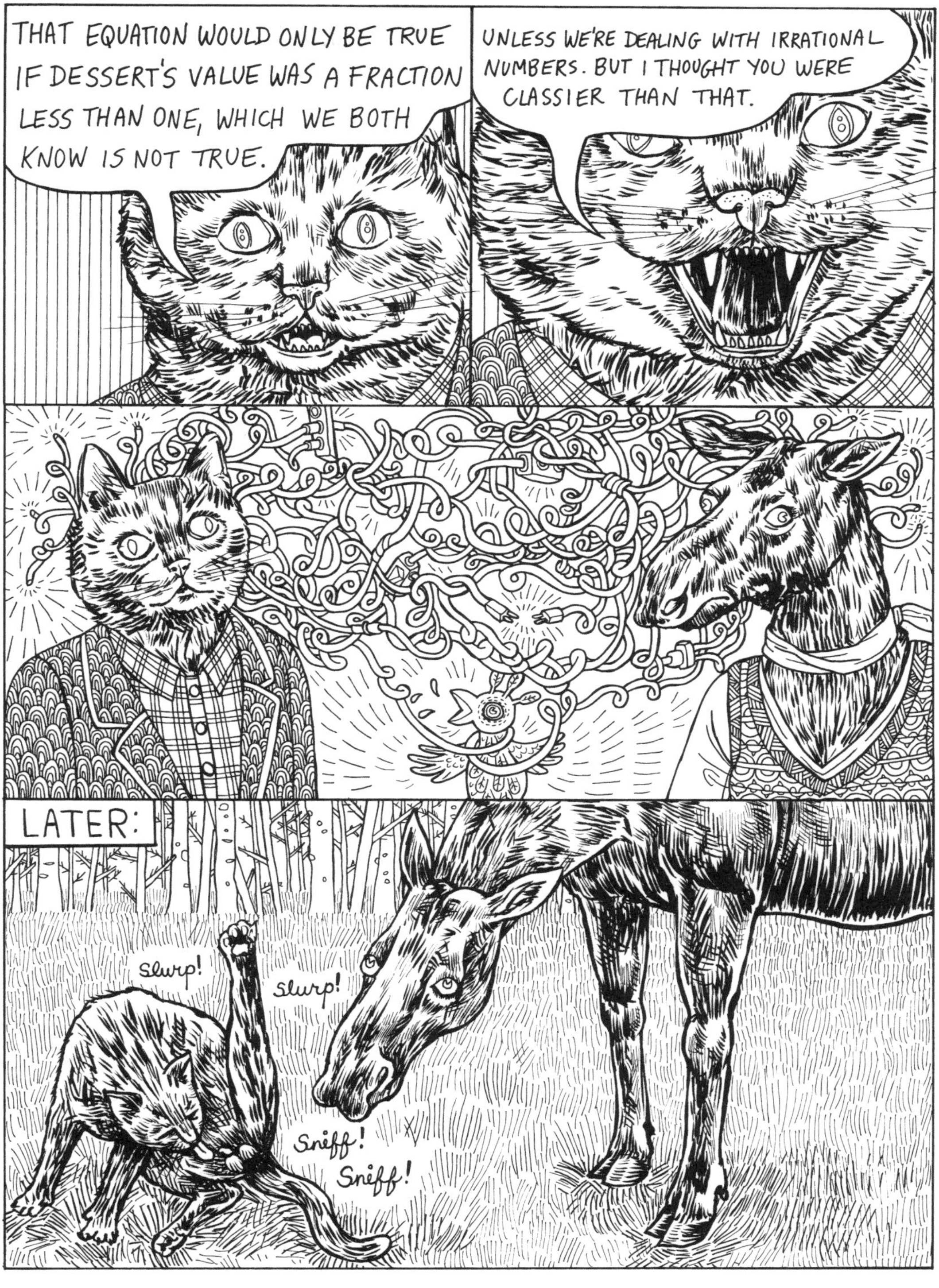
THAT EQUATION WOULD ONLY BE TRUE IF DESSERT'S VALUE WAS A FRACTION LESS THAN ONE, WHICH WE BOTH KNOW IS NOT TRUE.
UNLESS WE'RE DEALING WITH IRRATIONAL NUMBERS. BUT I THOUGHT YOU WERE CLASSIER THAN THAT.
LATER:
Slurp!
Slurp!
Sniff!
Sniff!

IS IT SCARY OR CUTE?

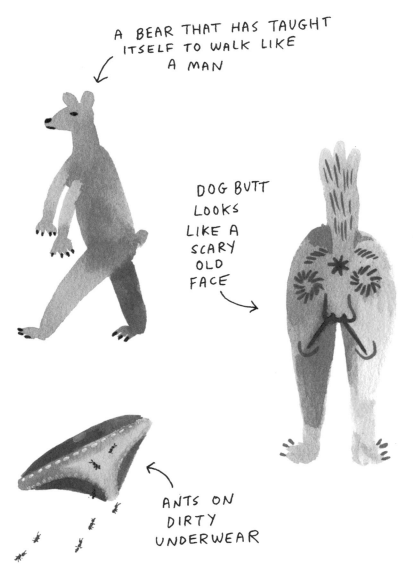

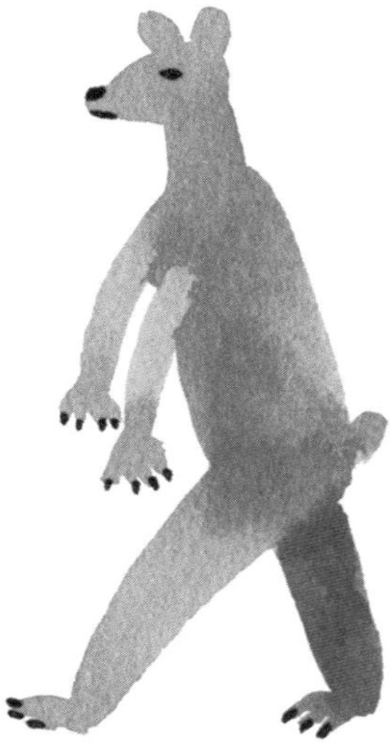
A BEAR THAT HAS TAUGHT ITSELF TO WALK LIKE A MAN

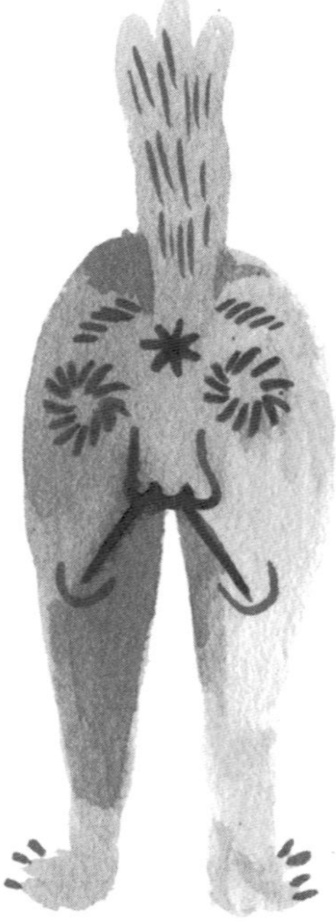
DOG BUTT LOOKS LIKE A SCARY OLD FACE

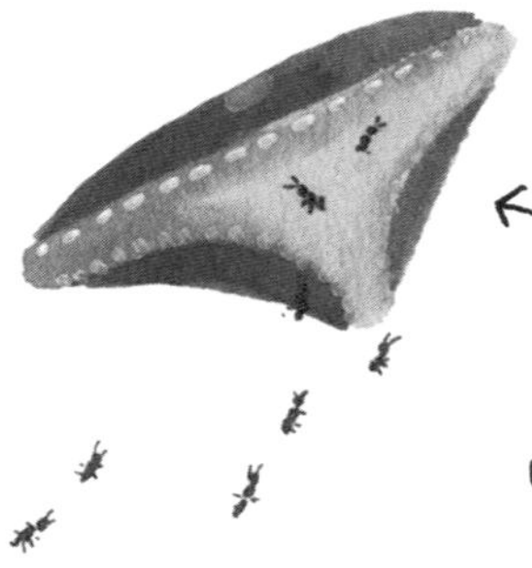
ANTS ON DIRTY UNDERWEAR

ANSWER: ALL SCARY

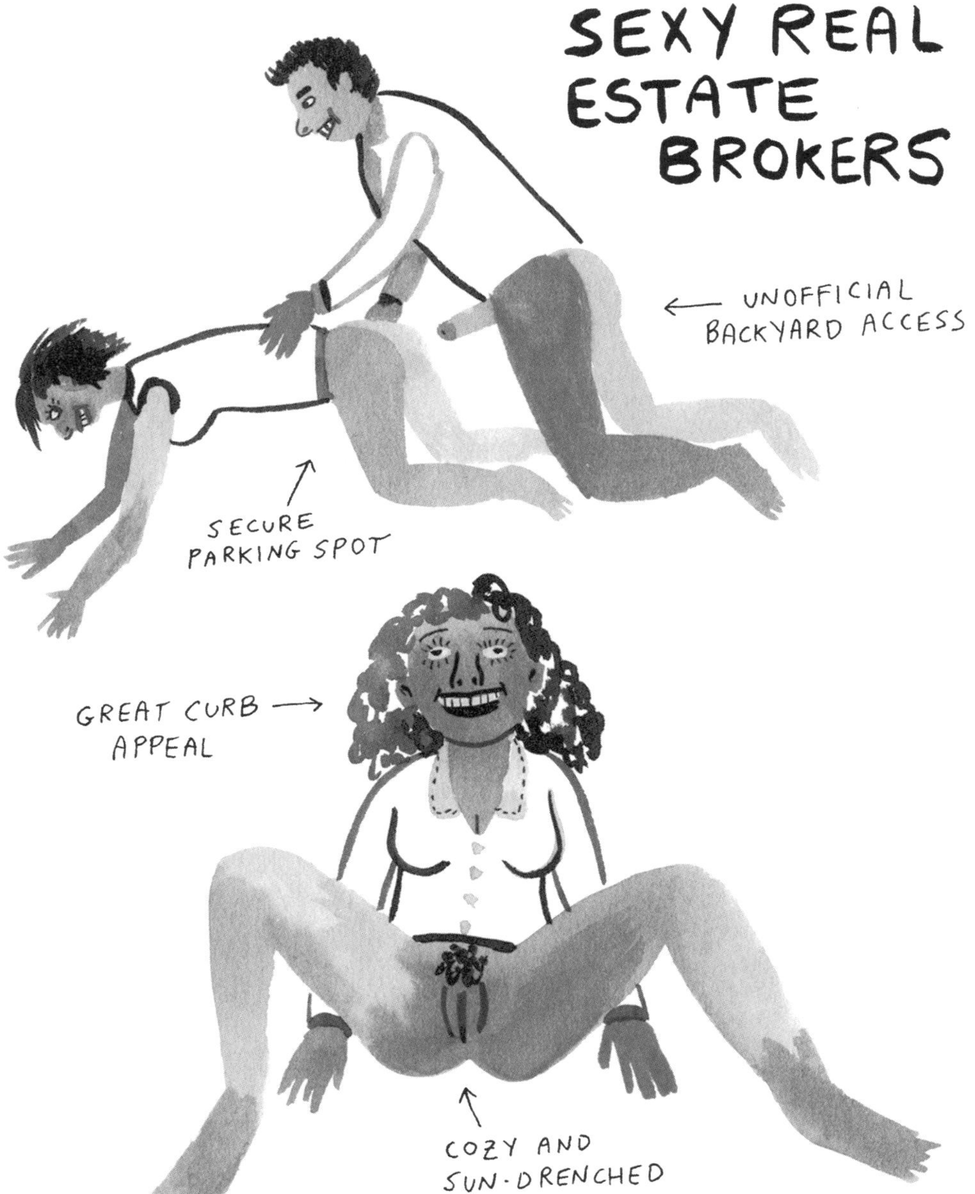
SEXY REAL ESTATE BROKERS
UNOFFICIAL BACKYARD ACCESS
SECURE PARKING SPOT
GREAT CURB APPEAL
COZY AND SUN-DRENCHED

GET EXCITED FOR

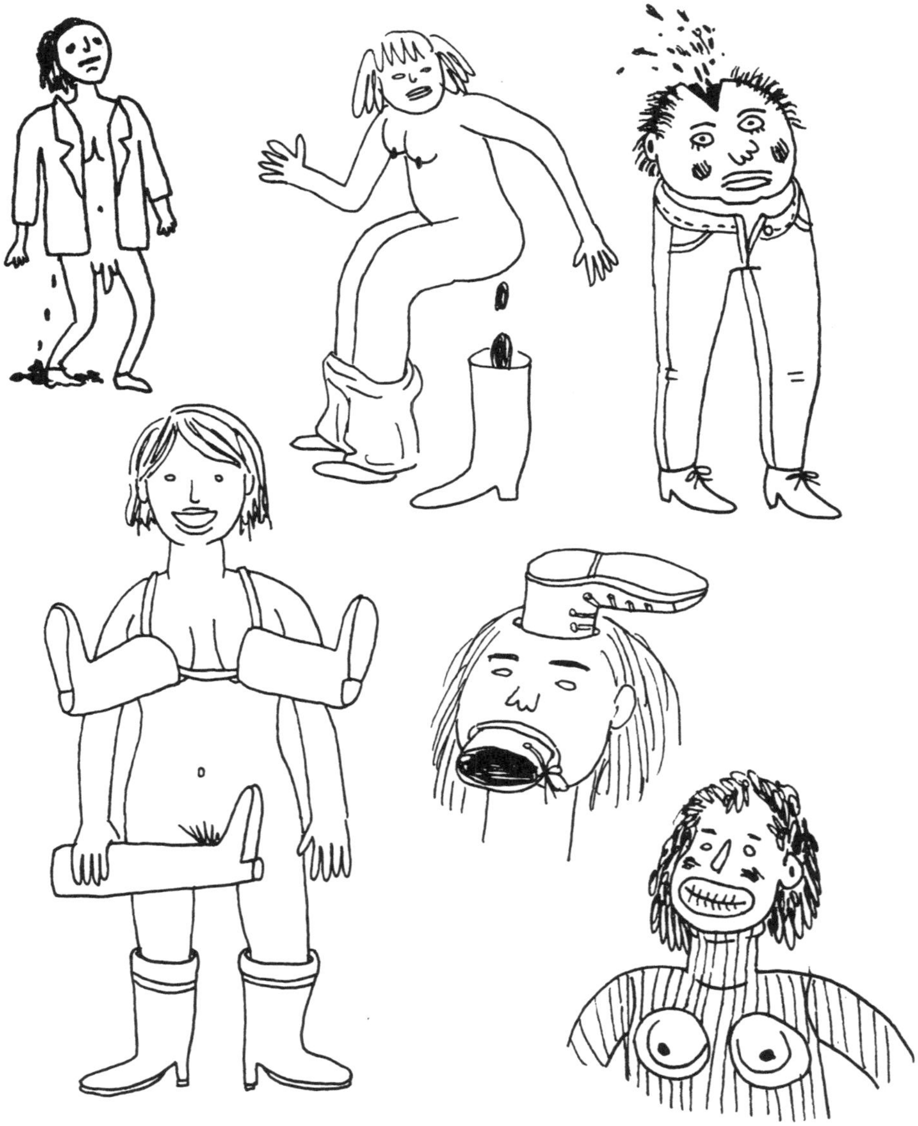

FALL FASHIONS!

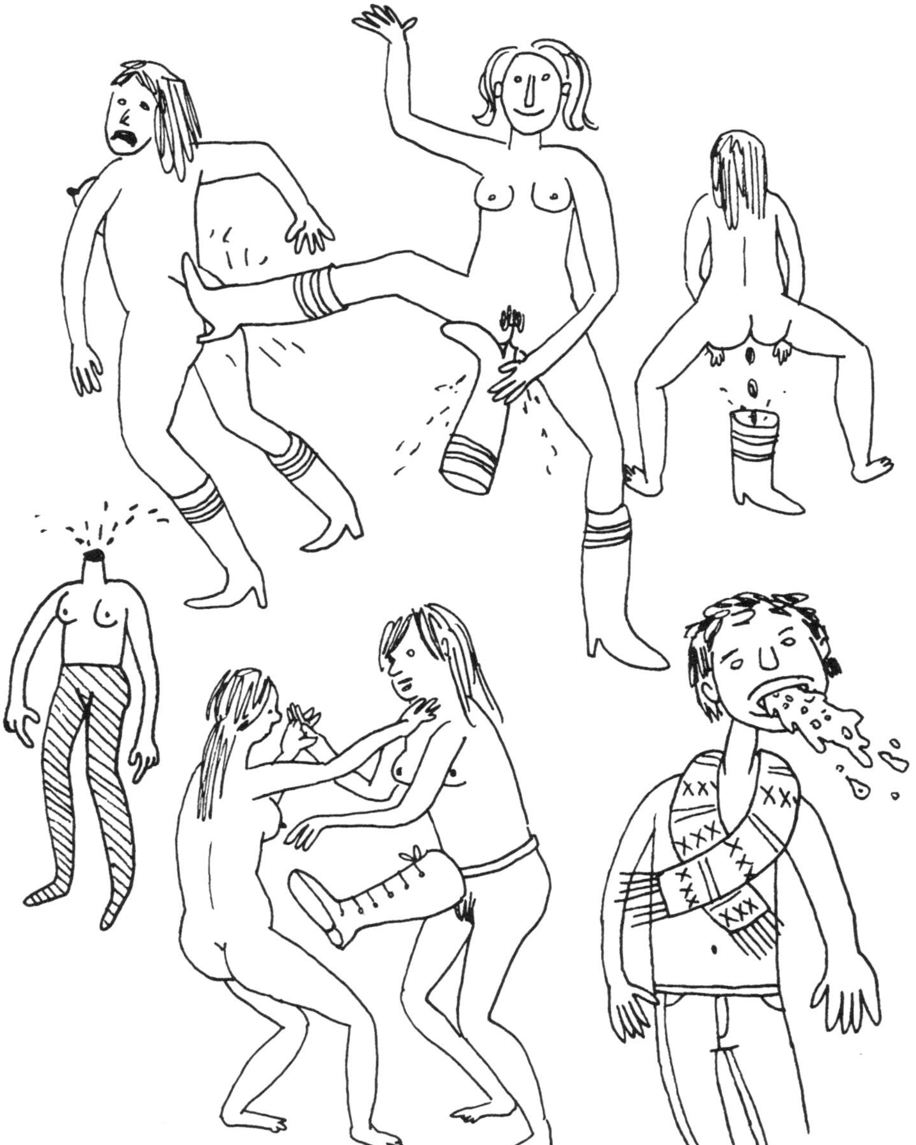

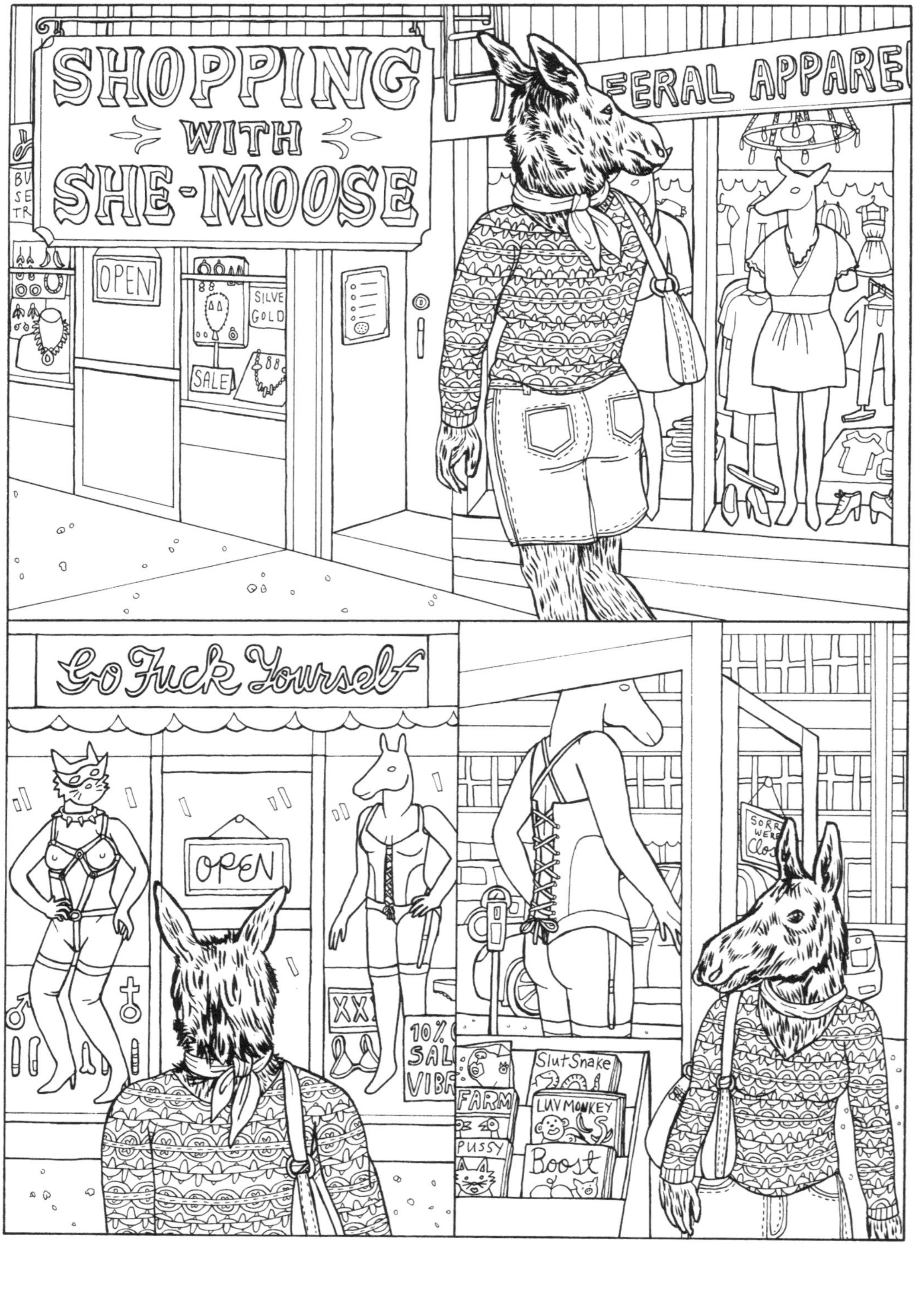

SHOPPING WITH SHE-MOOSE
FERAL APPARE
OPEN
SILVE GOLD
SALE
Go Fuck Yourself
OPEN
XX
10% SAL VIBR
SlutSnake
FARM
LUV MONKEY
PUSSY
Boost

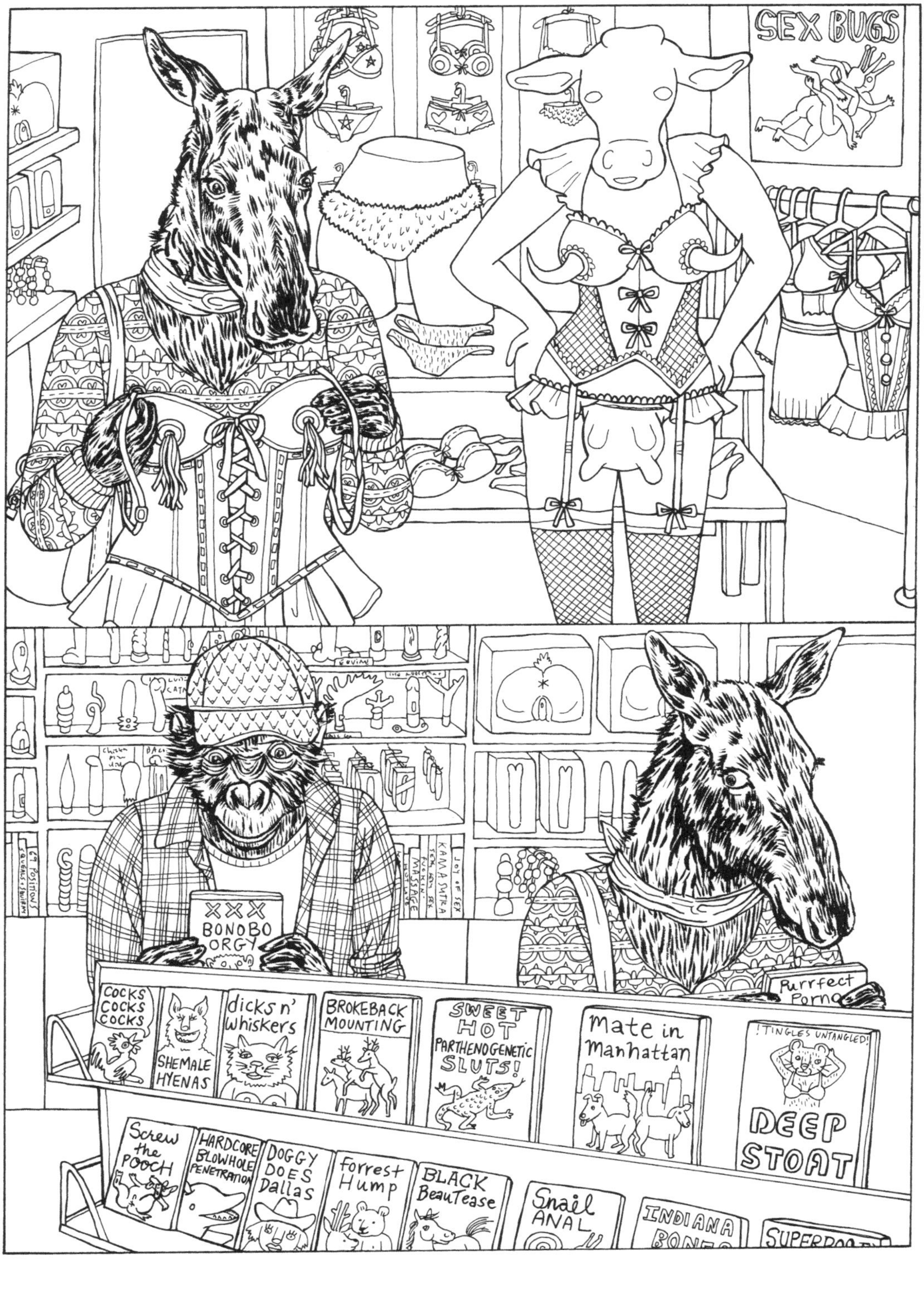
SEX BUGS
KAMA SUTRA
JOY OF SEX
XXX
BONOBO ORGY
Purrfect Porno
COCKS COCKS COCKS
SHEMALE HYENAS
dicks n' whiskers
BROKEBACK MOUNTING
SWEET HOT PARTHENOGENETIC SLUTS!
mate in manhattan
!TINGLES UNTANGLED!
DEEP STOAT
Screw the POOCH
HARDCORE BLOWHOLE PENETRATION
DOGGY DOES Dallas
Forrest Hump
BLACK BeauTease
Snail ANAL
INDIANA

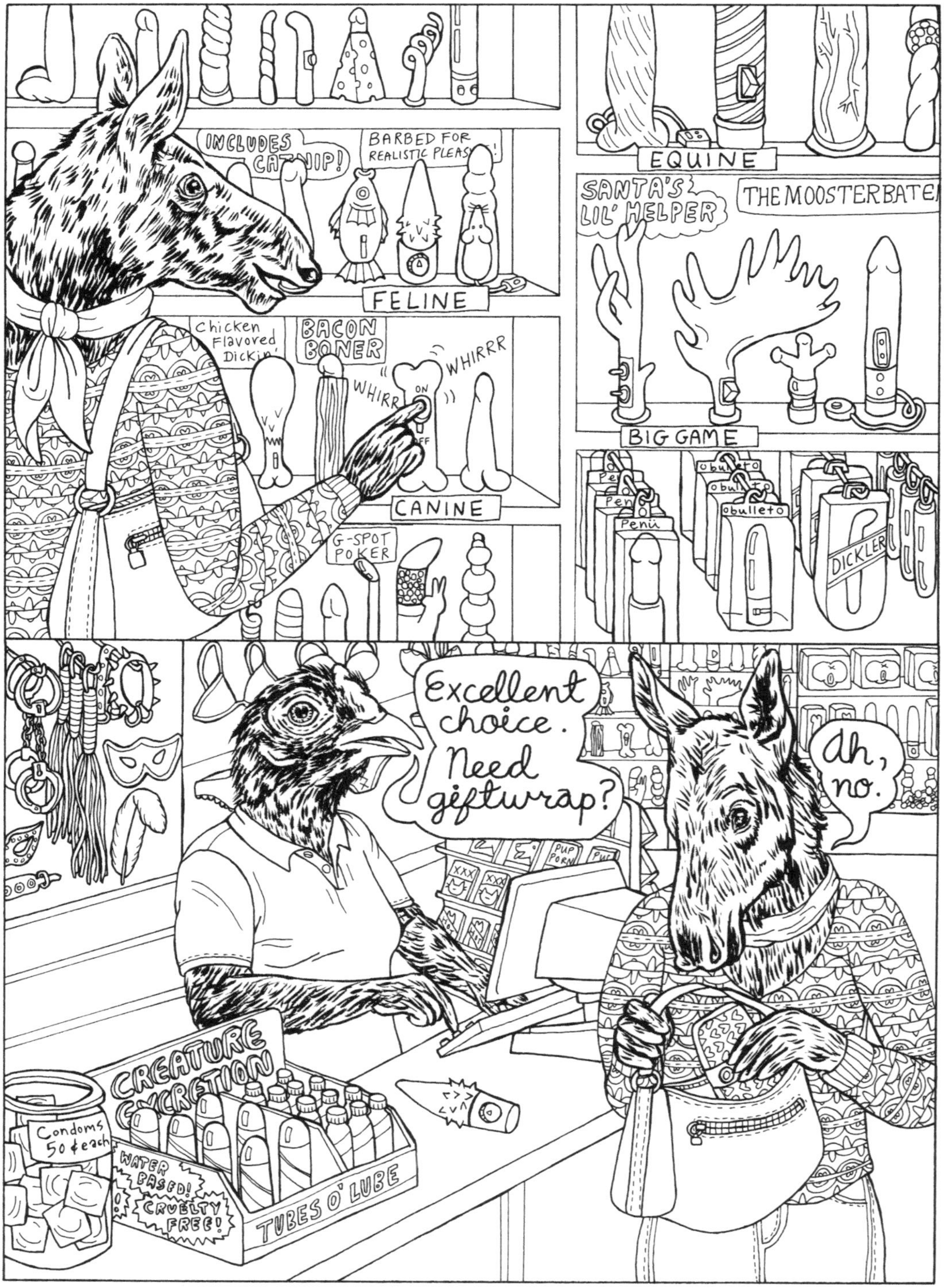

INCLUDES CATNIP!
BARBED FOR REALISTIC
FELINE
EQUINE
SANTA'S LIL' HELPER
THE MOOSTERBATE
BIG GAME
Chicken Flavored Dickin'
BACON BONER
WHIRRR
ON
WHIRR
OFF
CANINE
G-SPOT POKER
Penü
bullet
DICKLER
Excellent choice. Need giftwrap?
Ah, no.
PUP PORN
XXX
CREATURE EXCRETION
Condoms 50¢ each
WATER BASED! CRUELTY FREE!
TUBES O' LUBE

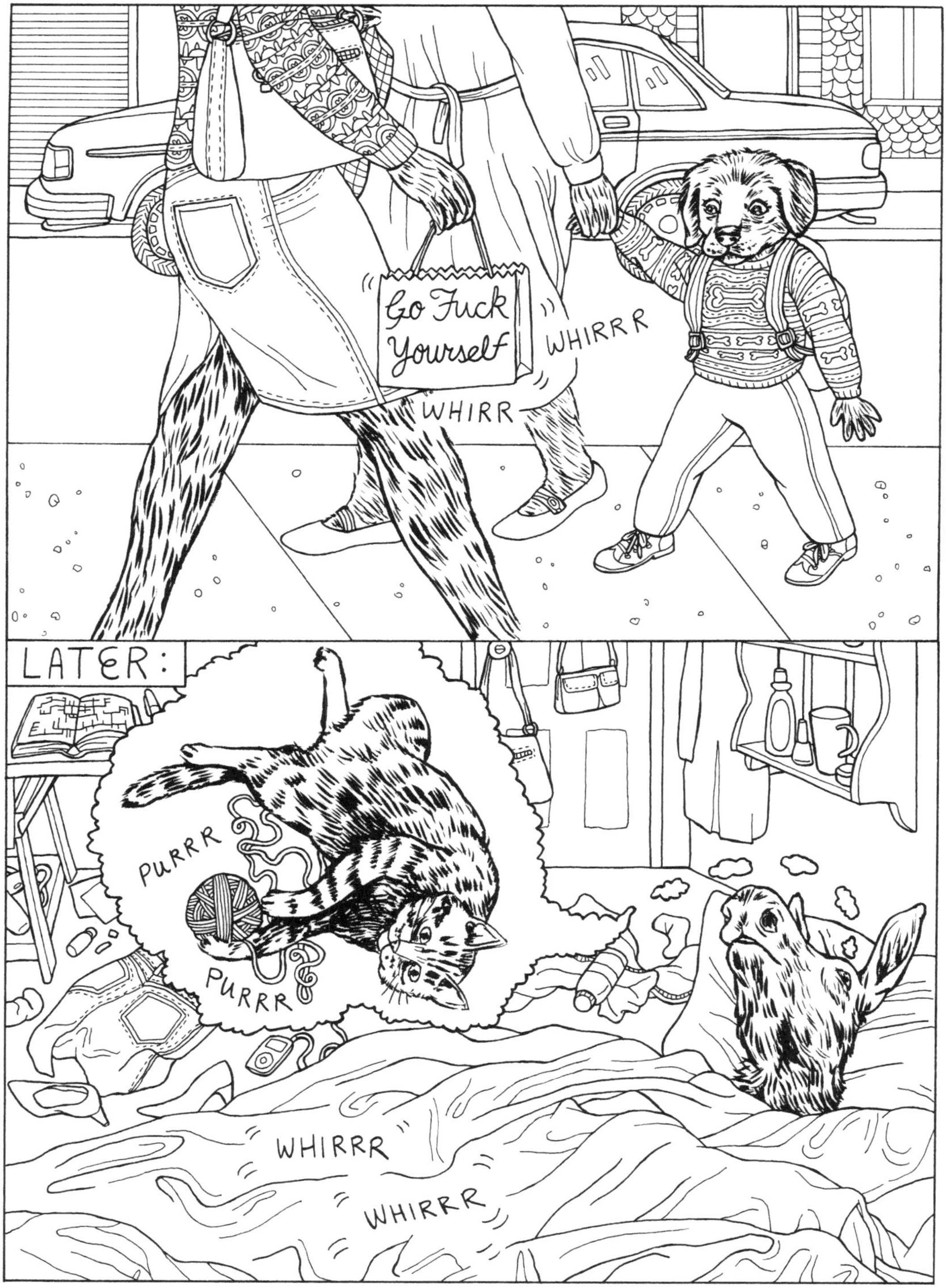
Go Fuck Yourself
WHIRRR
WHIRR
LATER:
PURRR
PURRRR
WHIRRR
WHIRRR

A TYPICAL WEEK

MONDAY : ON THE WAY TO WORK, MY FOOT STARTED ITCHING SO BADLY I THOUGHT I MIGHT HAVE TO CRASH (AND SCRATCH THE ITCH WITH BURNING DEBRIS).

cooked chick'n bones

TUESDAY : INDY ATE A COOKED CHICKEN AND HAD TO GO TO THE ANIMAL HOSPITAL.

WEDNESDAY : OUR NEIGHBOR AT WORK GAVE ME SOME FRUIT. HIS GIFT DID NOT SEEM INNOCENT.

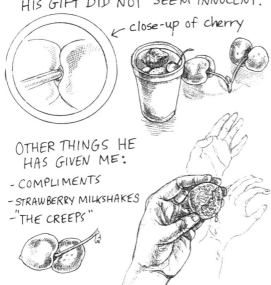

← close-up of cherry

OTHER THINGS HE HAS GIVEN ME:
- COMPLIMENTS
- STRAWBERRY MILKSHAKES
- "THE CREEPS"

THURSDAY : SUBMITTED A COMIC TO NICKELODEON KIDS MAGAZINE

Find the hidden Hamburgers!

FRIDAY: I WENT TO THE DENTIST AND THOUGHT ABOUT ORAL SEX SO I WOULD FEEL LESS NERVOUS.

Your teeth are going to ROT out of your slutty little mouth, you stupid fucking whore.

Don't Ferget to FLOSS!

SATURDAY: THOUGHT UP SOME INVENTIONS.

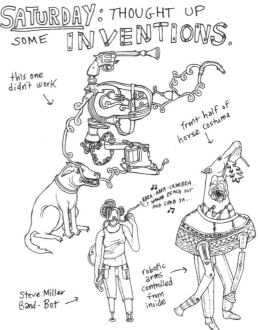

this one didn't work

front half of horse costume

♪ CABRA-ABRA-CADABRA... CABRA REACH OUT I WANNA REACH OUT AND GRAB YA... ♪

Steve Miller Band-Bot →

robotic arms controlled from inside

SUNDAY: BOUGHT OVERALL SHORTS FOR $1.00 AND THE TAG CALLED THEM "TEEN BIBS"

Also, I just realized all of the buttons have "NO" engraved into them.

TEEN BIBS

NEXT MONDAY: MOM SENT ME AN EMAIL TITLED "*Amazing Slideshow of*

Eagles Fishing!" THAT DID NOT DISAPPOINT.

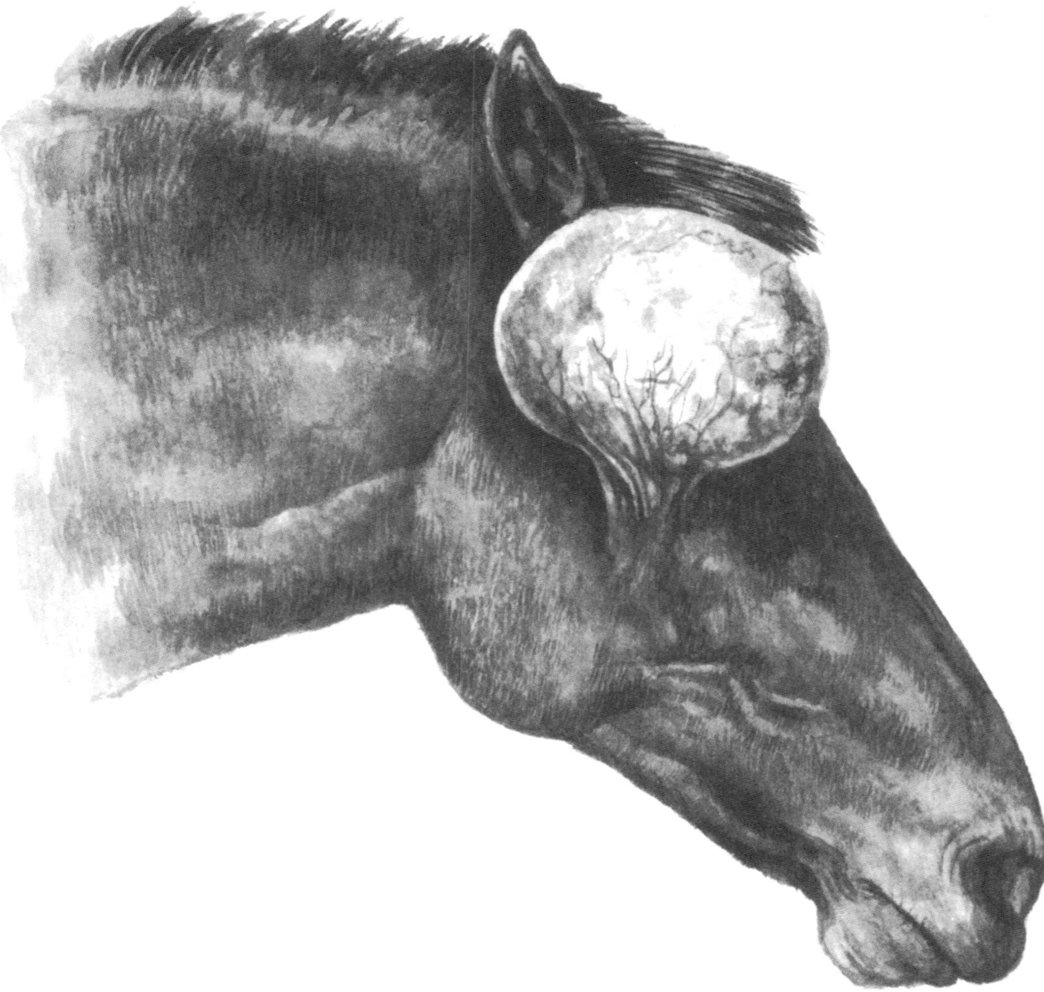

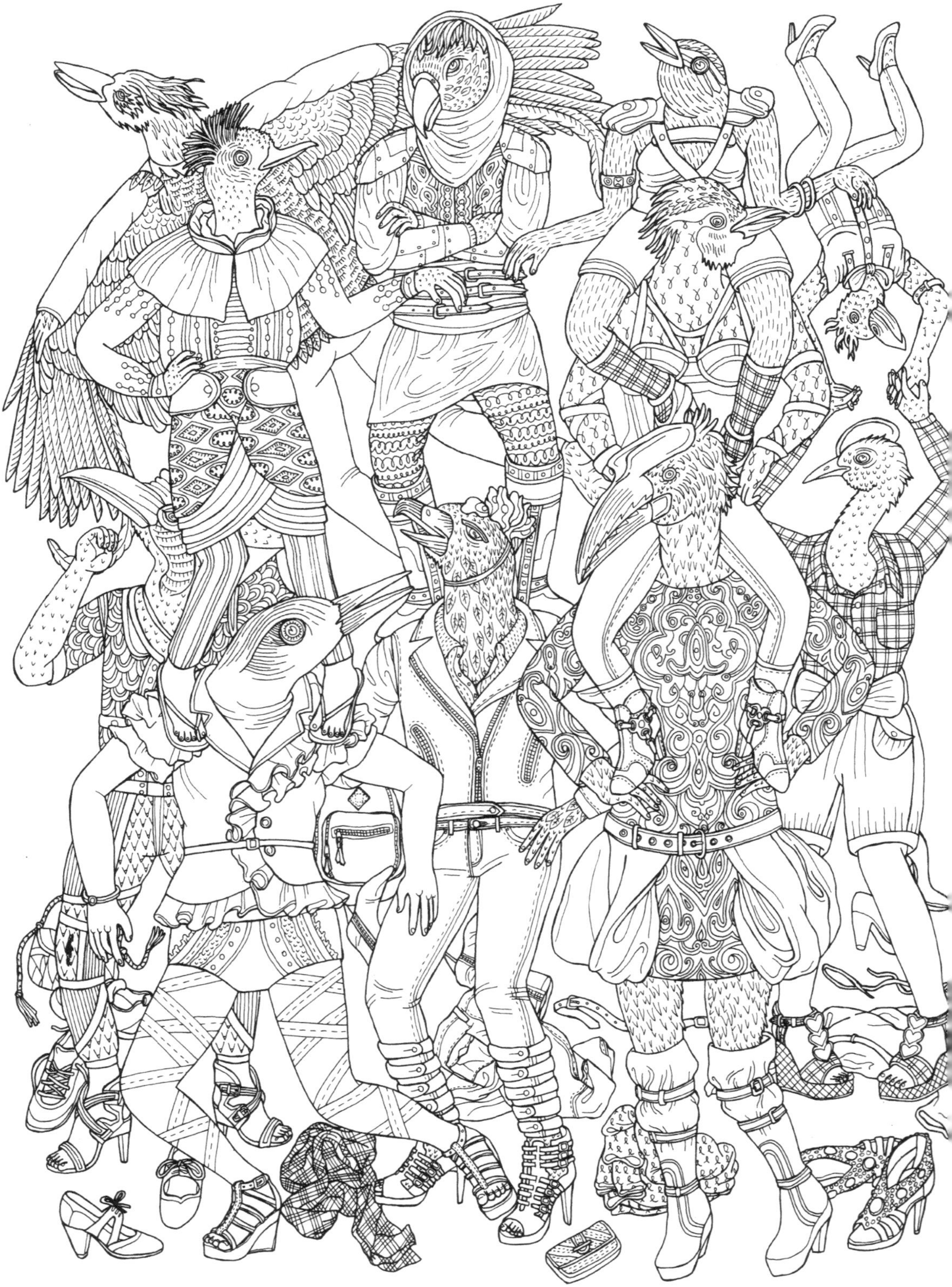

NORTH AMERICAN WILDLIFE AND HATS

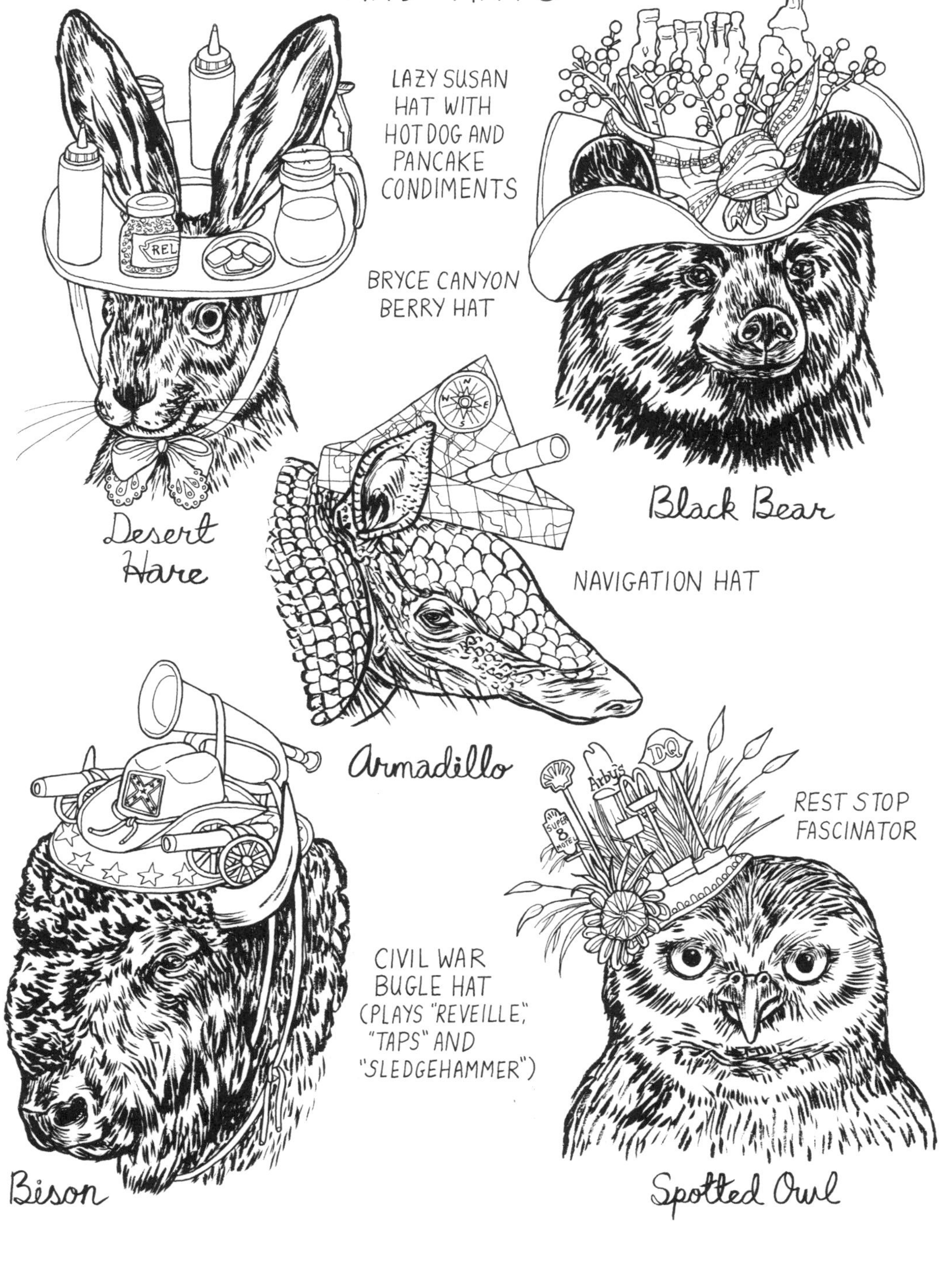

LAZY SUSAN HAT WITH HOT DOG AND PANCAKE CONDIMENTS
Desert Hare
BRYCE CANYON BERRY HAT
Black Bear
NAVIGATION HAT
Armadillo
CIVIL WAR BUGLE HAT (PLAYS "REVEILLE," "TAPS" AND "SLEDGEHAMMER")
Bison
REST STOP FASCINATOR
Spotted Owl

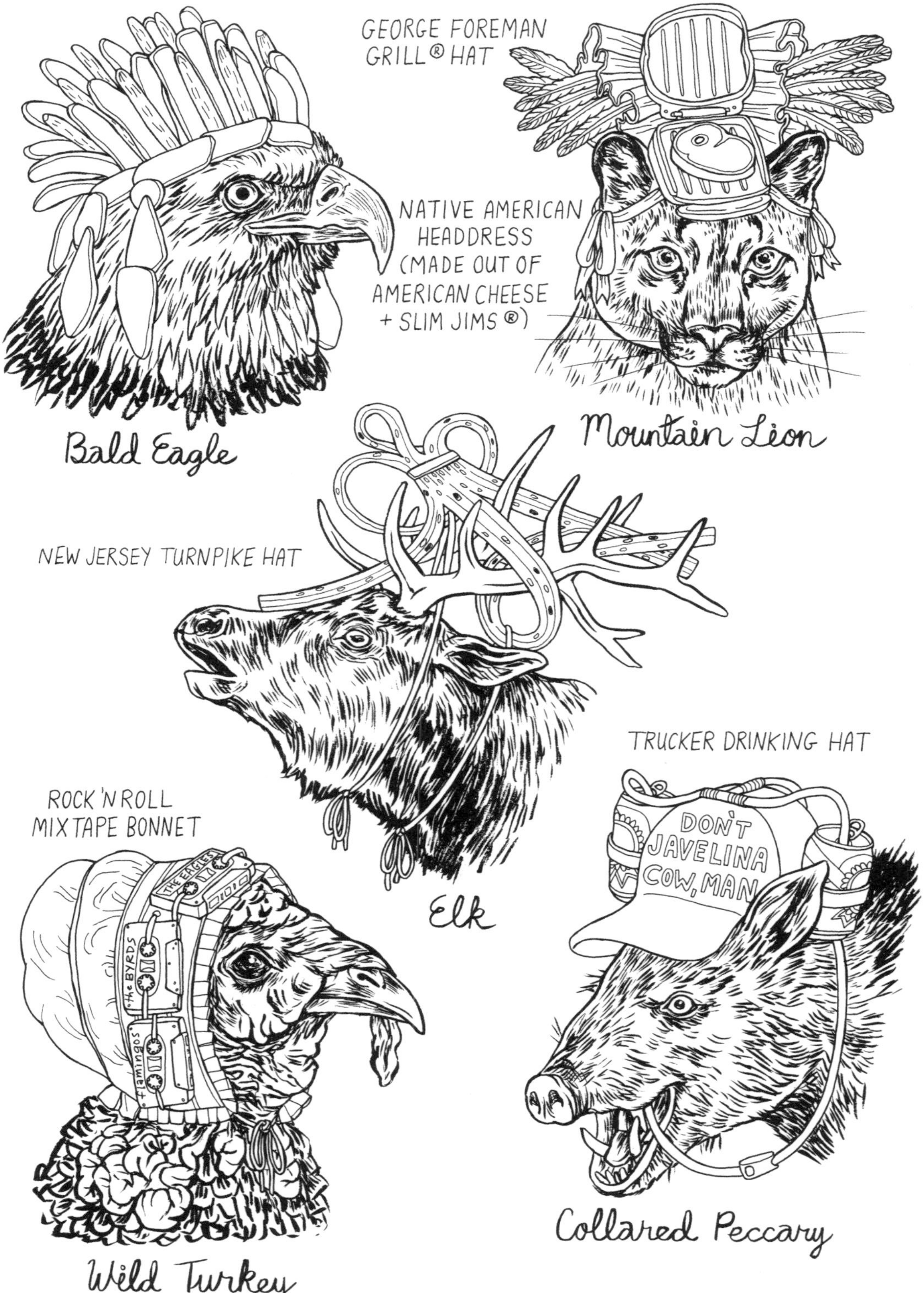

GEORGE FOREMAN GRILL® HAT
NATIVE AMERICAN HEADDRESS (MADE OUT OF AMERICAN CHEESE + SLIM JIMS ®)
Bald Eagle
Mountain Lion
NEW JERSEY TURNPIKE HAT
Elk
TRUCKER DRINKING HAT
DON'T JAVELINA COW, MAN
ROCK 'N ROLL MIXTAPE BONNET
THE EAGLES
the BYRDS
Wild Turkey
Collared Peccary

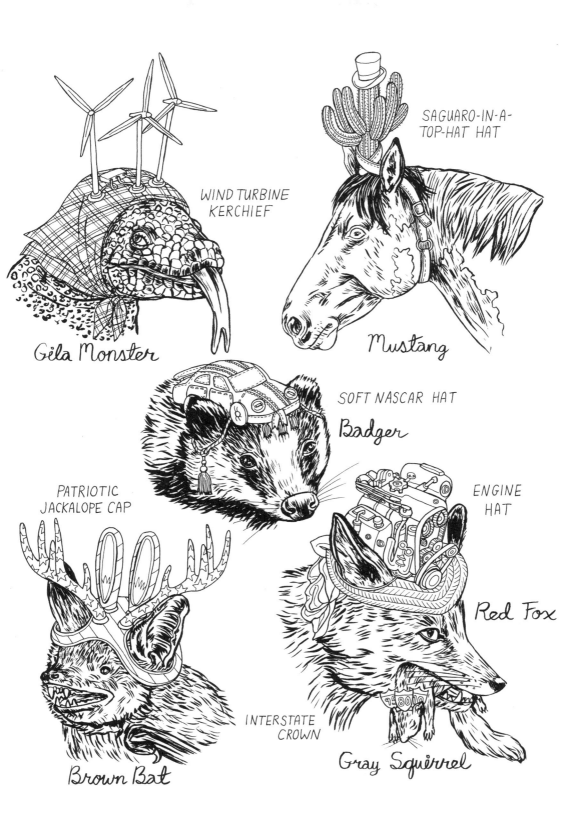

WIND TURBINE KERCHIEF

Gila Monster

SAGUARO-IN-A-TOP-HAT HAT

Mustang

SOFT NASCAR HAT

Badger

PATRIOTIC JACKALOPE CAP

ENGINE HAT

Red Fox

INTERSTATE CROWN

Brown Bat

Gray Squirrel

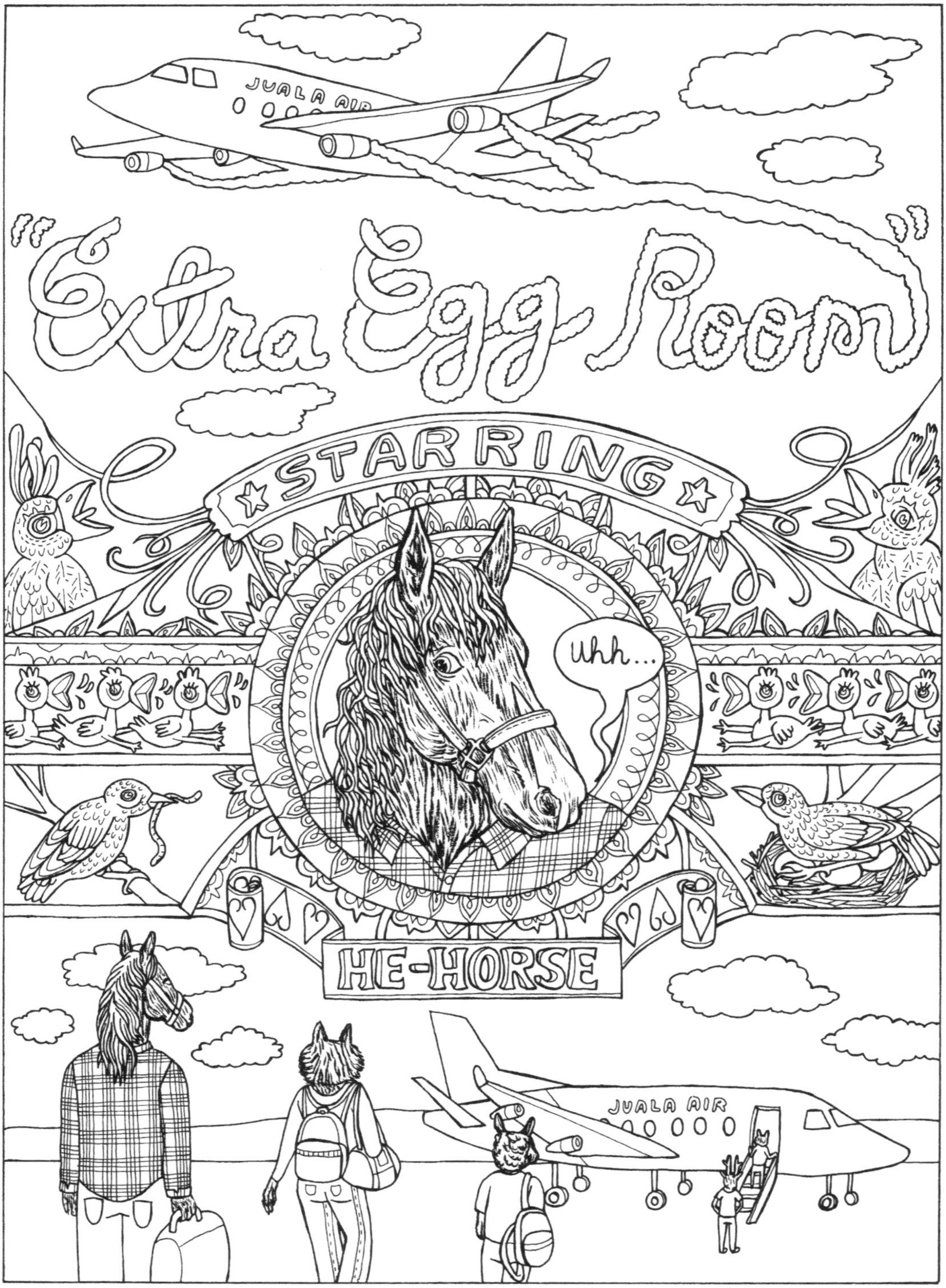
JUALA AIR
"Extra Egg Room"
STARRING
Uhh...
HE-HORSE
JUALA AIR

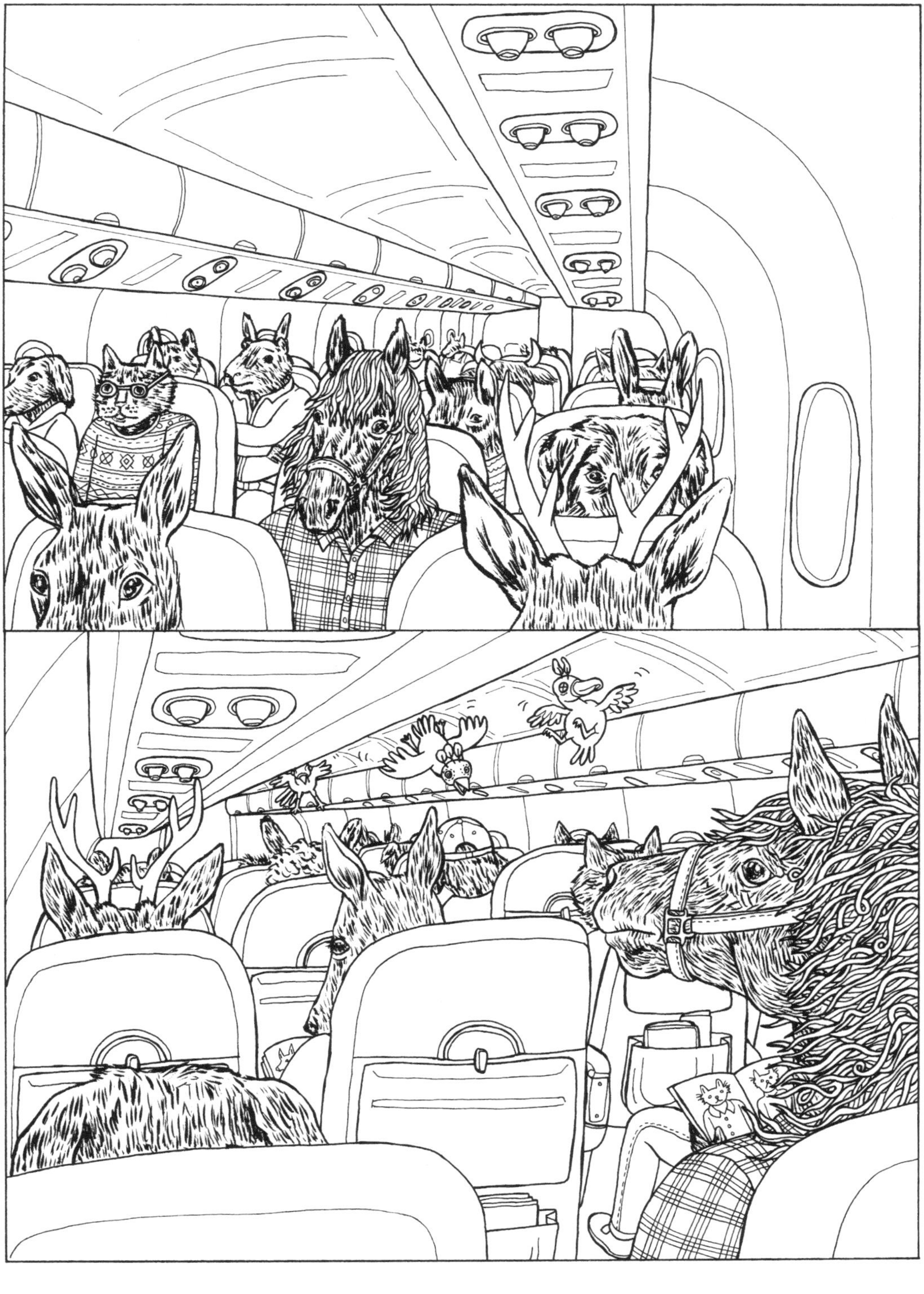

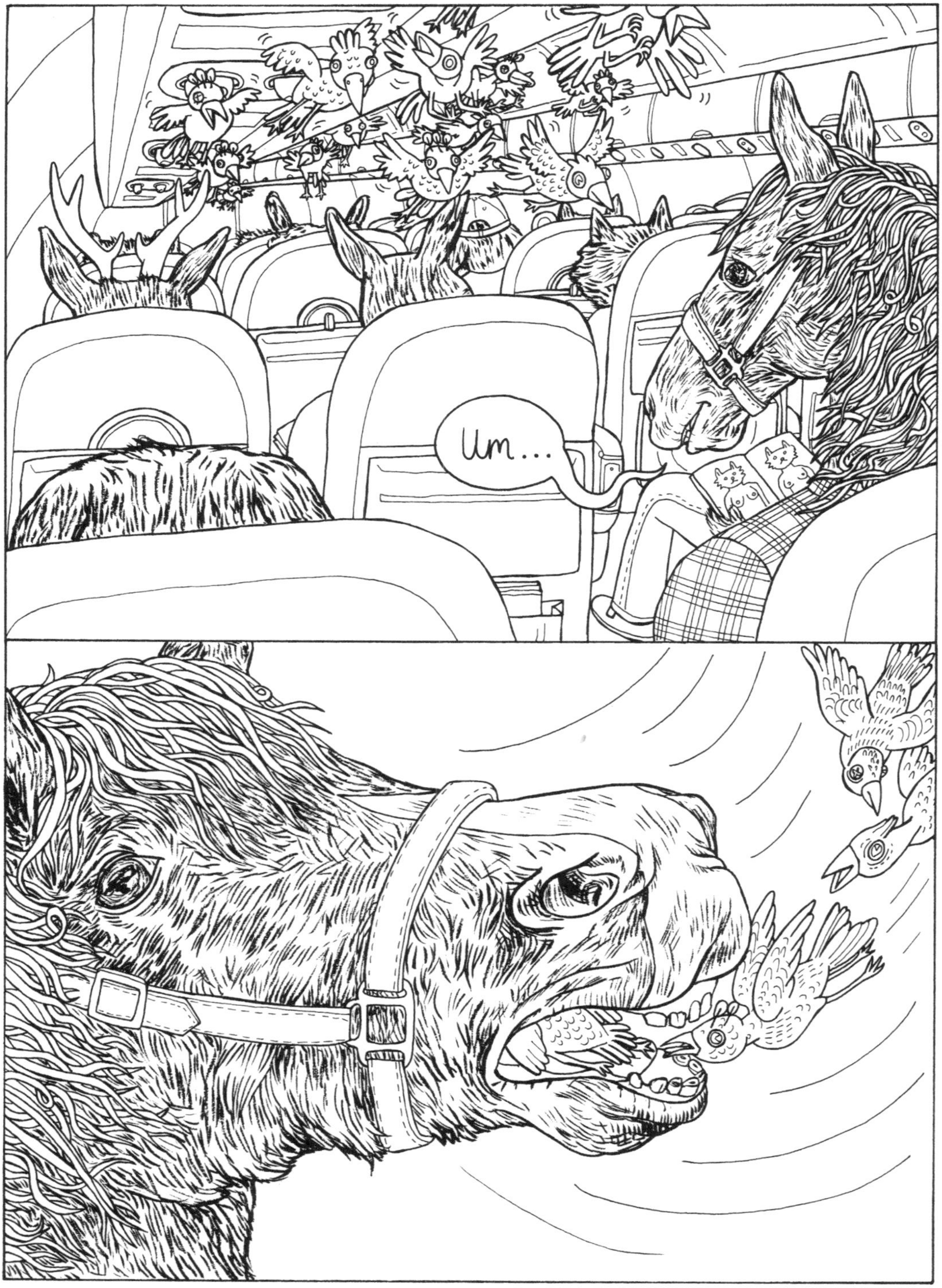
Um...

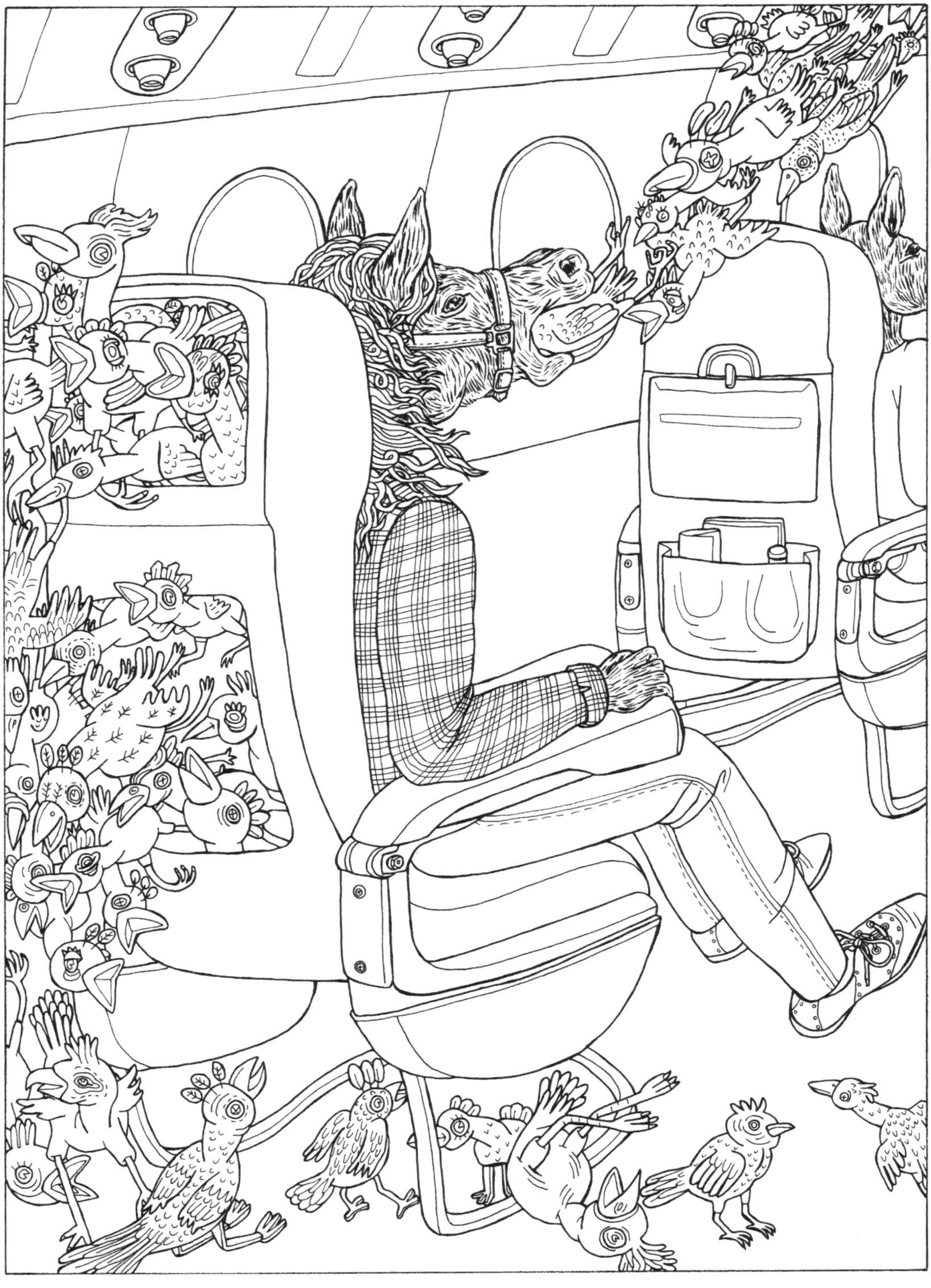

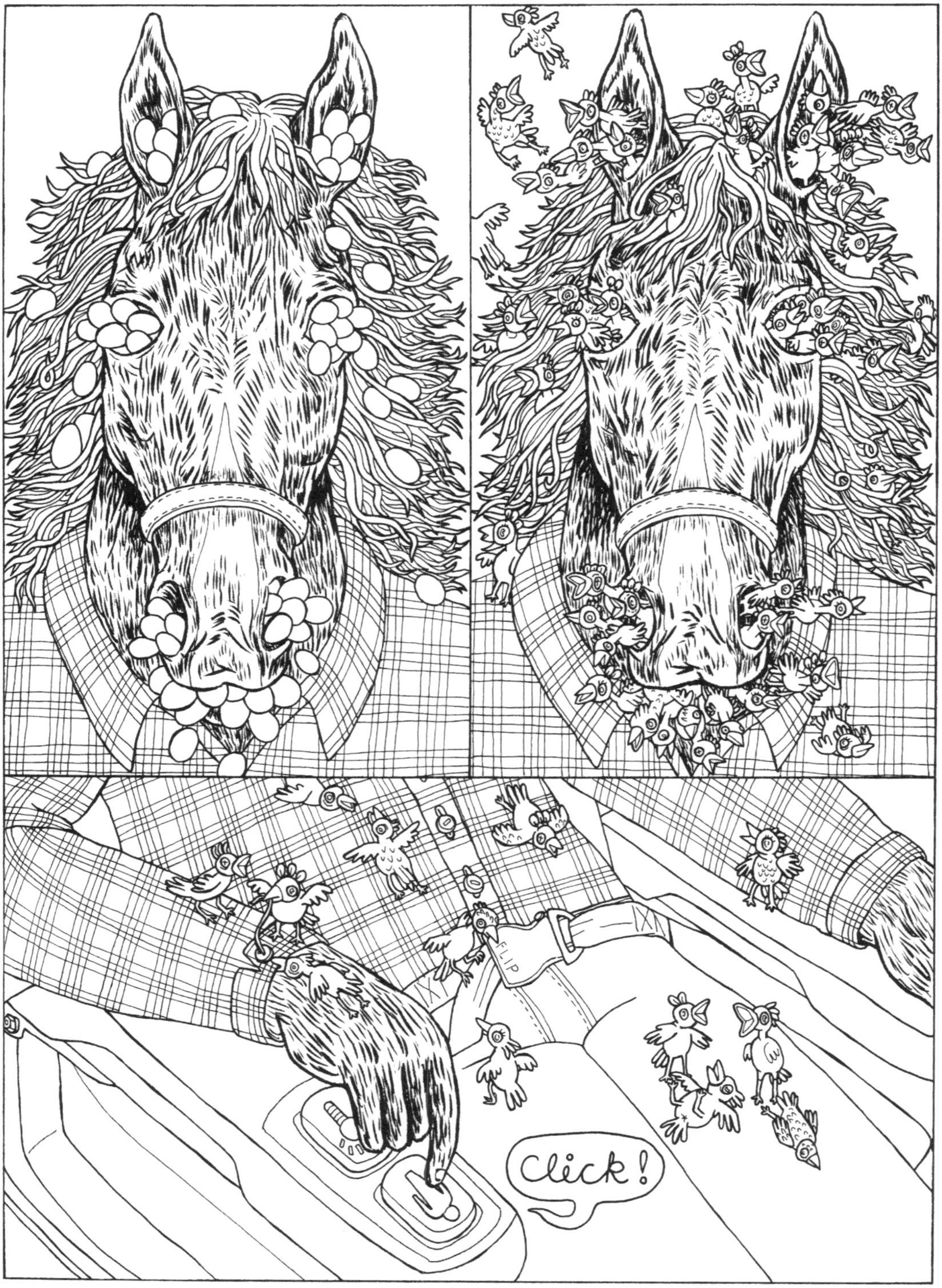
FLIP
Click!

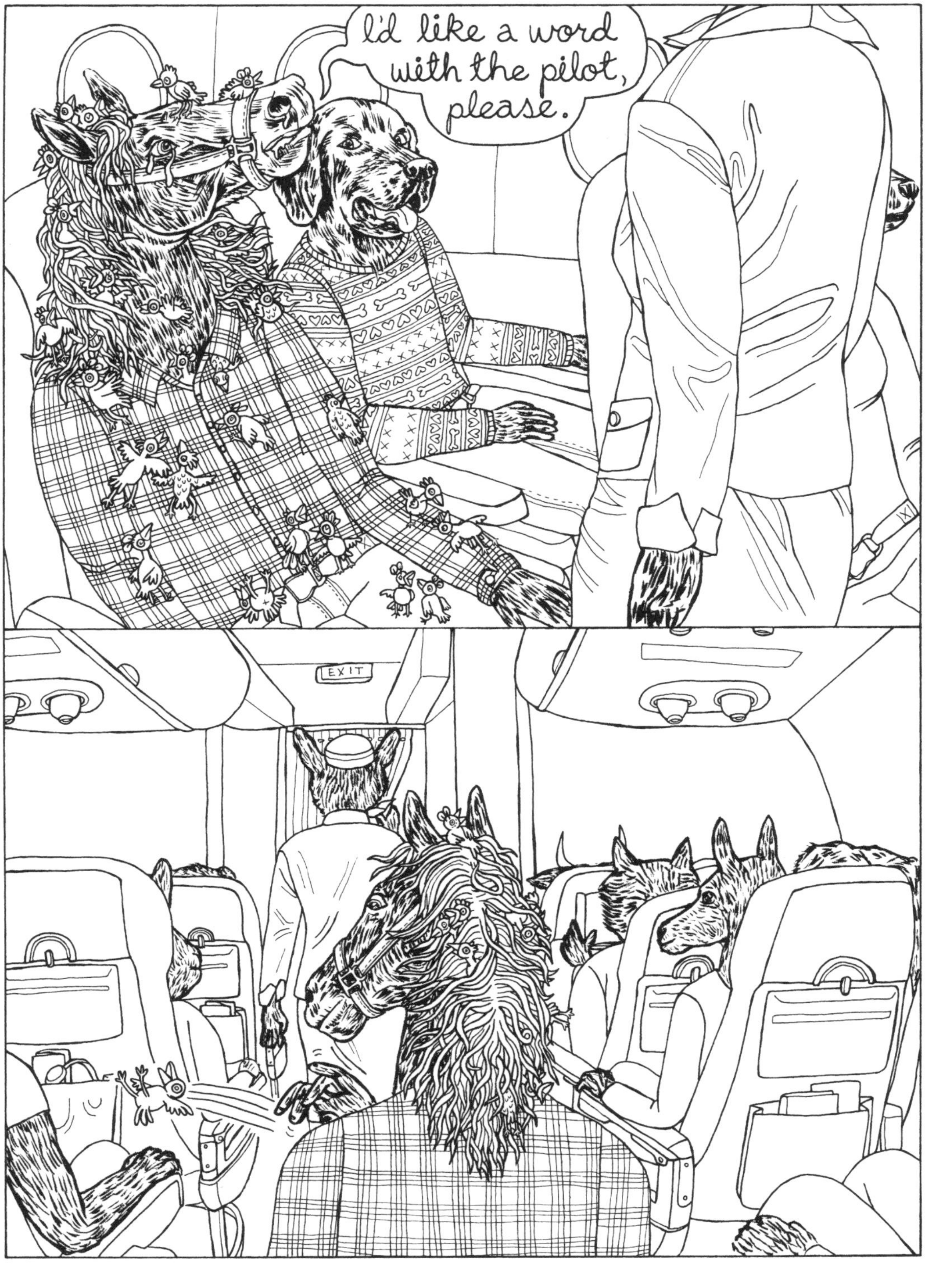
I'd like a word with the pilot, please.

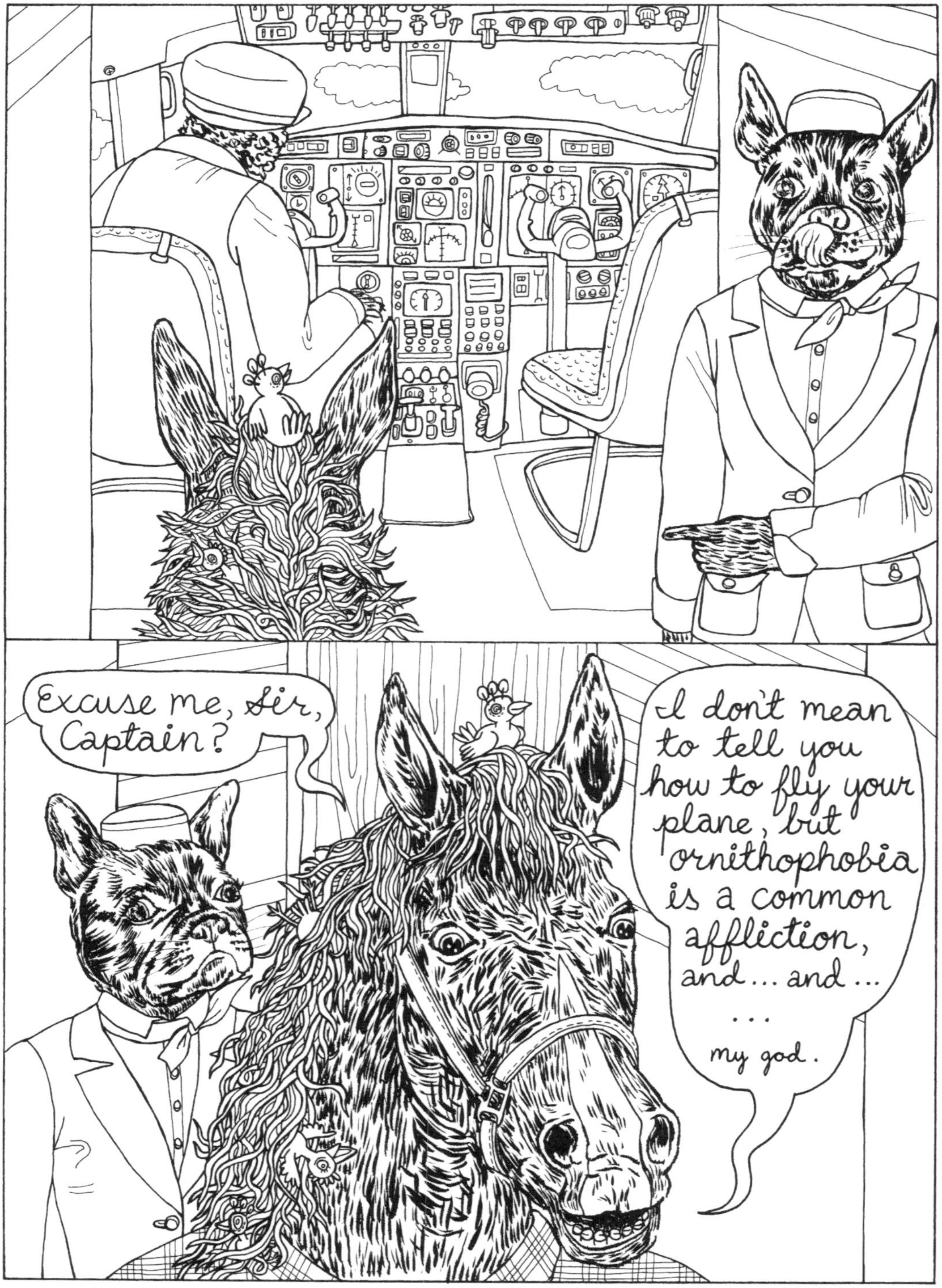
Excuse me, Sir, Captain?
I don't mean to tell you how to fly your plane, but ornithophobia is a common affliction, and... and... ... my god.

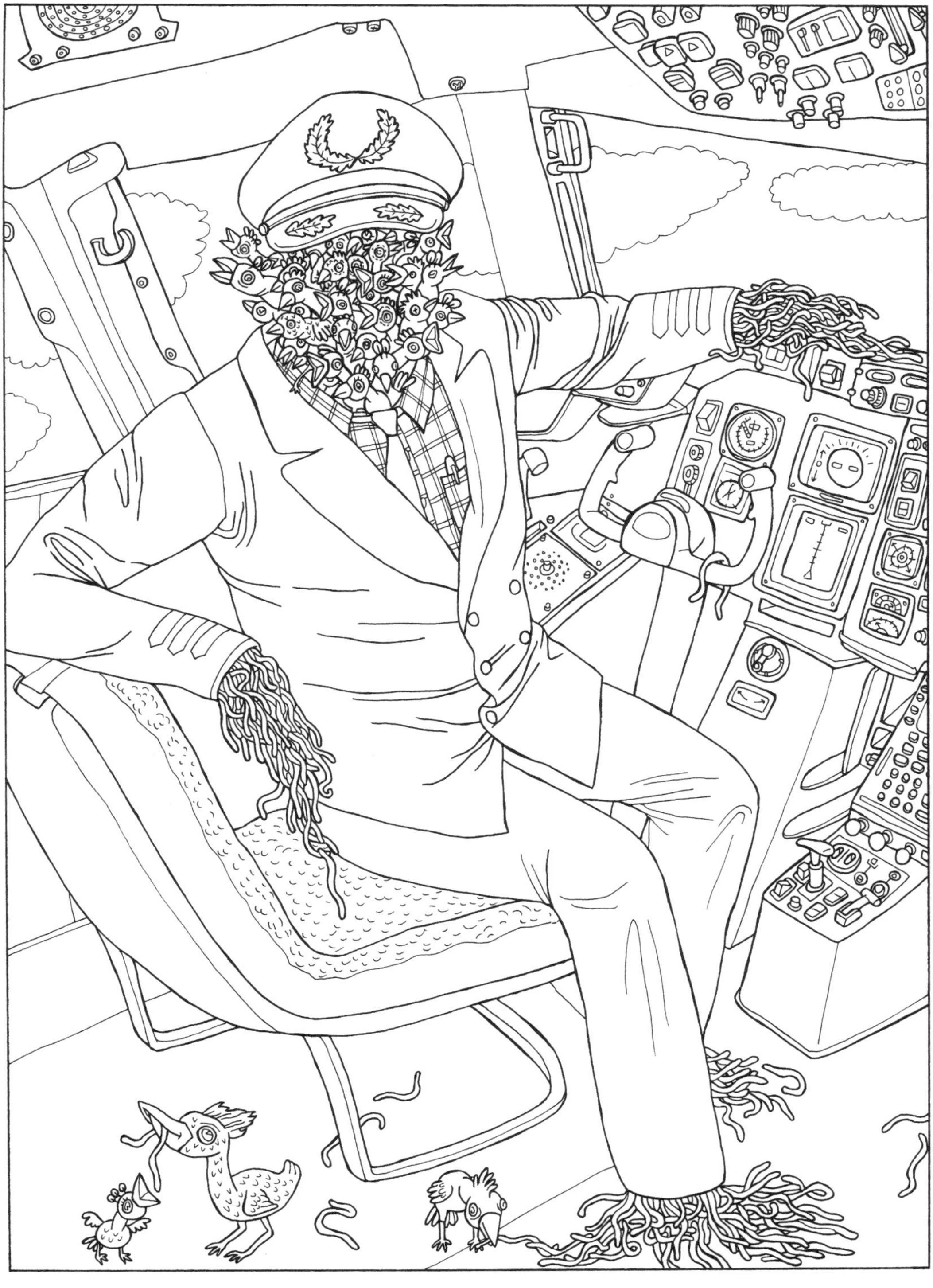

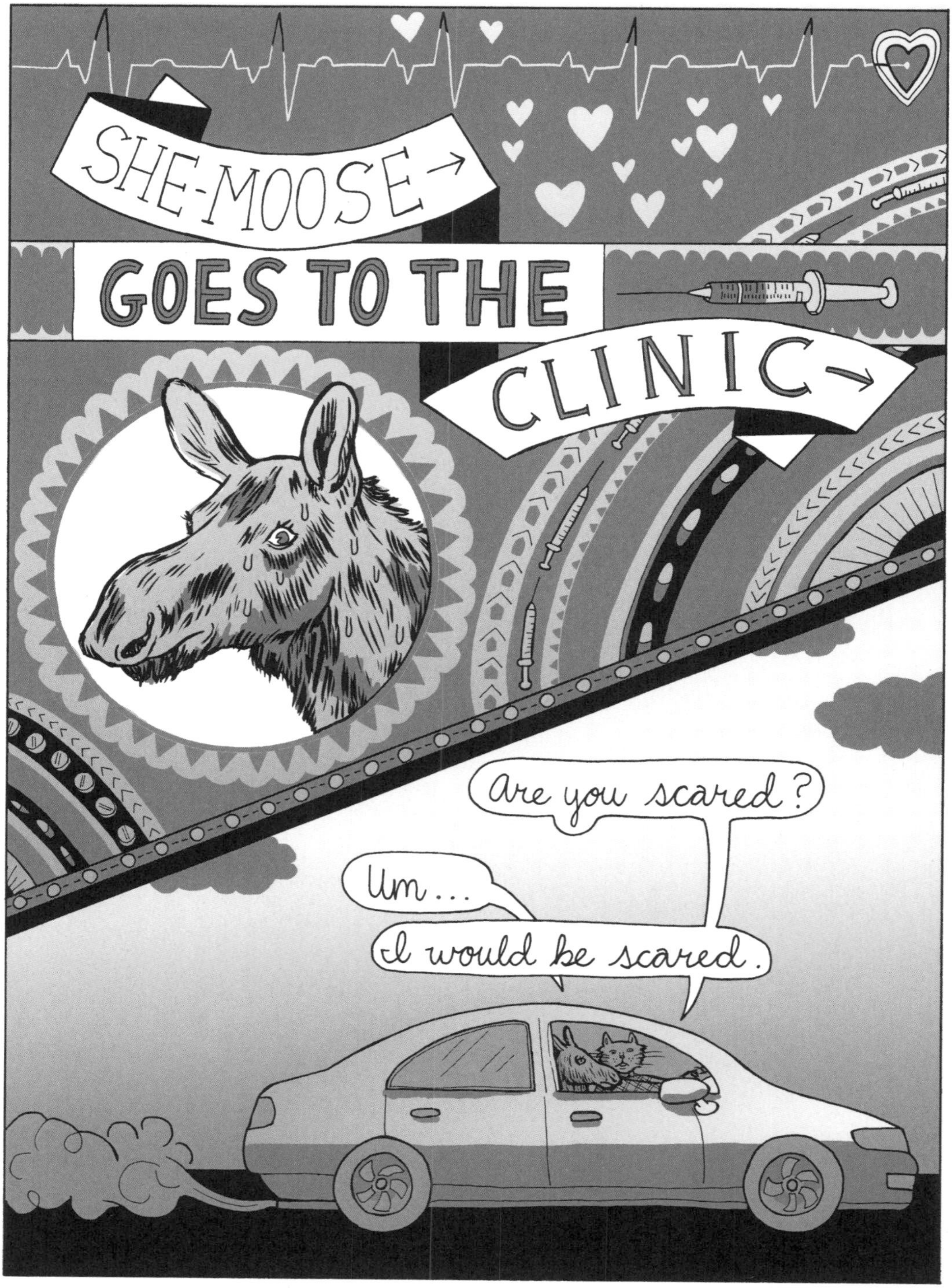
SHE-MOOSE
GOES TO THE
CLINIC
Are you scared?
Um...
I would be scared.

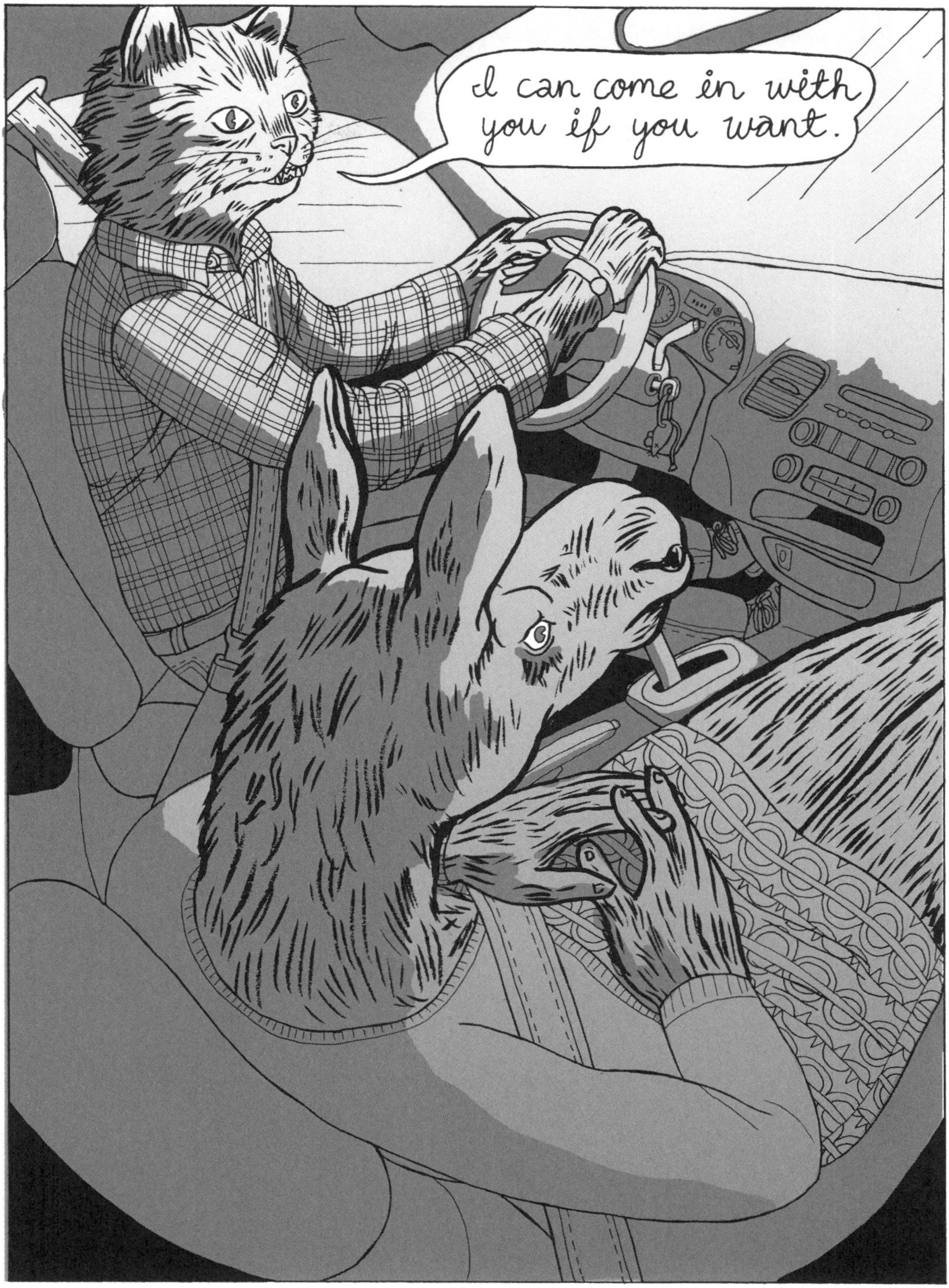
I can come in with you if you want.

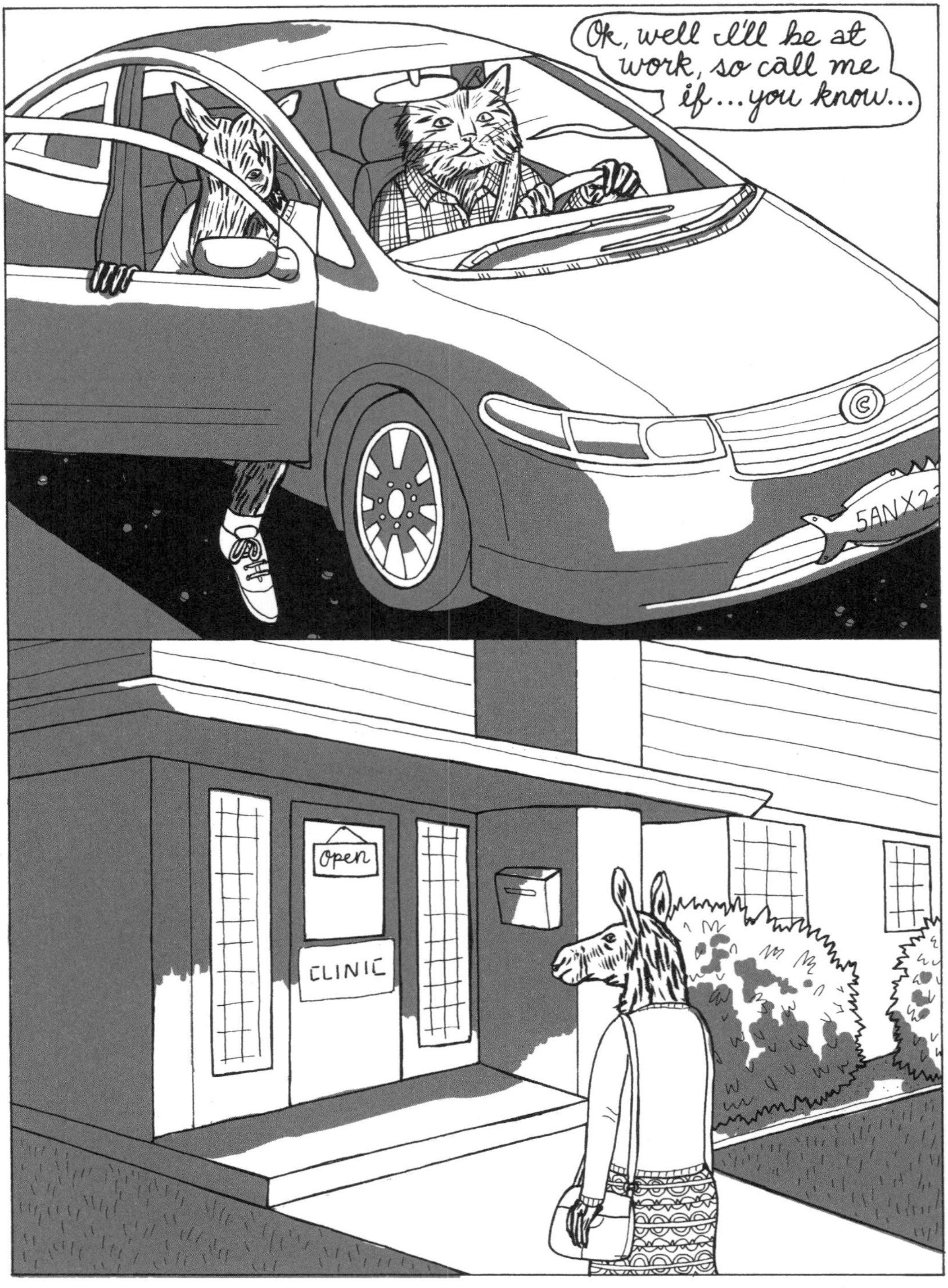
Ok, well I'll be at work, so call me if... you know...
5ANX23
Open
CLINIC

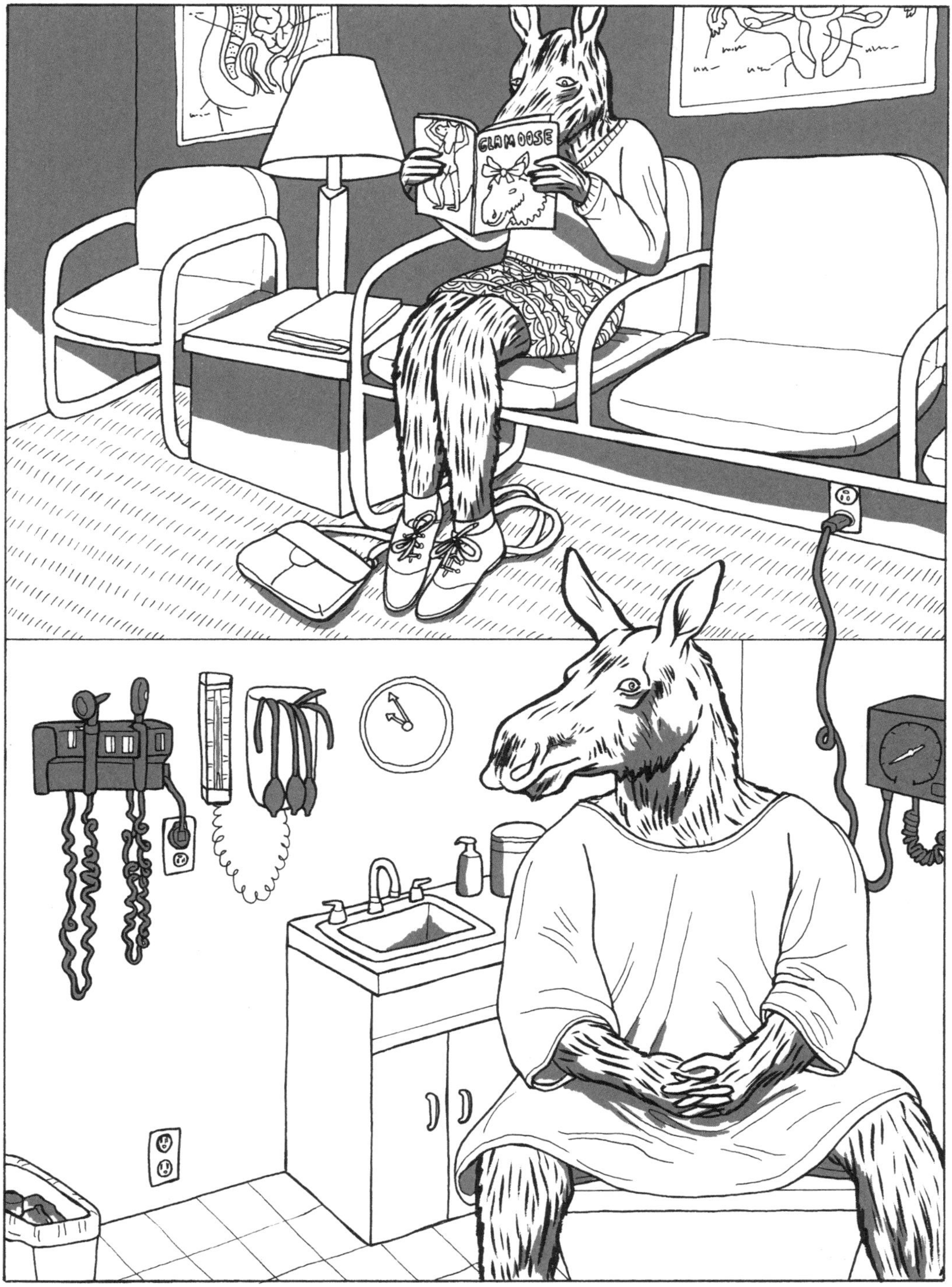
GLAMOOSE

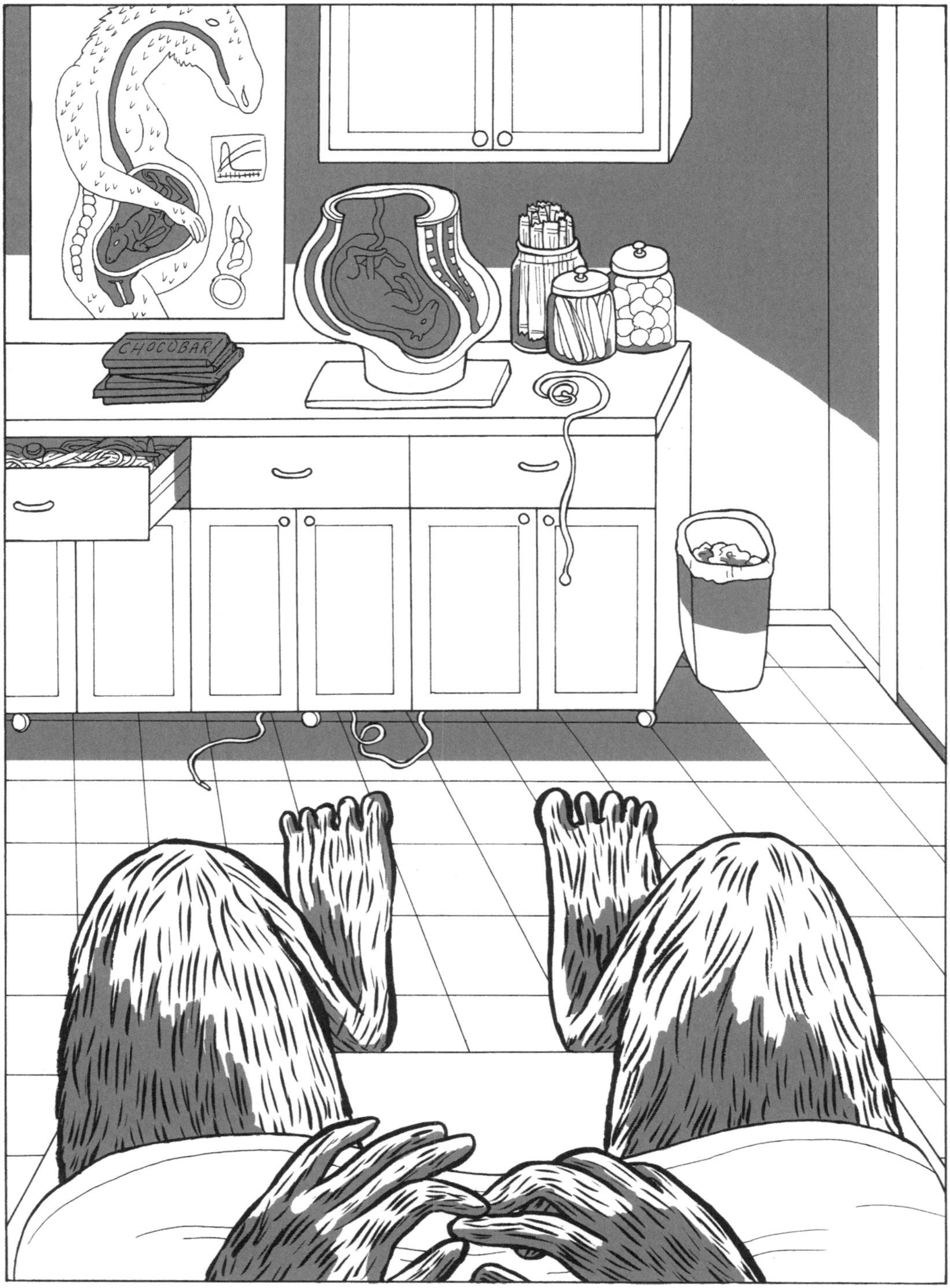
CHOCOBAR!

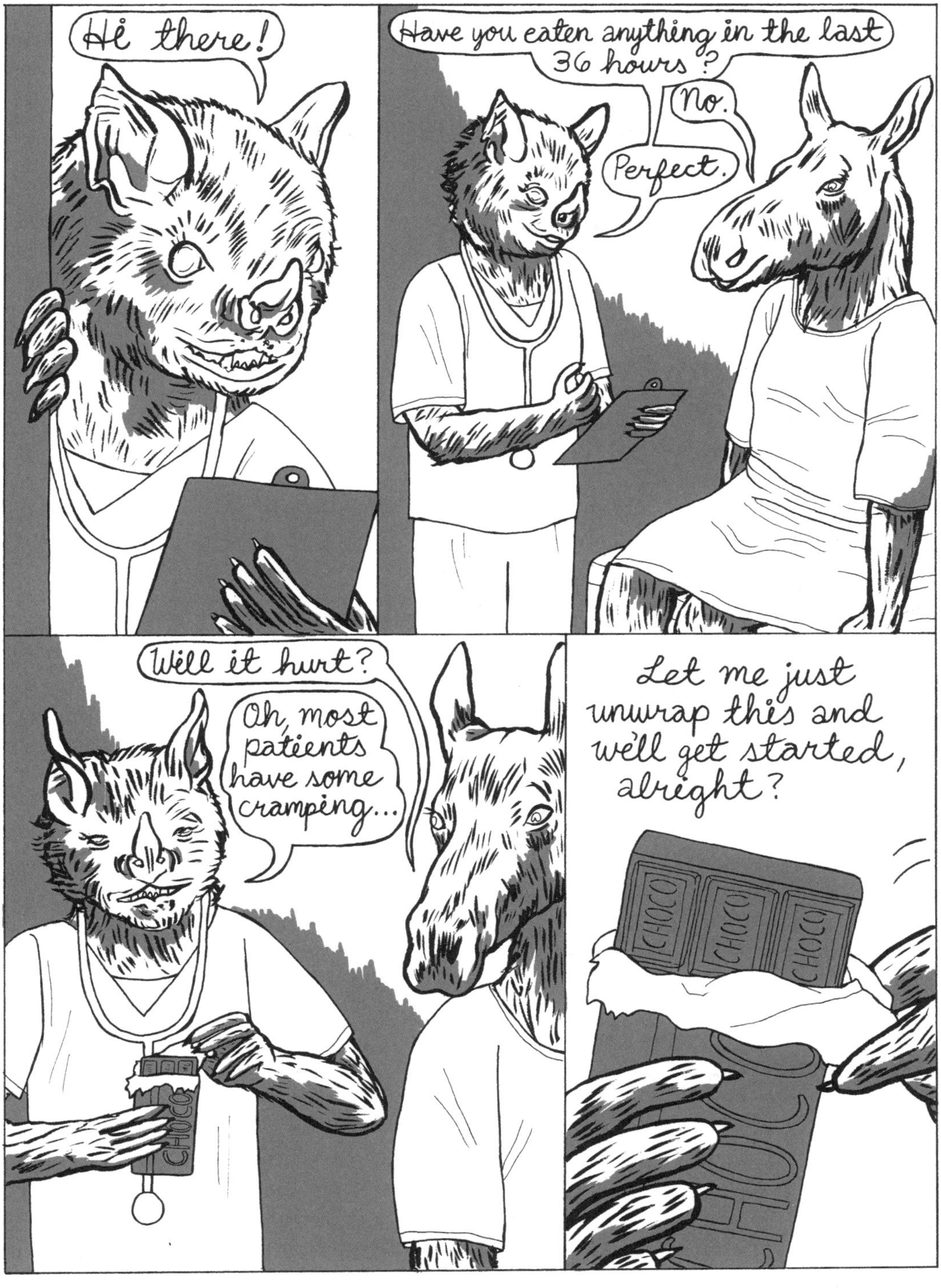
Hi there!
Have you eaten anything in the last 36 hours?
No.
Perfect.
Will it hurt?
Oh, most patients have some cramping...
CHOCO
Let me just unwrap this and we'll get started, alright?
CHOCO
CHOCO
CHOCO

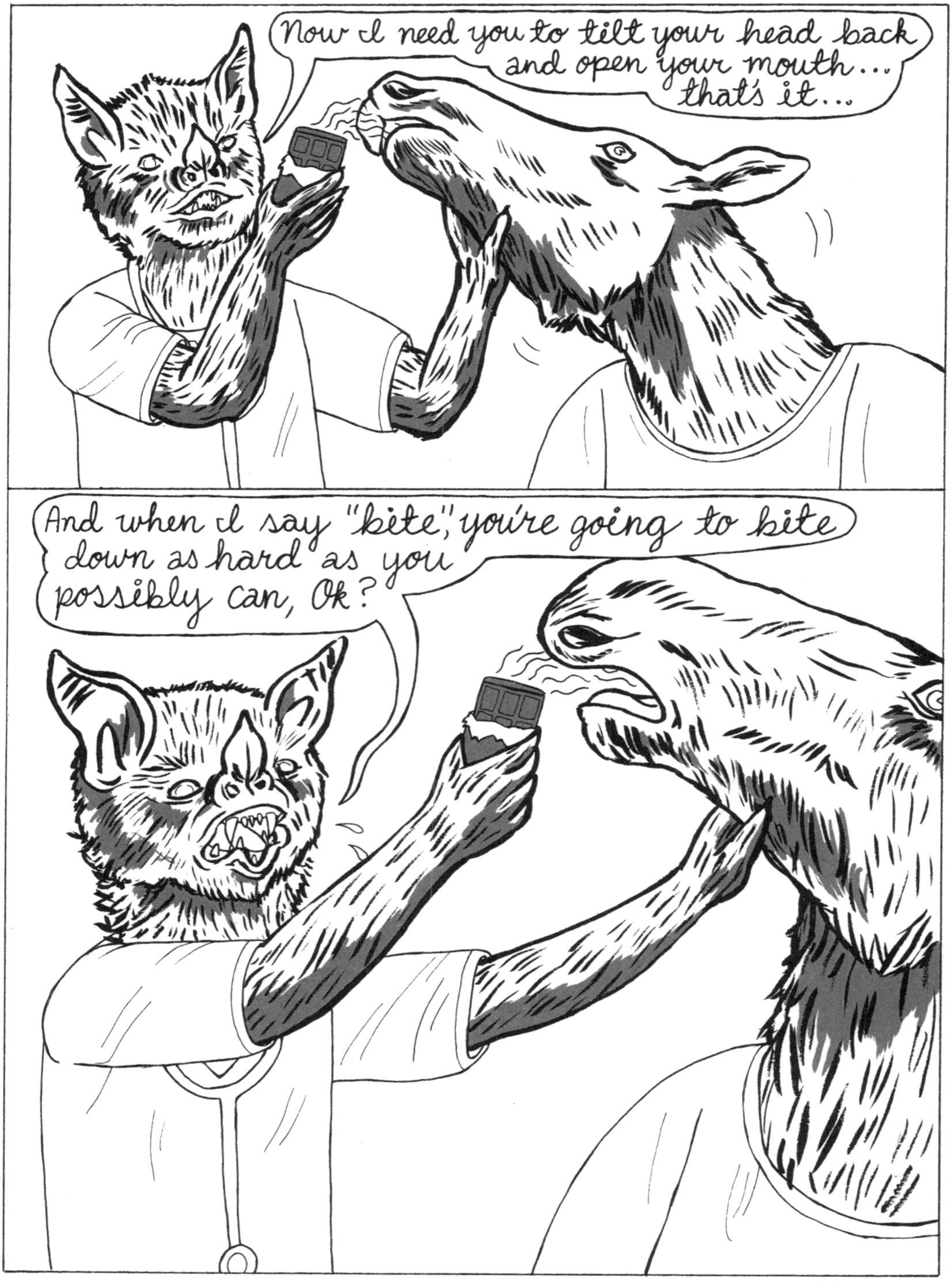
Now I need you to tilt your head back and open your mouth... that's it...
And when I say "bite," you're going to bite down as hard as you possibly can, Ok?

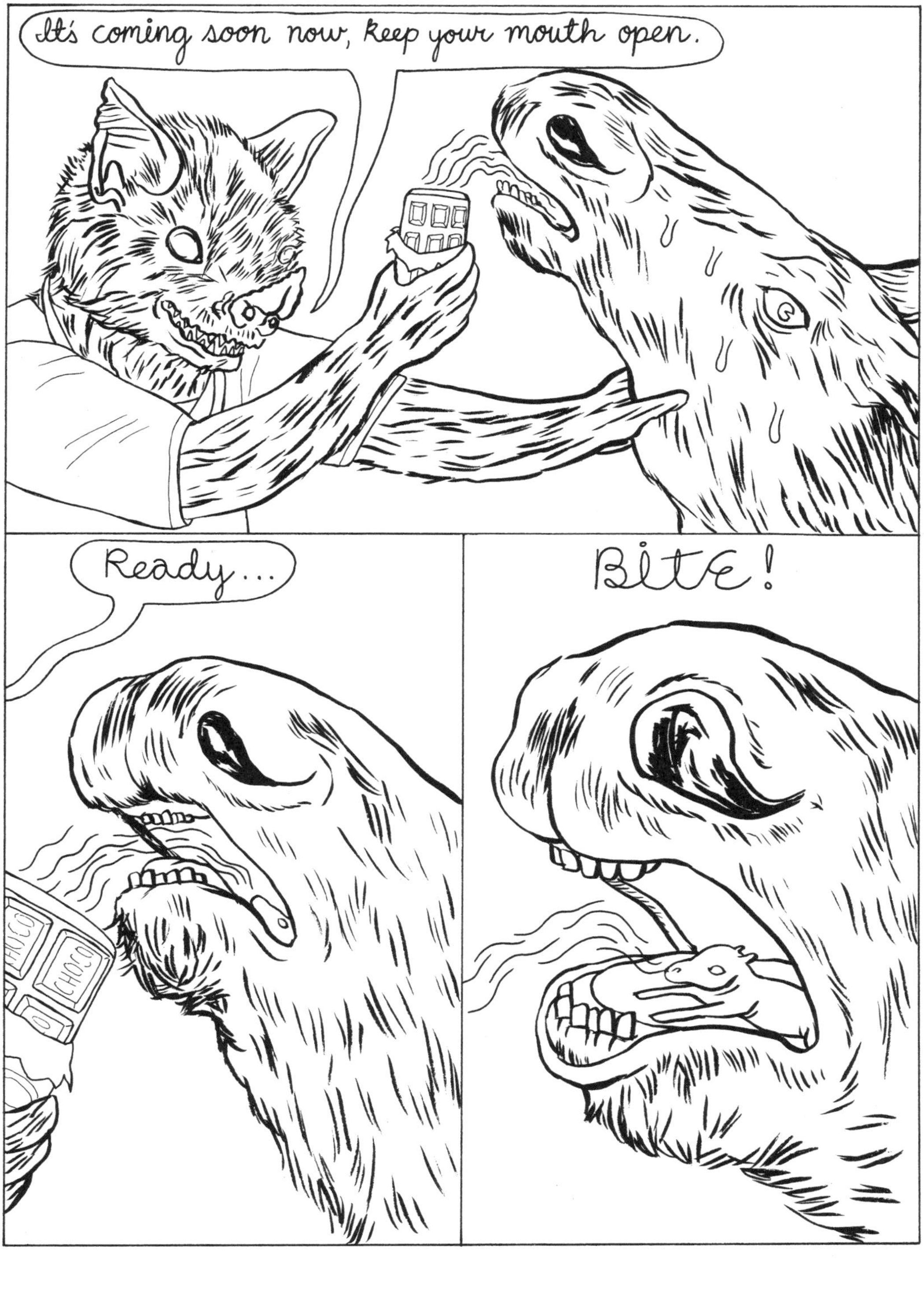
It's coming soon now, keep your mouth open.
Ready...
BITE!
CHOCO
CHOCO

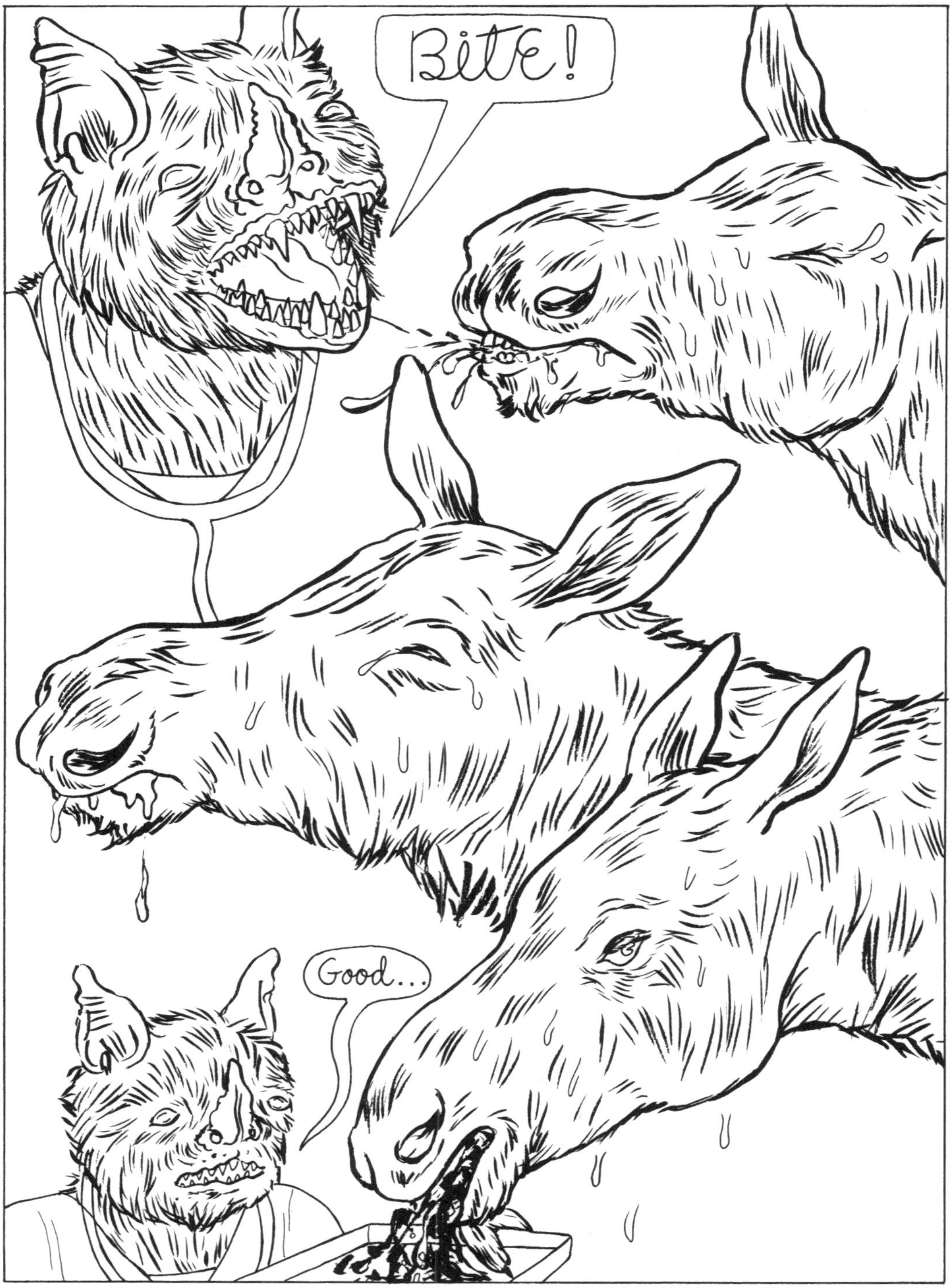
BITE!
Good...

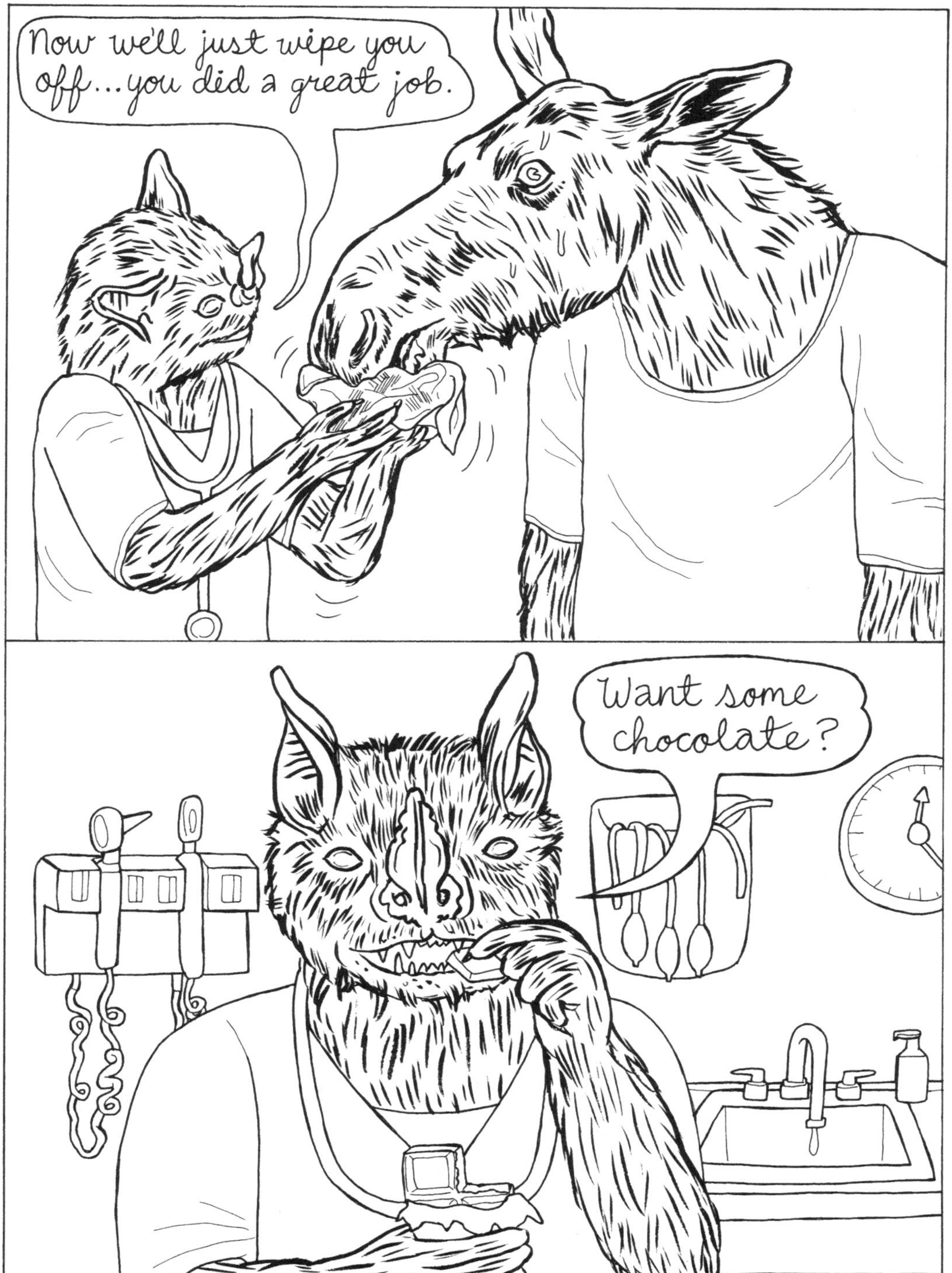
Now we'll just wipe you off... you did a great job.
Want some chocolate?

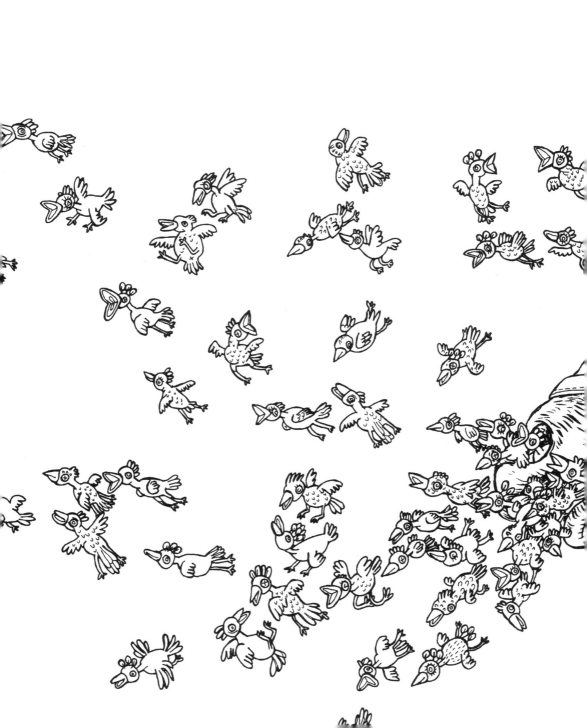

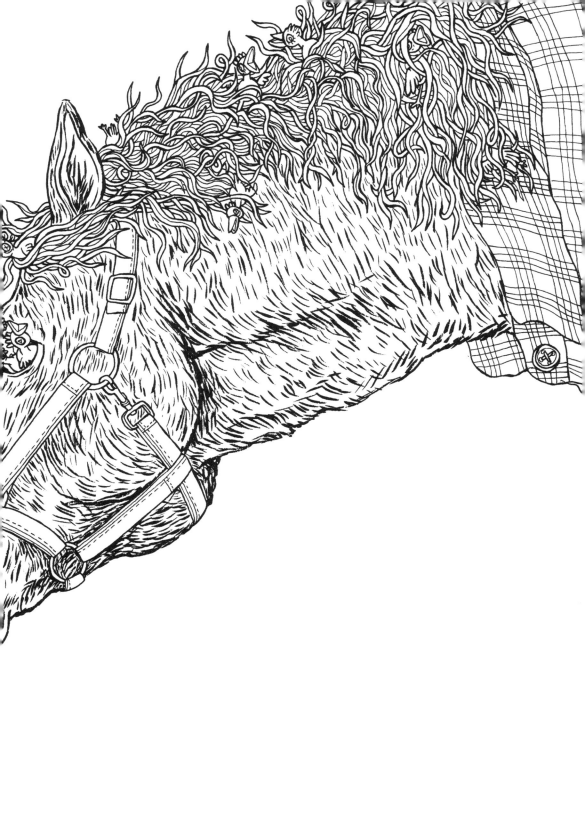

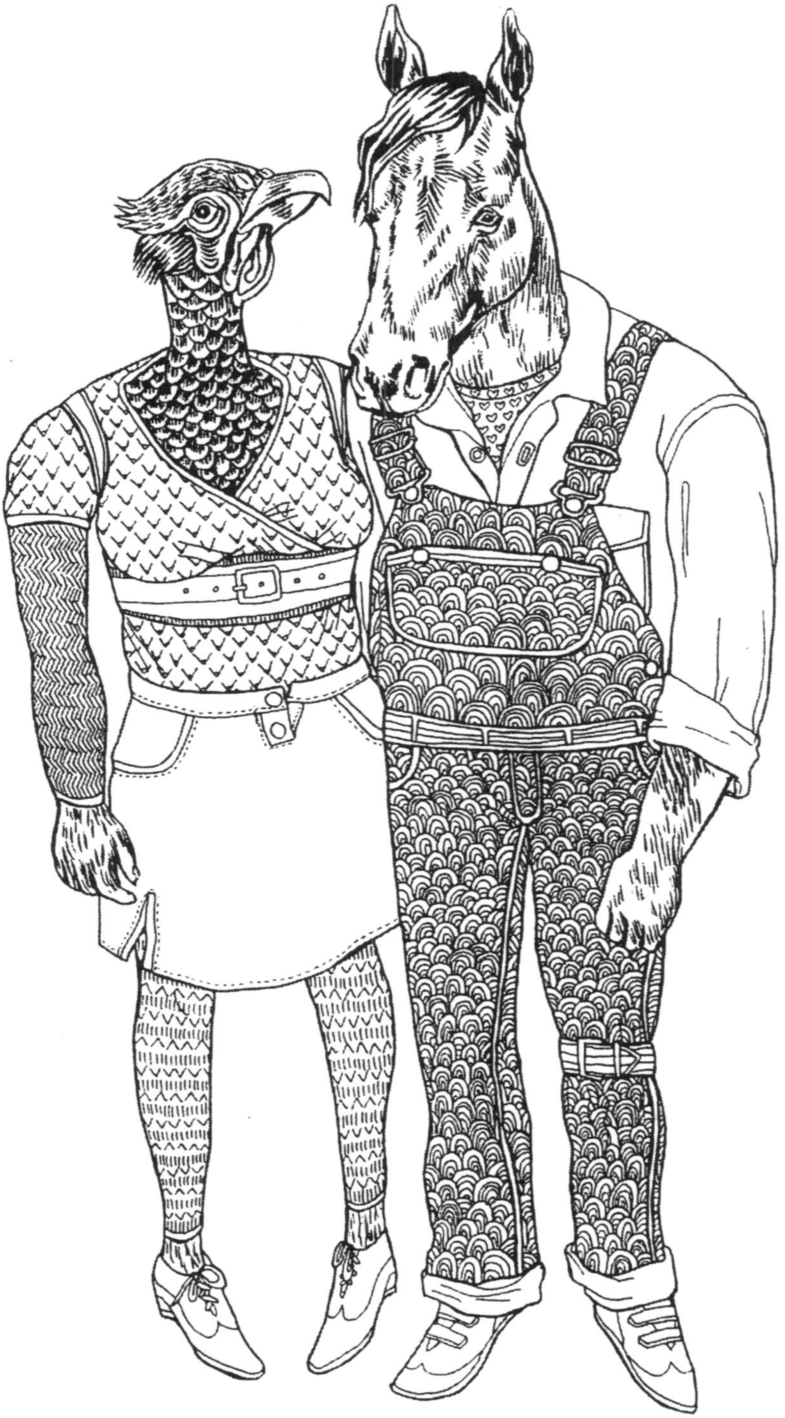

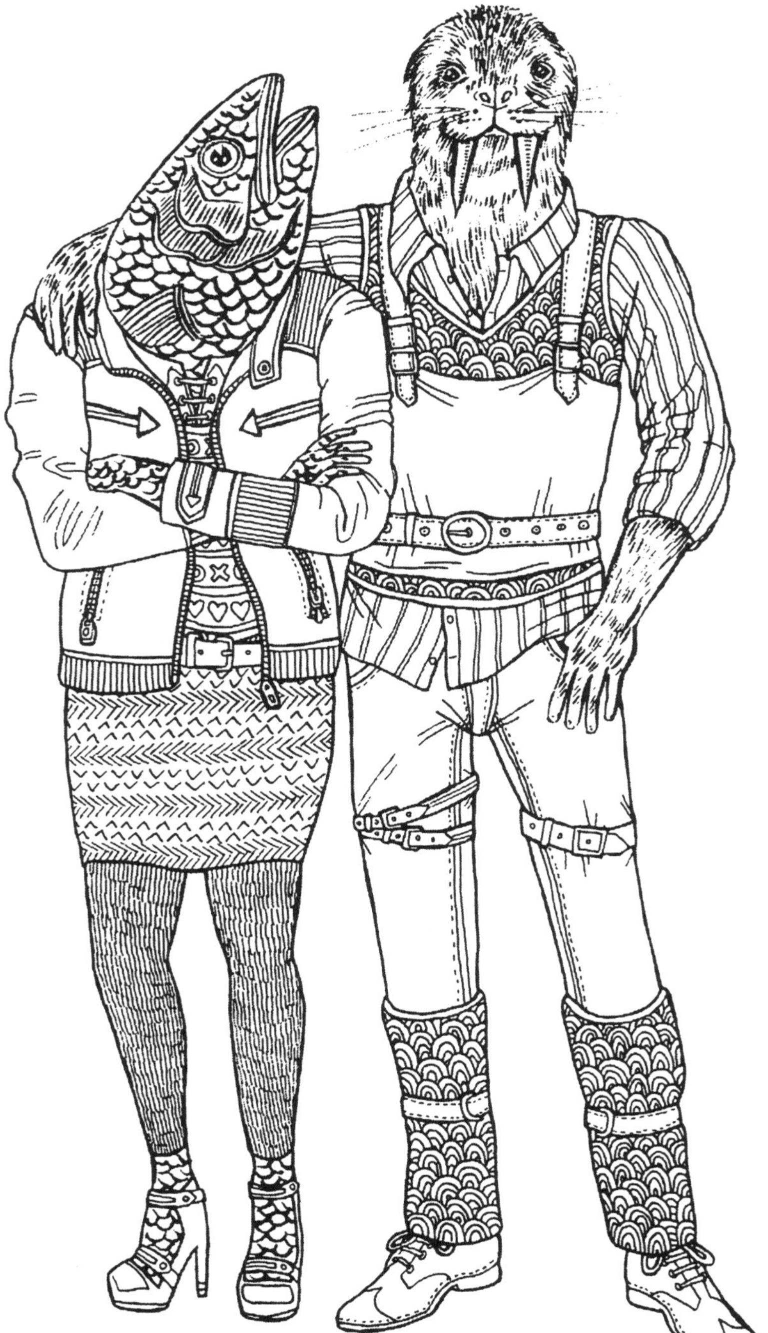

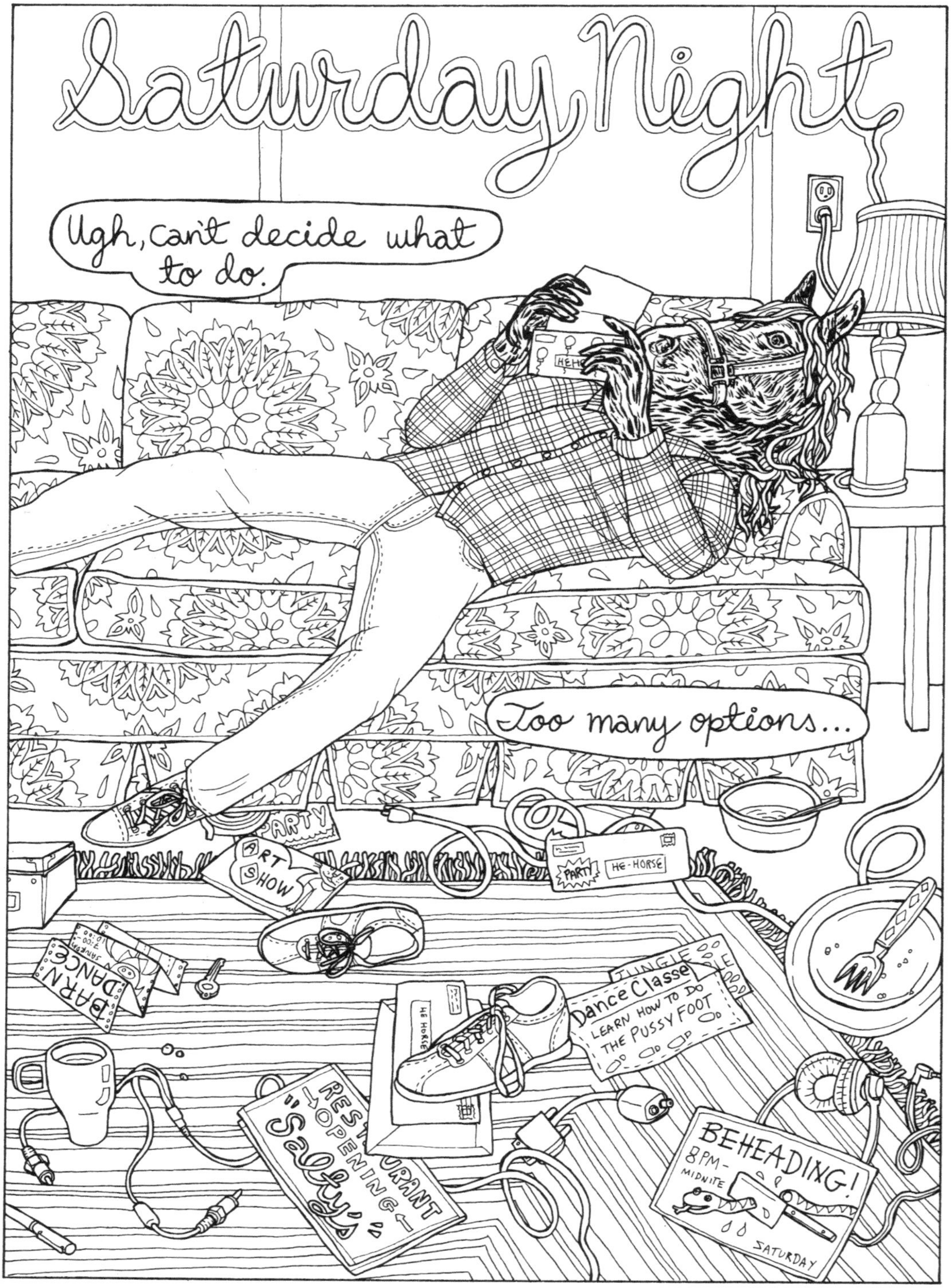
Saturday Night
Ugh, can't decide what to do.
Too many options...
PARTY
ART SHOW
PARTY
HE-HORSE
BARN DANCE
Dance Classe
LEARN HOW TO DO THE PUSSY FOOT
RESTAURANT OPENING
BEHEADING!
8PM-
MIDNITE
SATURDAY

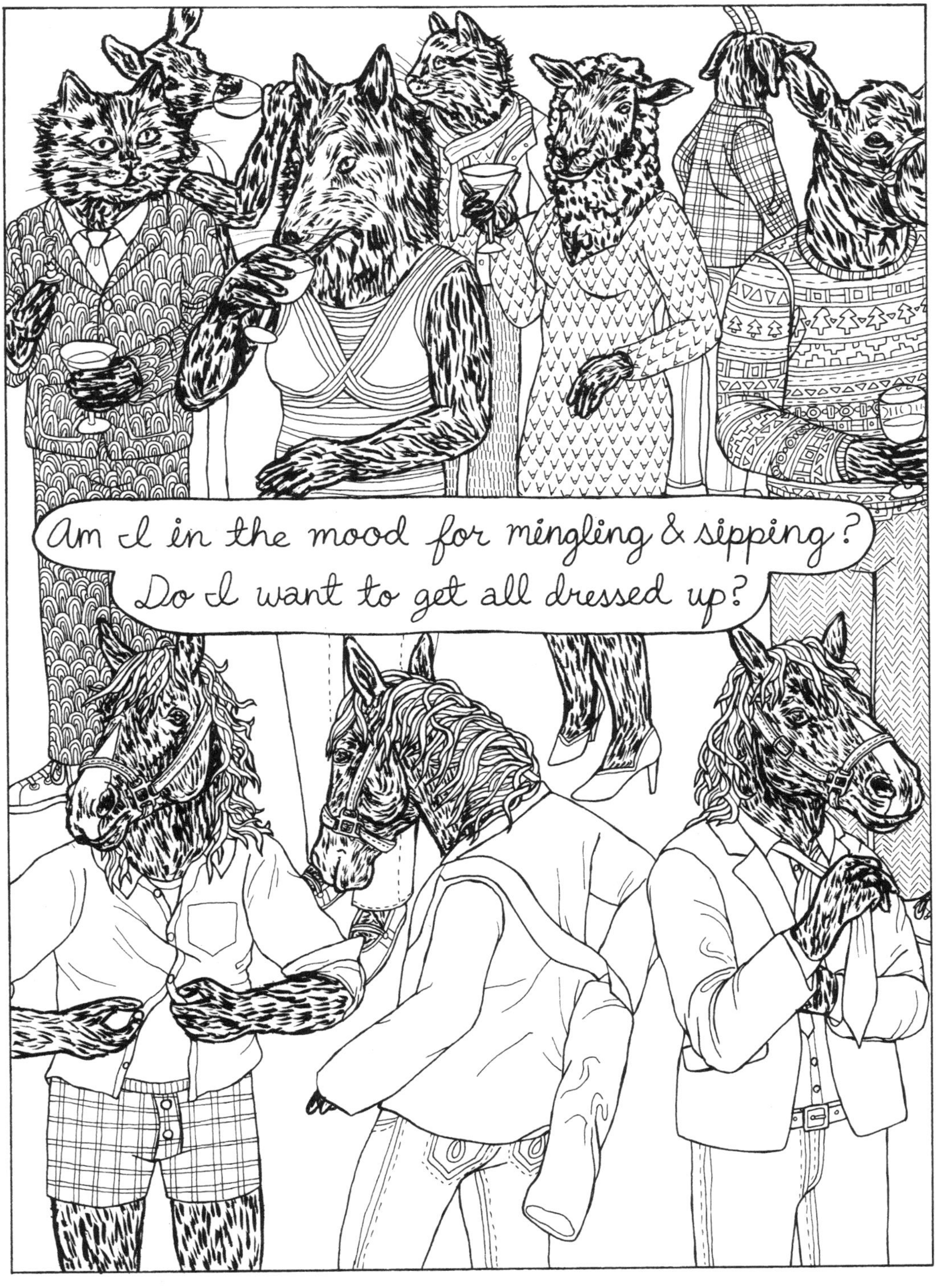
Am I in the mood for mingling & sipping?
Do I want to get all dressed up?

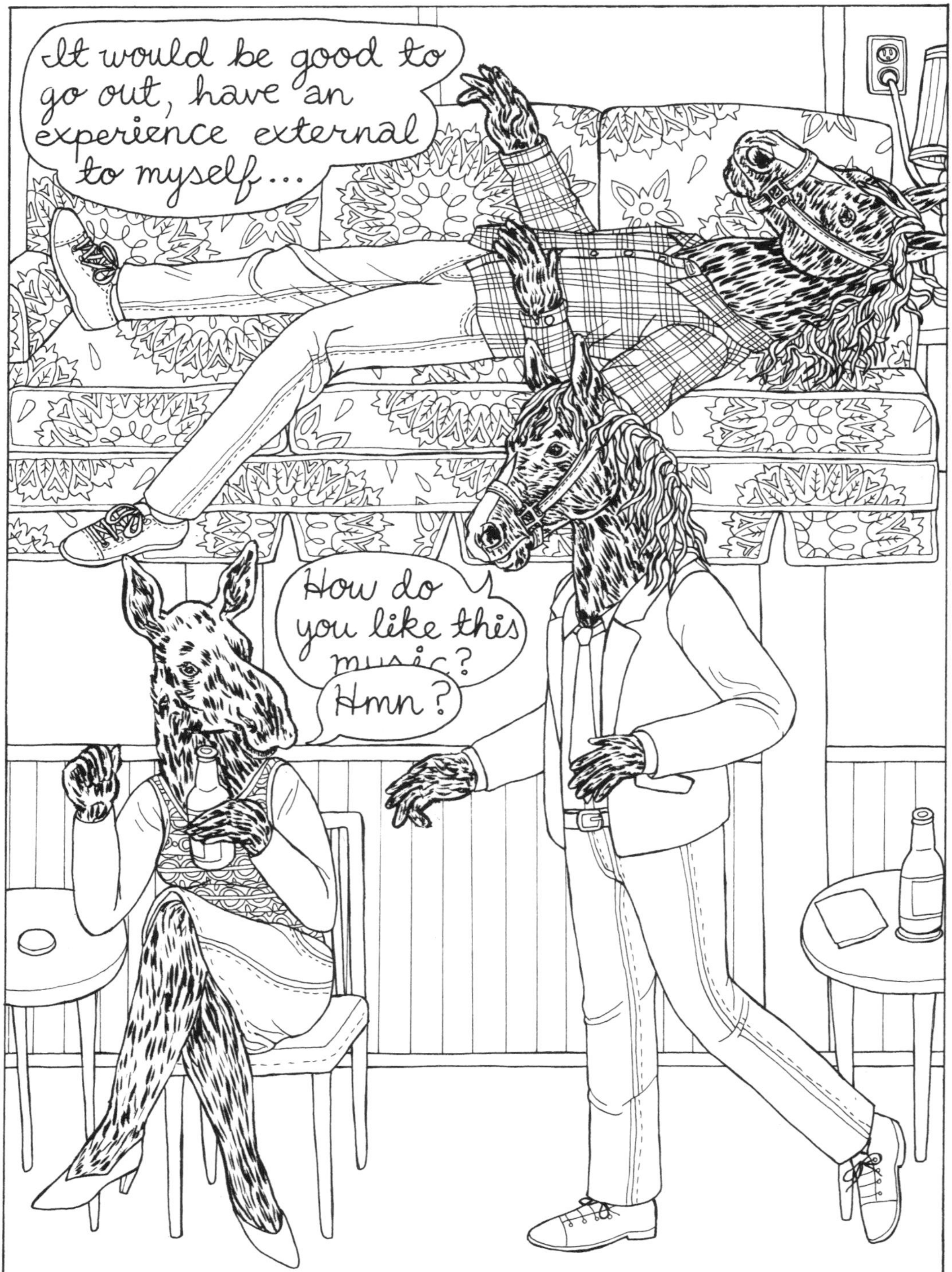
It would be good to go out, have an experience external to myself...
How do you like this music?
Hmn?

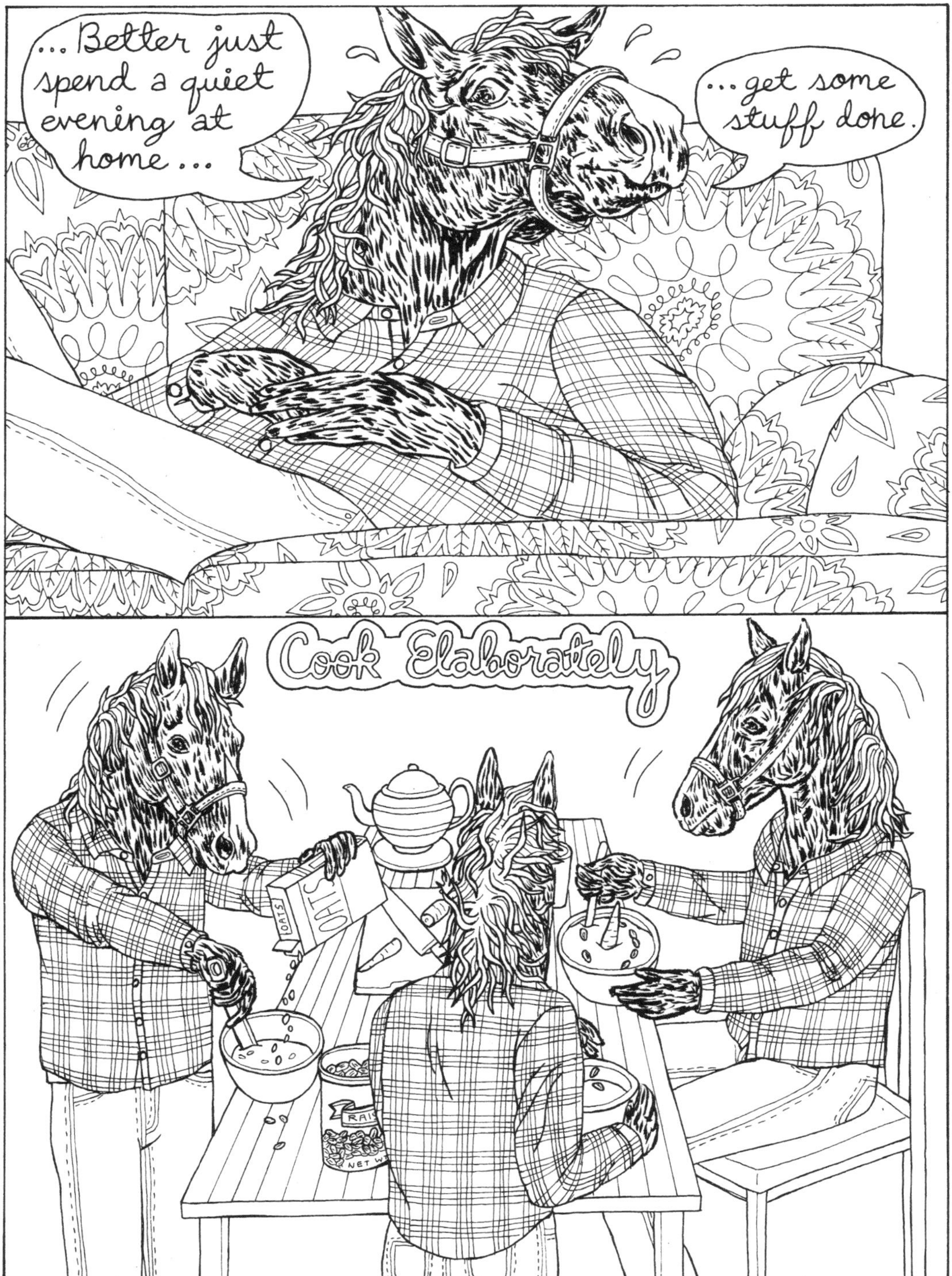
...Better just spend a quiet evening at home...
...get some stuff done.
Cook Elaborately
OATS
OATS
RAI
NET W

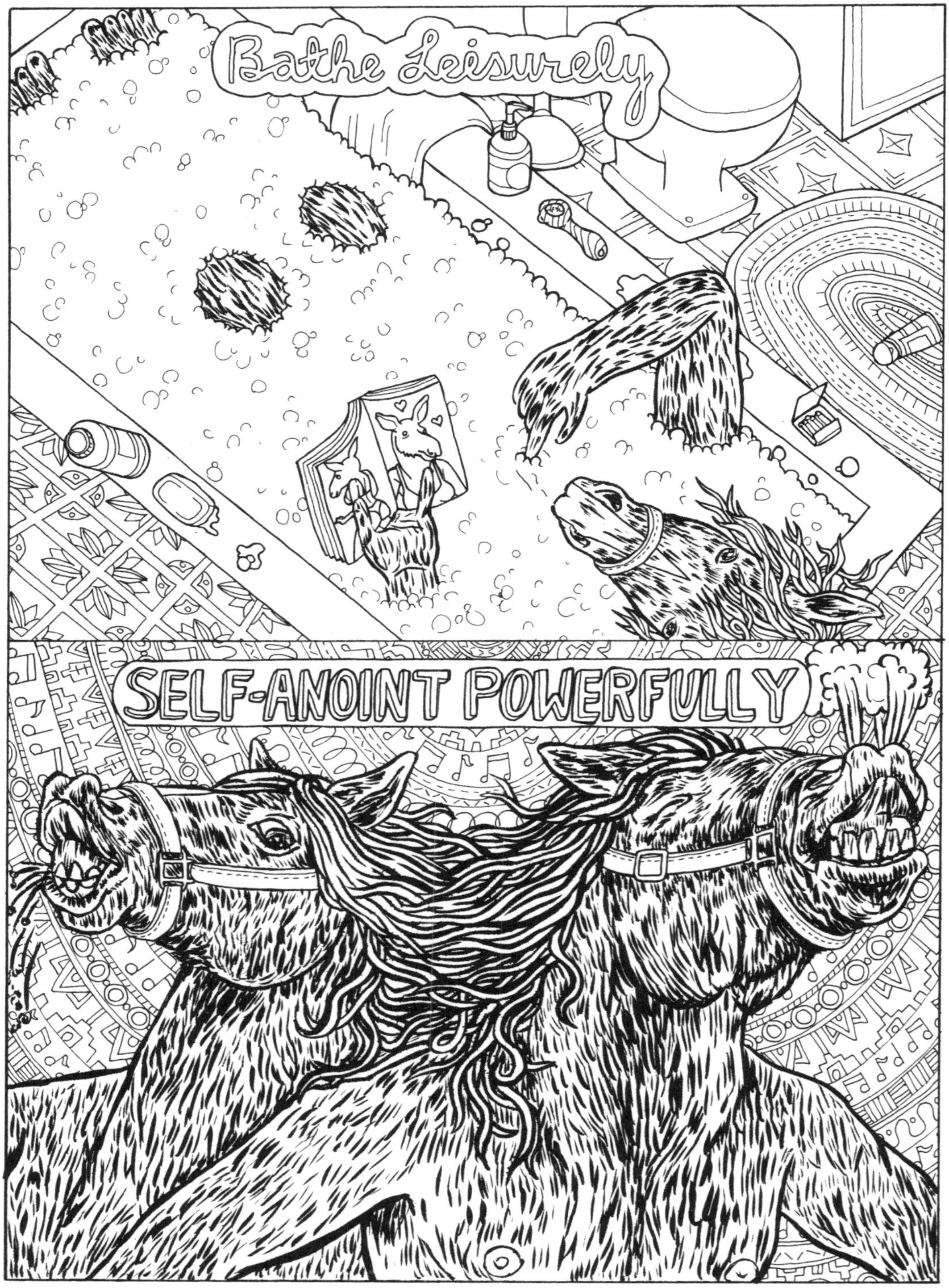

Bathe Leisurely
SELF-ANOINT POWERFULLY

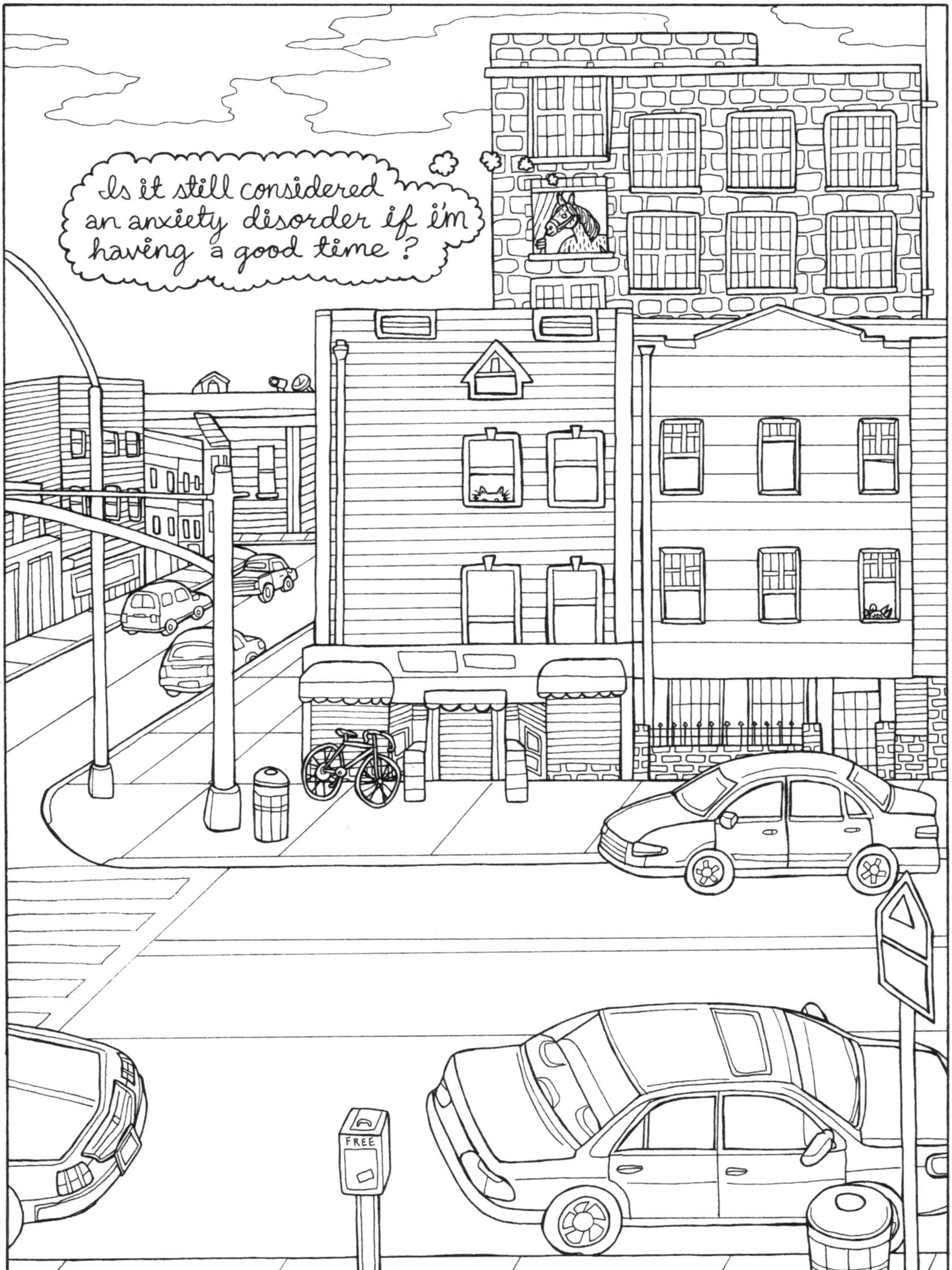
Is it still considered an anxiety disorder if i'm having a good time?
FREE

PIGEONS ARE NOT JUST RATS WITH WINGS AND THIS ILLUSTRATION DEMONSTRATES THAT.

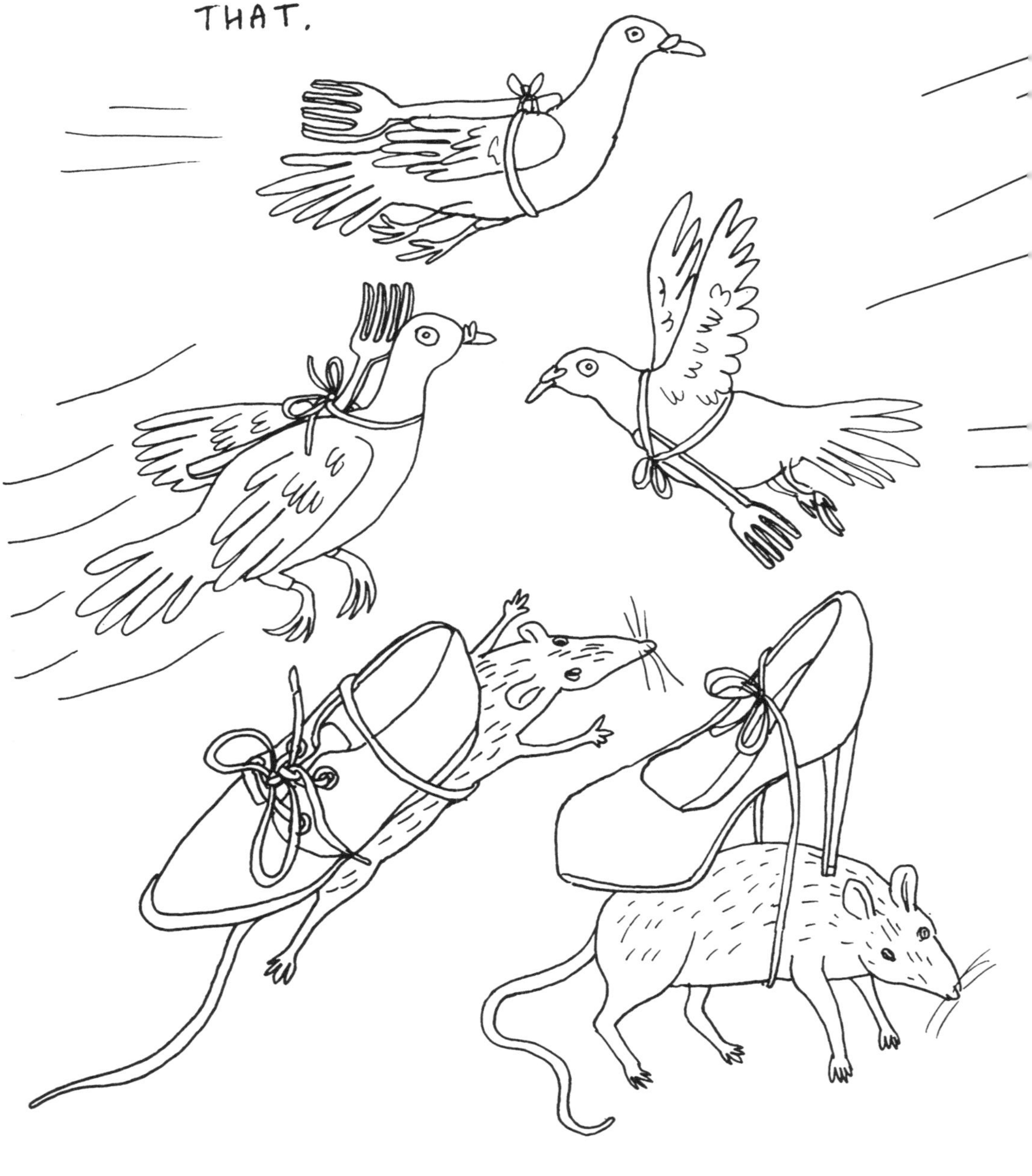

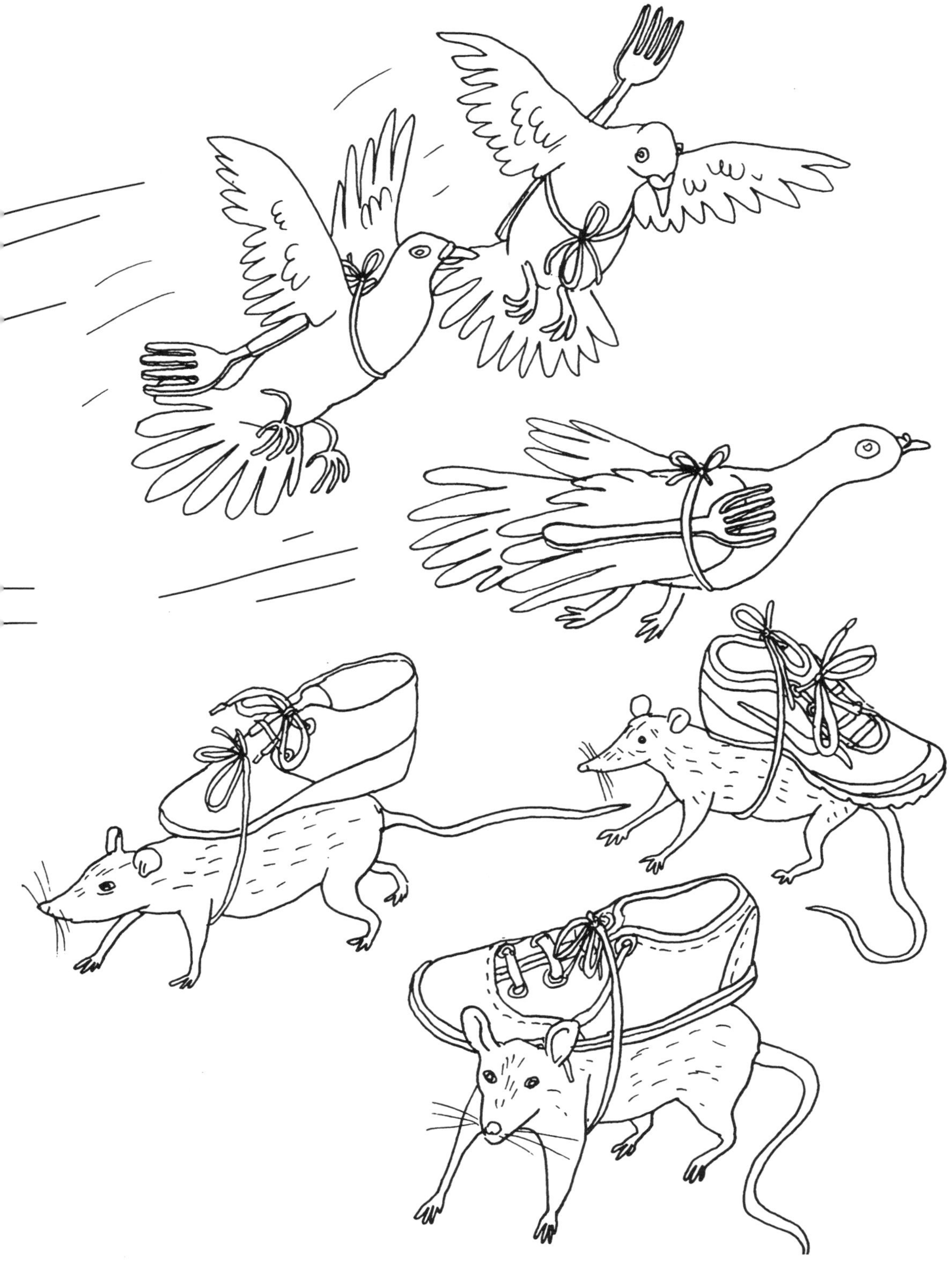

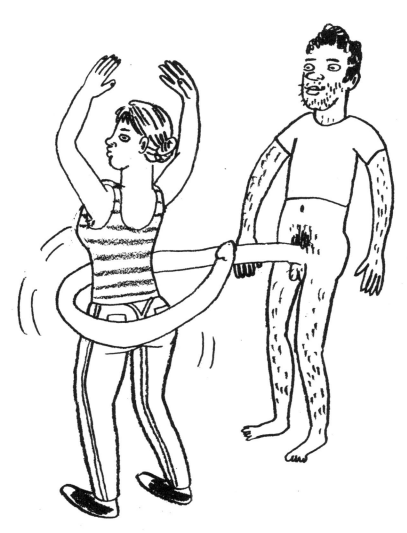

HERE'S HOW YOU COULD HULA HOOP
WITH A DICK IF YOU HAD TO

WHY ARE YOU SHITTING HERE
ARE YOU MAKING POO
PEE OR POO?
ARE YOU POOING
I CAN SMELL IT
WHAT ARE YOU DOING IN THERE
WILL YOU BE DONE POOPING SOON
ARE YOU CRAPPING RIGHT NOW
ARE YOU USING ALL THE TOILET PAPER
GROSS
HOW MANY POOS ARE YOU POOING
CAN I COME SEE YOUR POO

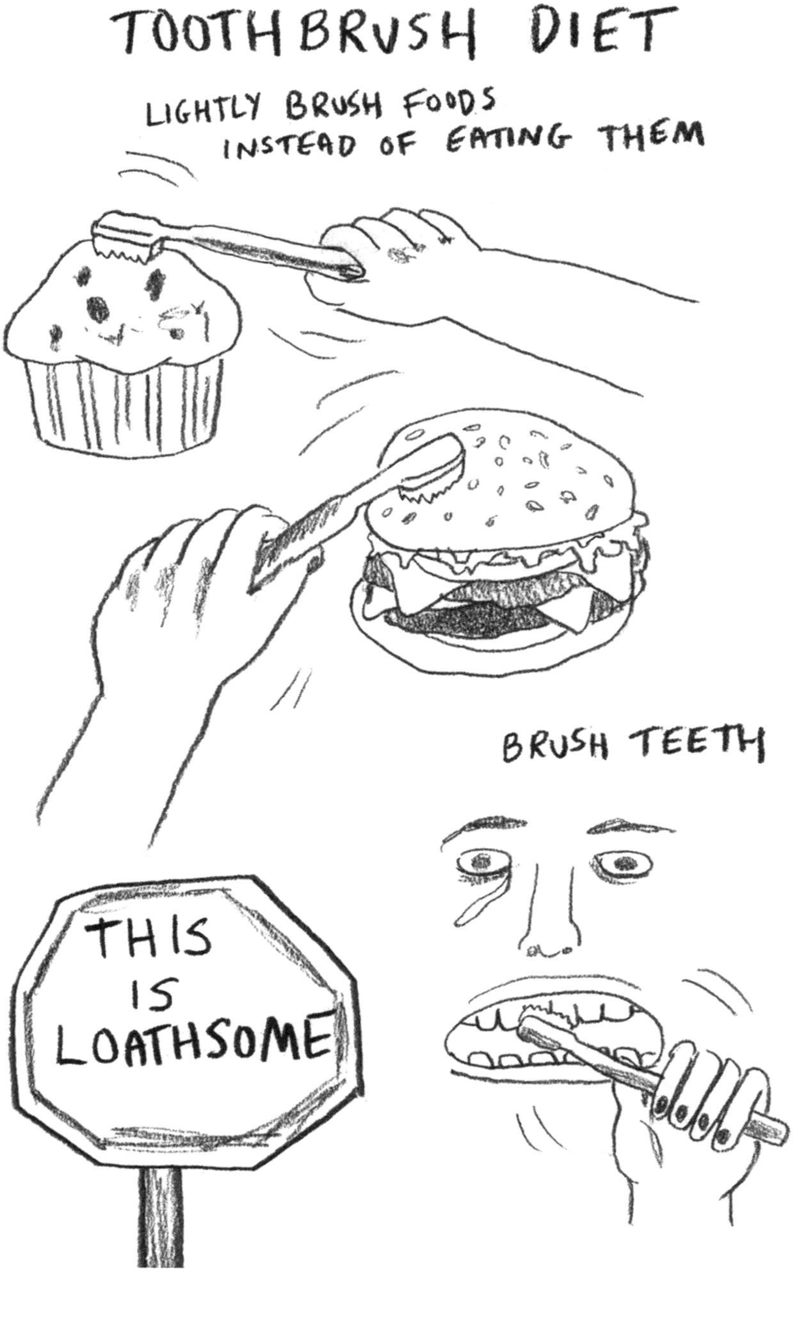
TOOTHBRUSH DIET
LIGHTLY BRUSH FOODS INSTEAD OF EATING THEM
BRUSH TEETH
THIS IS LOATHSOME

REJECTED RUDYARD KIPLING "JUST SO" STORIES

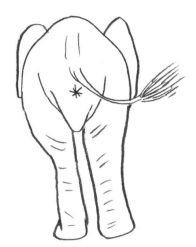

"HOW THE ELEPHANT'S BUTTHOLE GOT SO PINKISH-BROWN"

"HOW THE TIGER'S ASSHOLE GOT SO PINK"

"HOW THE DOG'S WATER GOT SO SLIMY"

"HOW THE COW'S BUTTHOLE GOT SO BEIGEY-PINK"

BAD PETS

① TINA, THE BITCHFISH

② FARTY FARTY FRUITBAT

③ BERNAPET PEEPERS

④ MACARONI PONY

⑤ BABY BIRD THAT FELL OUT OF A NEST

urrrghh

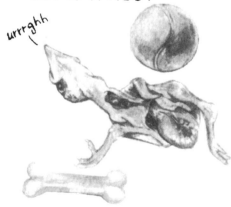

⑥ NARCOLEPTIC RODENTS WHO WISH YOU'D FUCK OFF

⑦ HAND-FACED DOGS

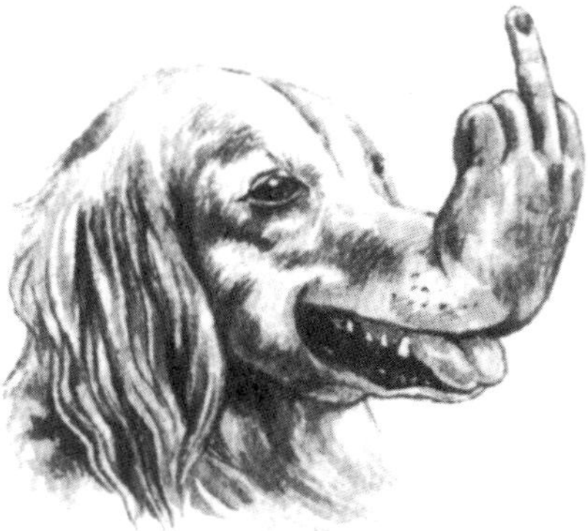

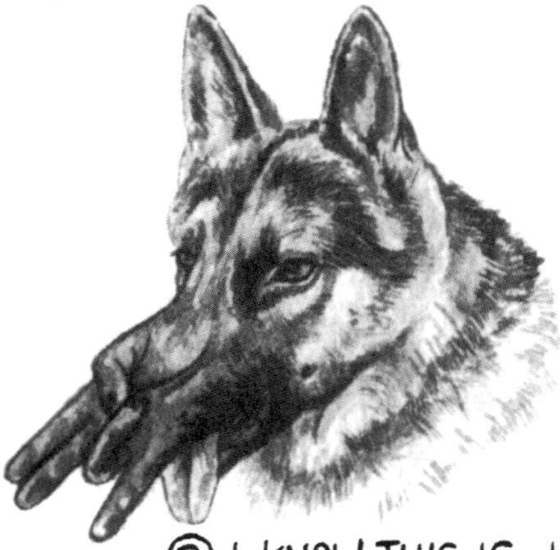

⑧ KITTEN TIED TO A PLATE OF MEDIOCRE FOOD

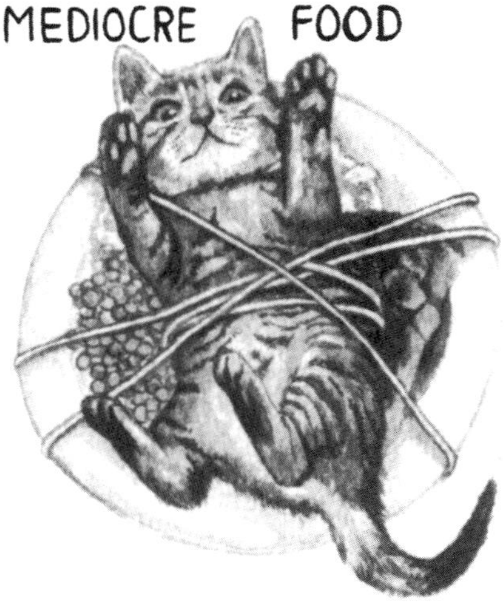

⑨ I KNOW THIS IS JUST A SANDWICH, BUT IT FEELS LIKE A PET

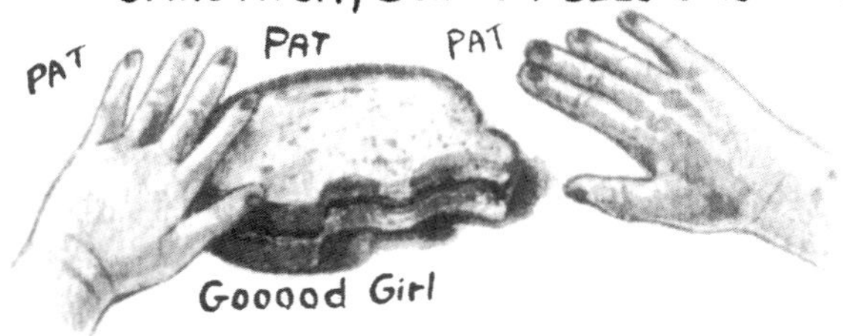
PAT
PAT
PAT
Gooood Girl

⑩ JAPANESE FOLD

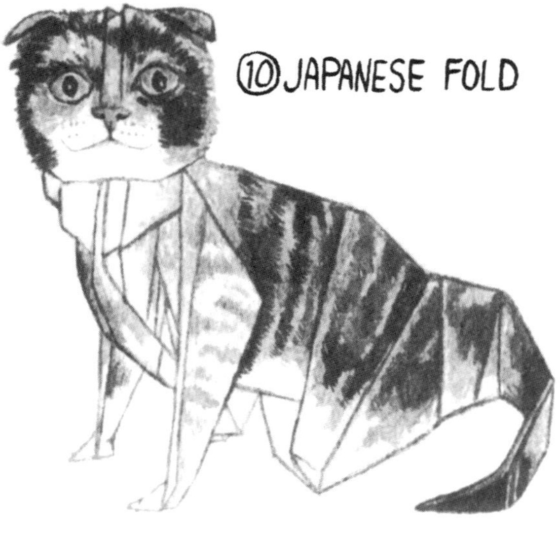

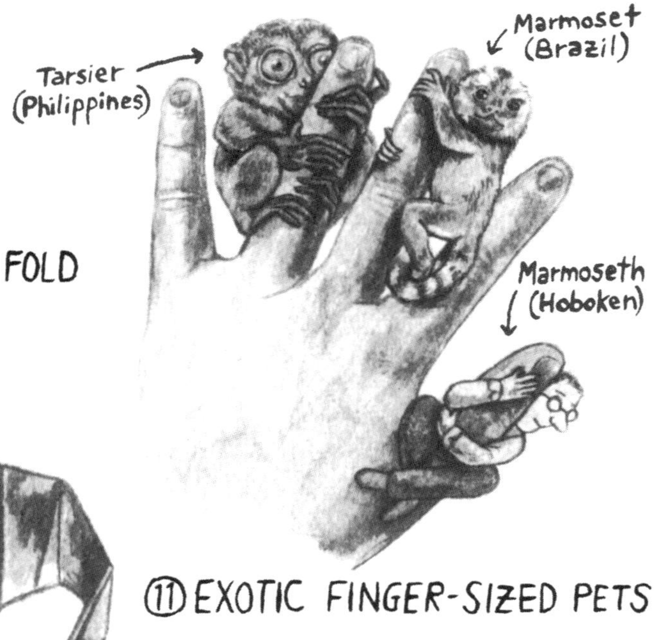
Tarsier
(Philippines)
Marmoset
(Brazil)
Marmoseth
(Hoboken)

⑪ EXOTIC FINGER-SIZED PETS

WORST SANDWICHES

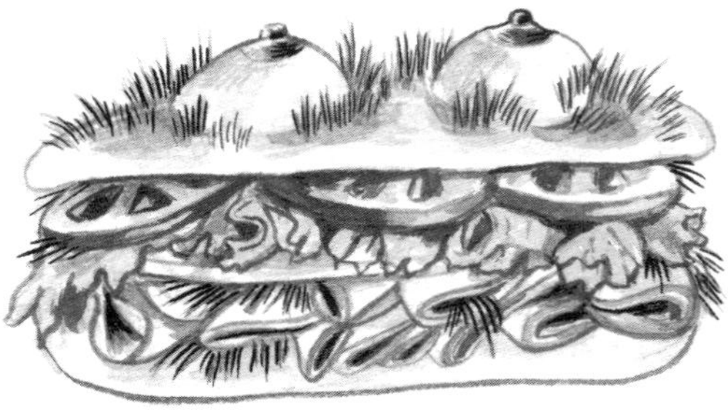

① SANDWICH WITH SECONDARY SEX CHARACTERISTICS

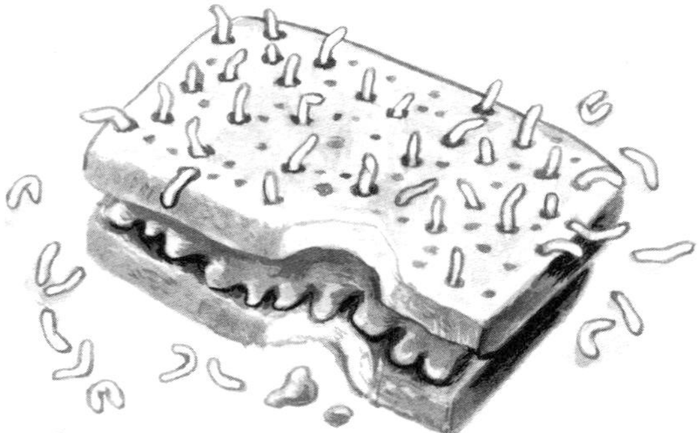

② PEANUT BUTTER SANDWICH THAT DOESN'T TASTE RIGHT

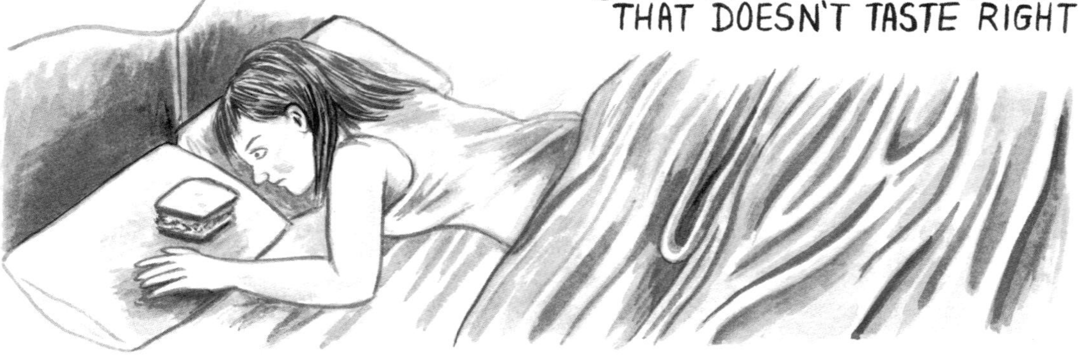

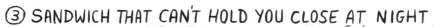

③ SANDWICH THAT CAN'T HOLD YOU CLOSE AT NIGHT

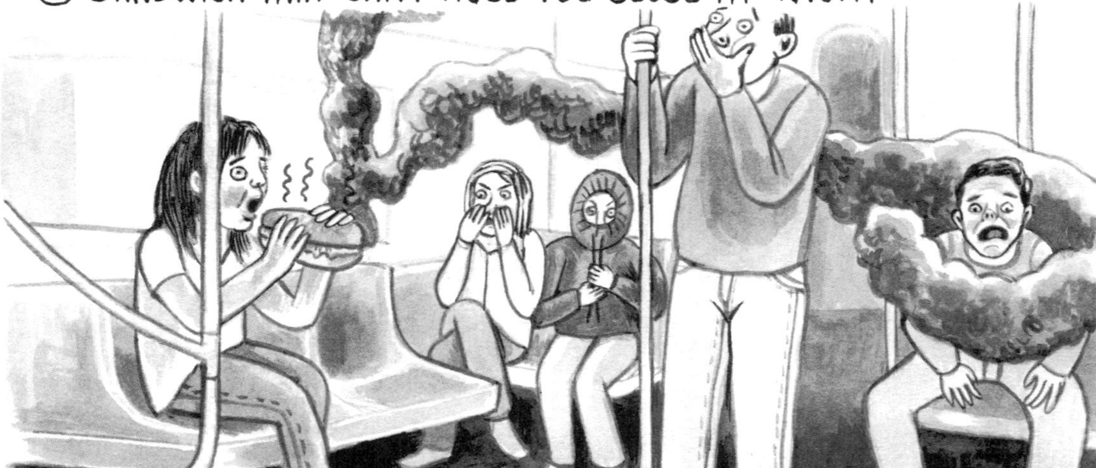

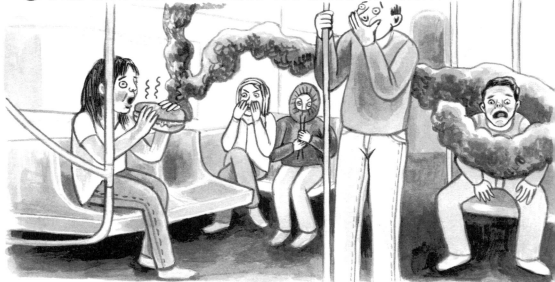

④ SANDWICH THAT MAKES ITS PRESENCE WELL-KNOWN TO NOSES

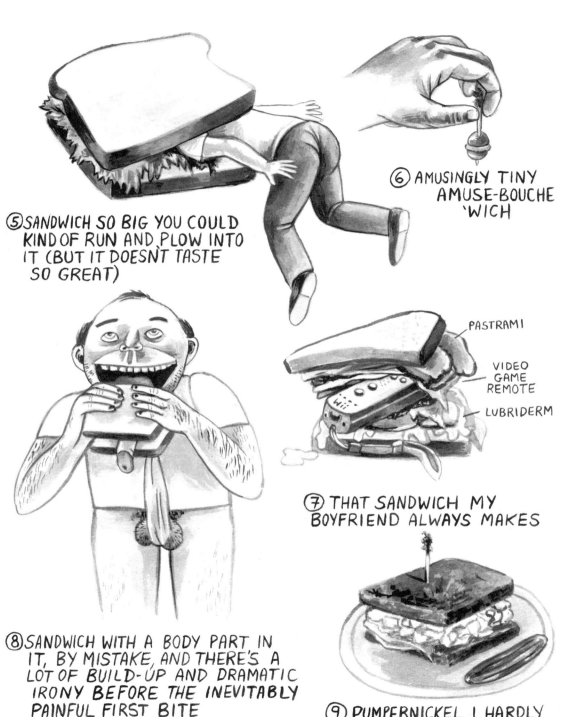

⑤ SANDWICH SO BIG YOU COULD KIND OF RUN AND PLOW INTO IT (BUT IT DOESN'T TASTE SO GREAT)

⑥ AMUSINGLY TINY AMUSE-BOUCHE 'WICH

PASTRAMI

VIDEO GAME REMOTE

LUBRIDERM

⑦ THAT SANDWICH MY BOYFRIEND ALWAYS MAKES

⑧ SANDWICH WITH A BODY PART IN IT, BY MISTAKE, AND THERE'S A LOT OF BUILD-UP AND DRAMATIC IRONY BEFORE THE INEVITABLY PAINFUL FIRST BITE

⑨ PUMPERNICKEL I HARDLY KNOW HER! (WITH EGG)

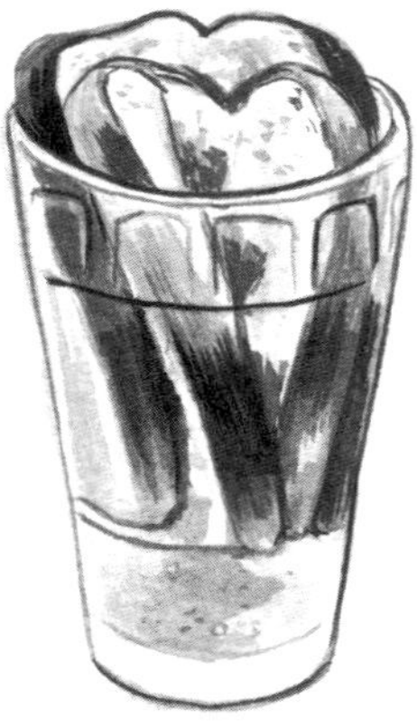

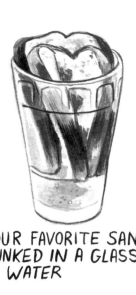

⑩ YOUR FAVORITE SANDWICH DUNKED IN A GLASS OF WATER

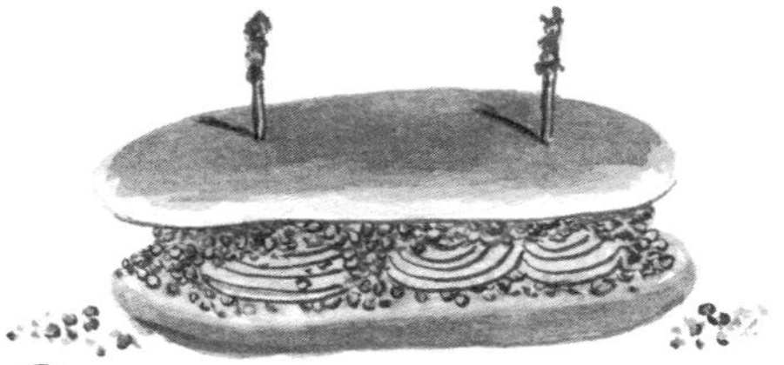

⑪ GRAVEL 'N ONIONS

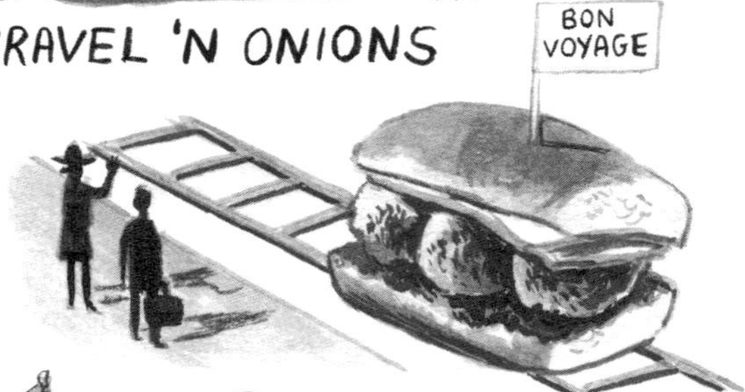
BON VOYAGE

⑫ DELICIOUS MEATWICH YOU LEFT ON THE TRAIN

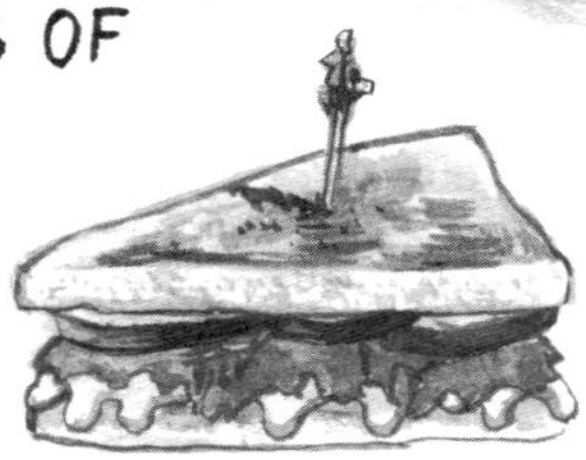

⑬ DIET B.L.T. WITH SLIM FAST® INSTEAD OF MAYO AND NOTHING INSTEAD OF BACON

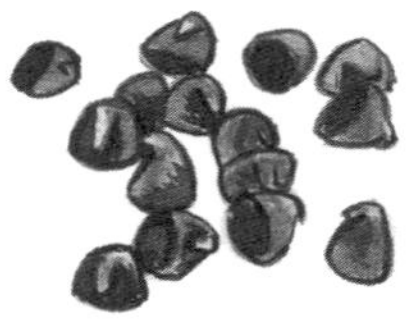

⑭ CHOCOLATE CHIPS ARE NOT A GOOD LUNCH

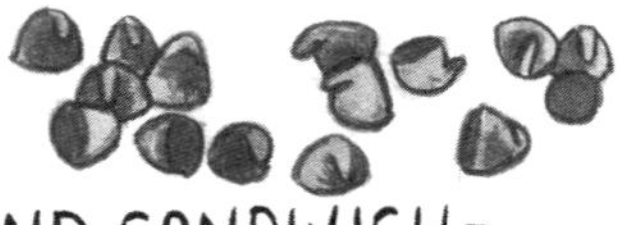

AND SANDWICH-FLAVORED CHIPS ARE TRYING TOO HARD

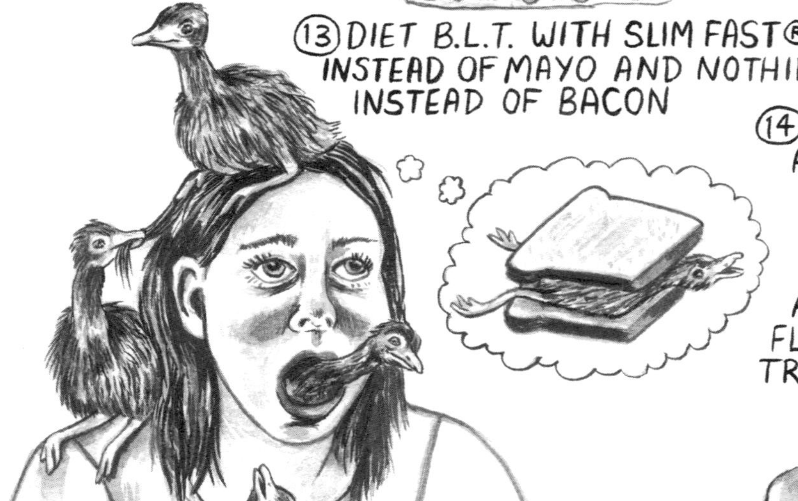

⑮ IT WOULD SUCK IF A FRIEND INVITED YOU OVER FOR SANDWICHES BUT YOU MISHEARD THEM AND THEY REALLY WANTED YOU TO LEND A HAND WITH A BAND OF BABY OSTRICHES

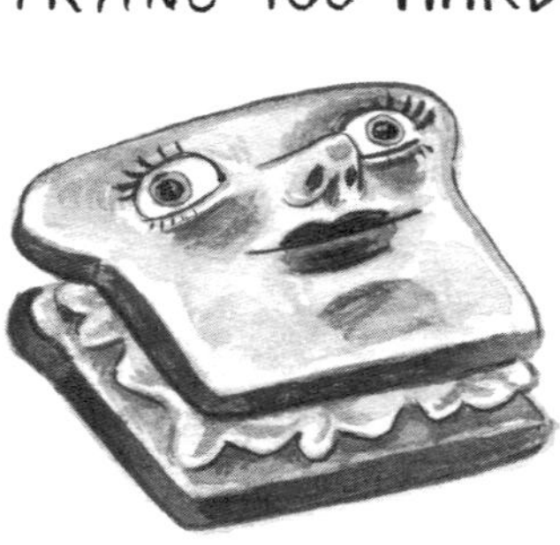

⑯ YOU ARE GREAT! BUT YOU WOULD BE A PRETTY BAD SANDWICH

HOW TO GET A HAIRCUT

ADMIT THAT YOUR HAIR COULD USE PROFESSIONAL HELP.

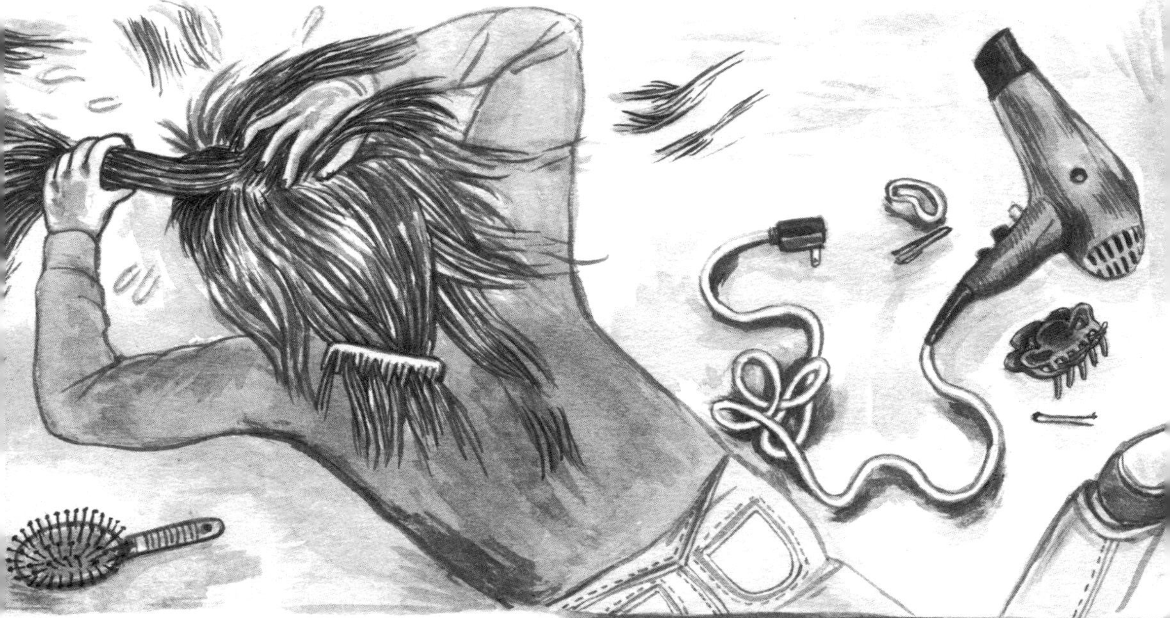

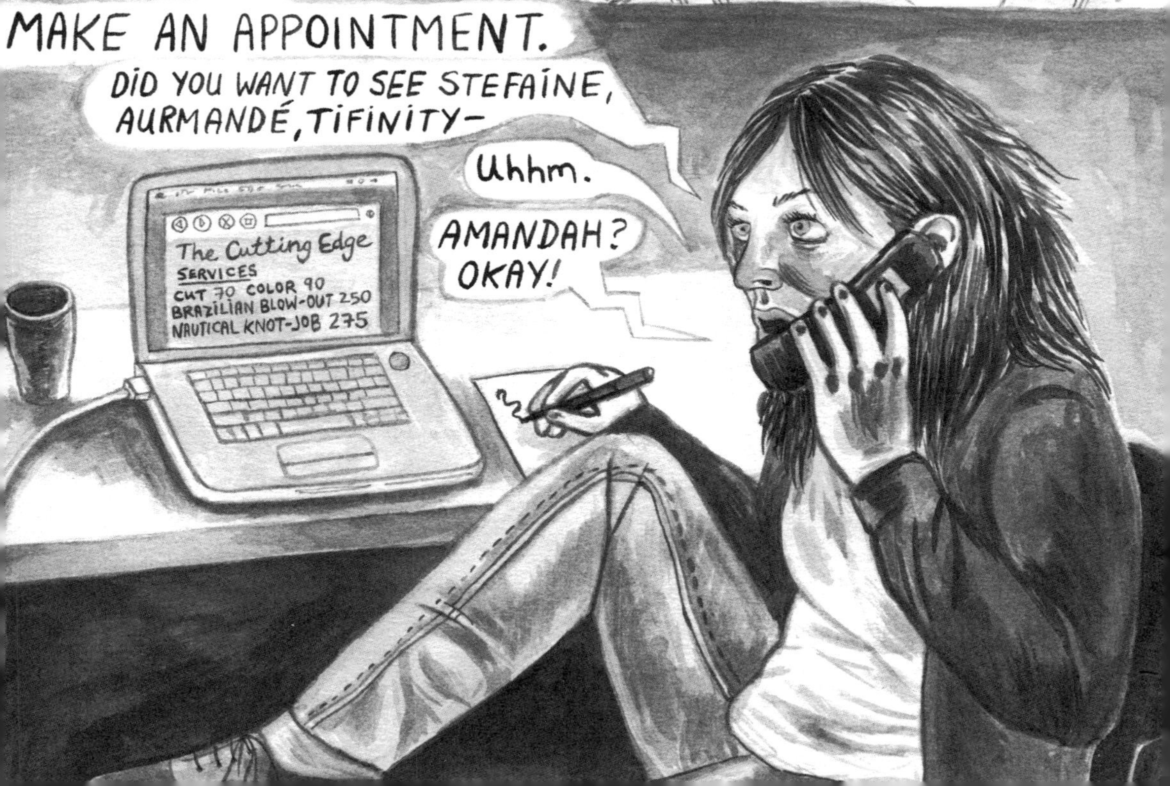
MAKE AN APPOINTMENT.
DID YOU WANT TO SEE STEFAÍNE, AURMANDÉ, TIFINITY–
Uhhm.
AMANDAH? OKAY!
The Cutting Edge
SERVICES
CUT 70 COLOR 90
BRAZILIAN BLOW-OUT 250
NAUTICAL KNOT-JOB 275

③ BROWSE THE SALON'S MAGAZINES FOR IDEAS OF HOW YOU'D LIKE YOUR HAIR TO LOOK.

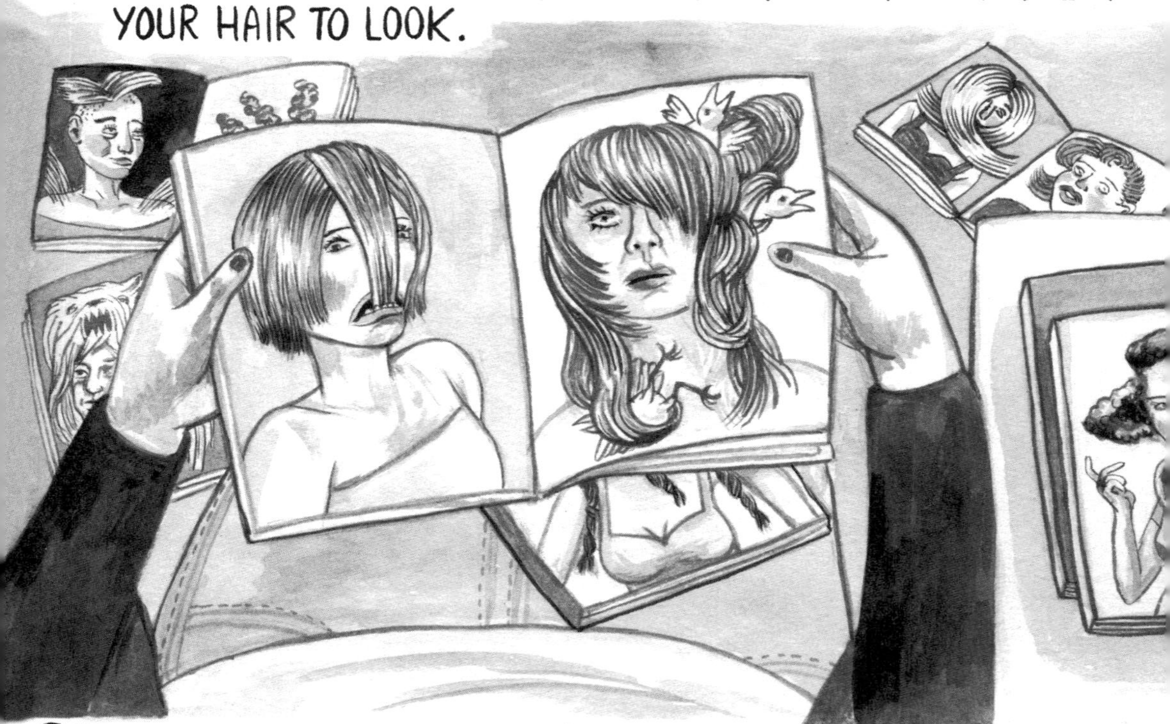

④ TRUST YOUR HAIRDRESSER'S OPINION.

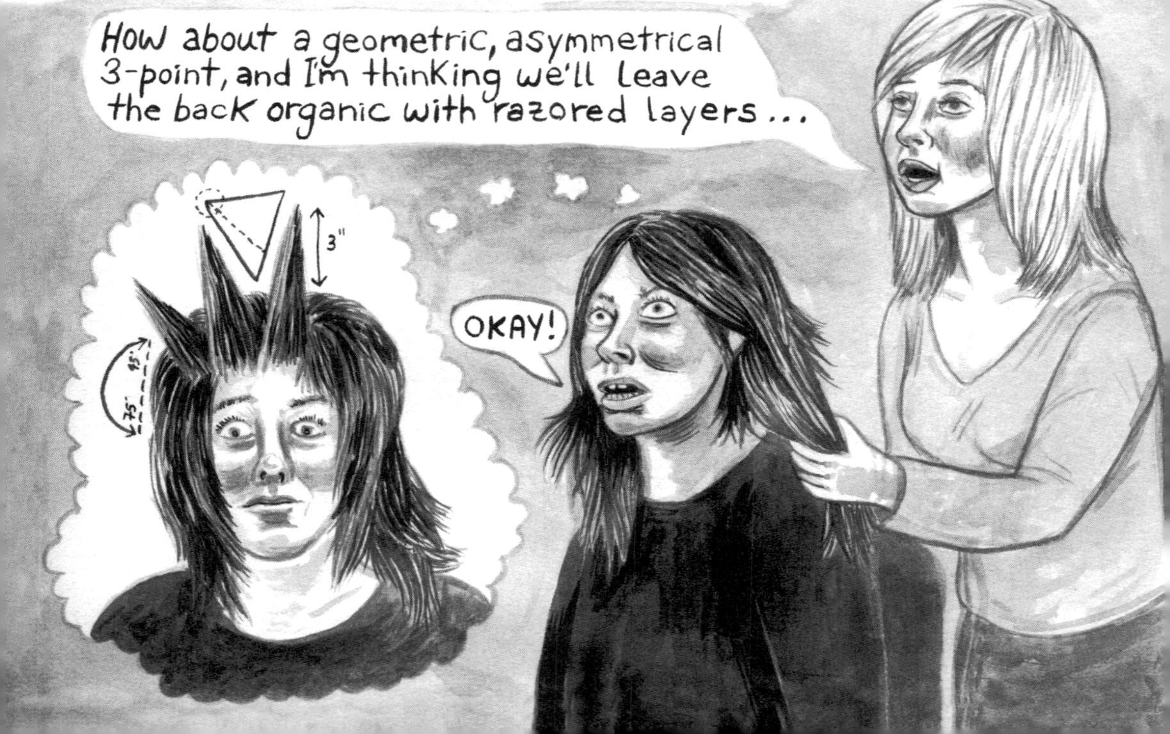

How about a geometric, asymmetrical 3-point, and I'm thinking we'll leave the back organic with razored layers...
3"
OKAY!

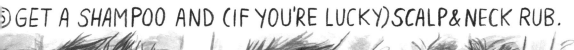

GET A SHAMPOO AND (IF YOU'RE LUCKY) SCALP & NECK RUB.

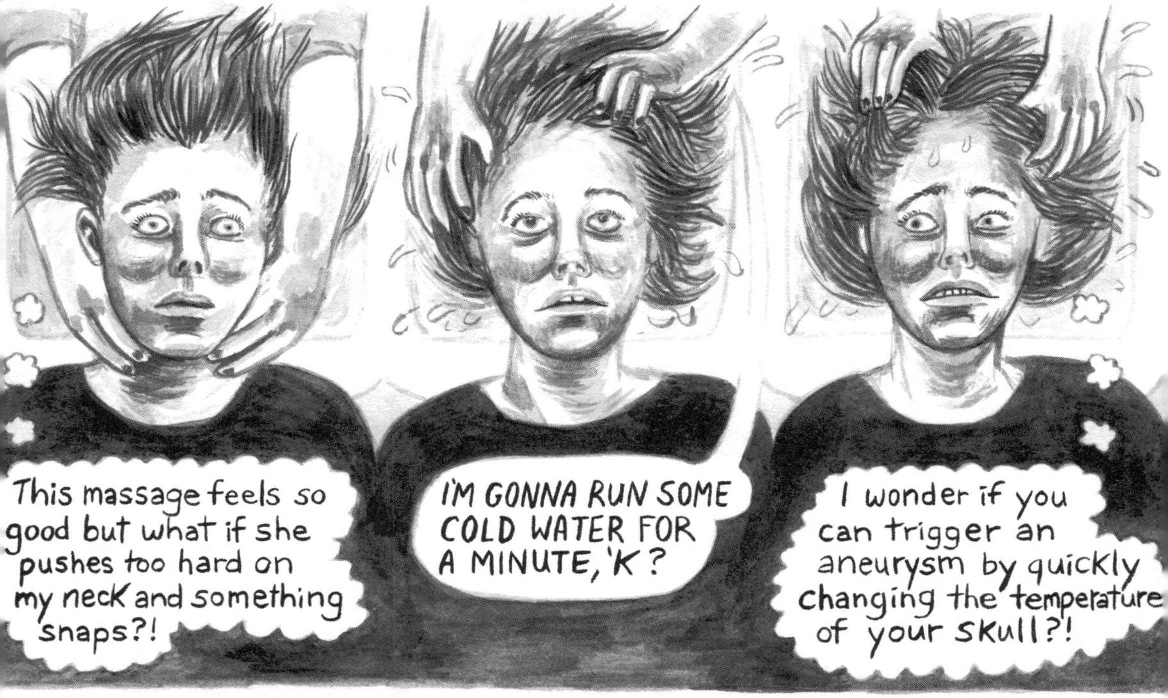

This massage feels so good but what if she pushes too hard on my neck and something snaps?!
I'M GONNA RUN SOME COLD WATER FOR A MINUTE, 'K?
I wonder if you can trigger an aneurysm by quickly changing the temperature of your skull?!

MOST SALONS WILL OFFER A BEVERAGE. CHOOSE WISELY.

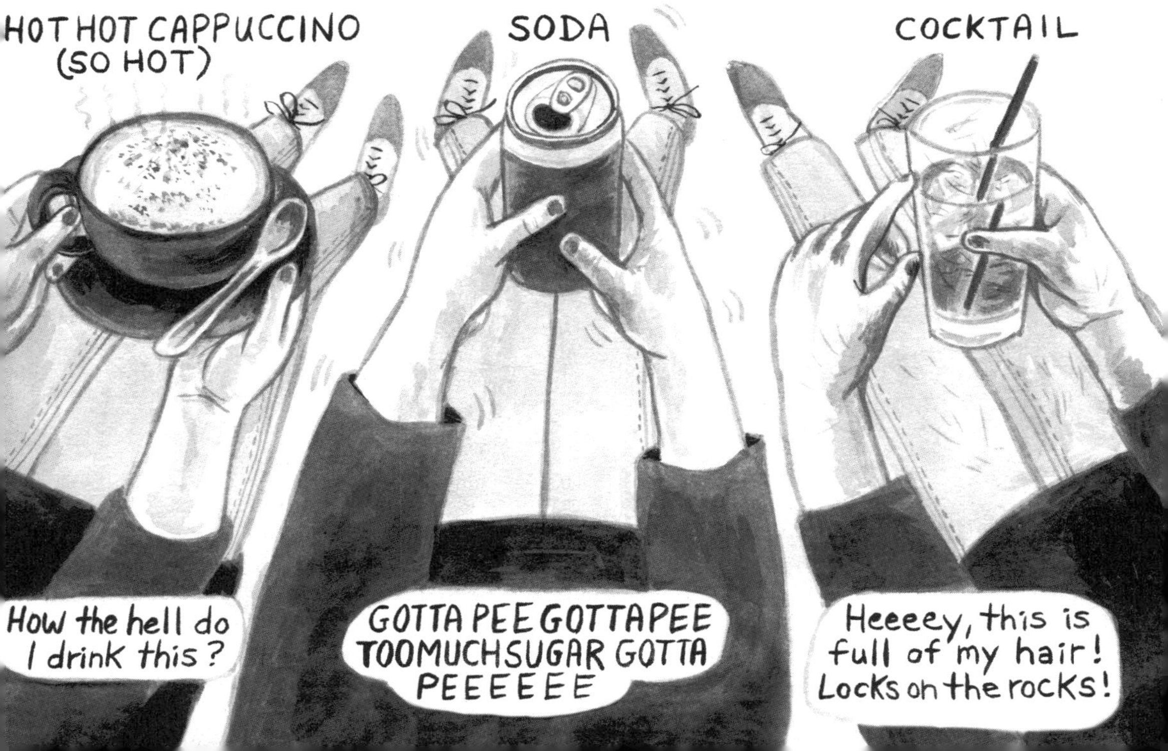

HOT HOT CAPPUCCINO (SO HOT)
SODA
COCKTAIL
How the hell do I drink this?
GOTTA PEE GOTTA PEE TOOMUCHSUGAR GOTTA PEEEEEE
Heeeey, this is full of my hair! Locks on the rocks!

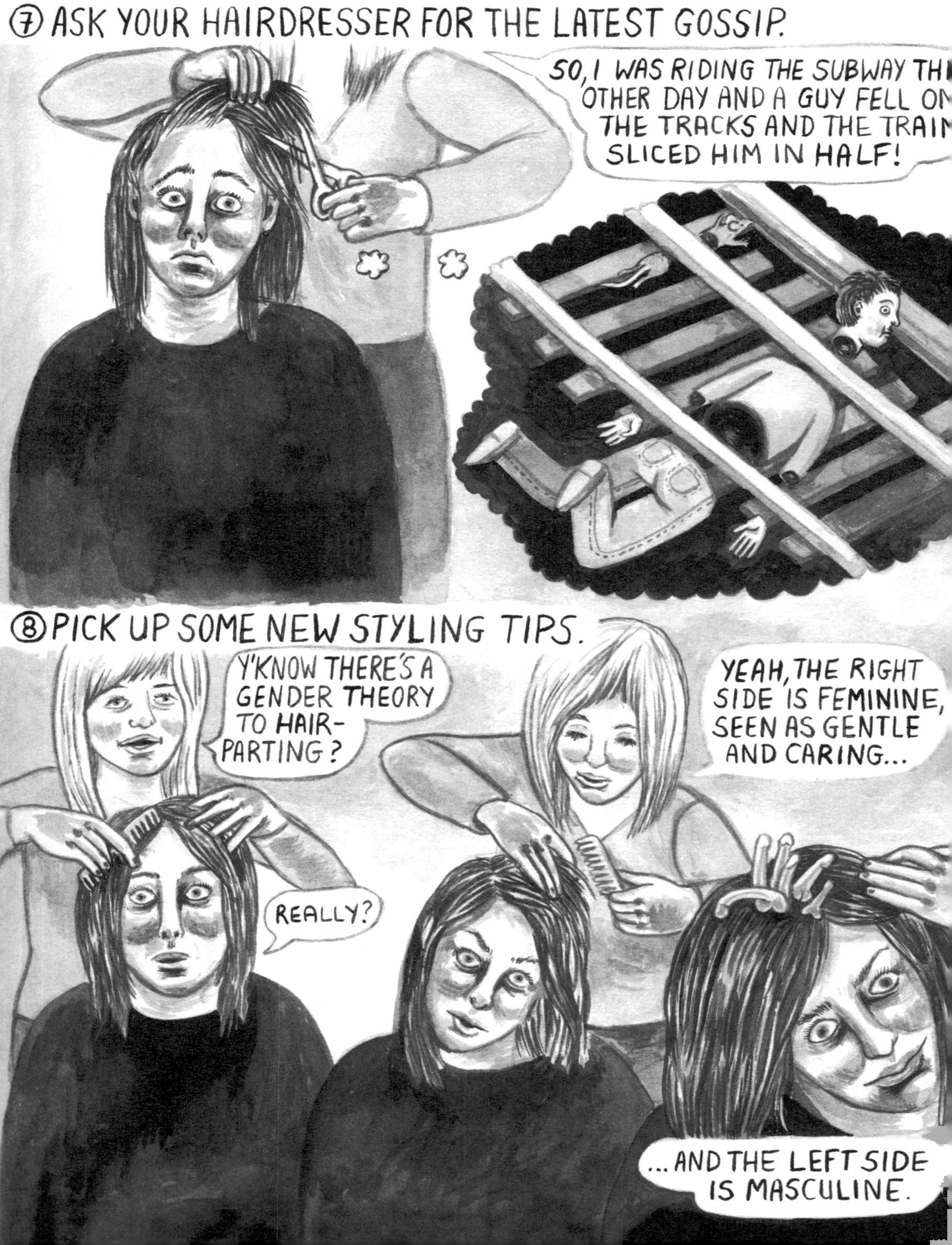
⑦ ASK YOUR HAIRDRESSER FOR THE LATEST GOSSIP.
SO, I WAS RIDING THE SUBWAY TH OTHER DAY AND A GUY FELL ON THE TRACKS AND THE TRAIN SLICED HIM IN HALF!
⑧ PICK UP SOME NEW STYLING TIPS.
Y'KNOW THERE'S A GENDER THEORY TO HAIR-PARTING?
REALLY?
YEAH, THE RIGHT SIDE IS FEMININE, SEEN AS GENTLE AND CARING...
...AND THE LEFT SIDE IS MASCULINE.

⑨ GET THE FINISHING TOUCHES.

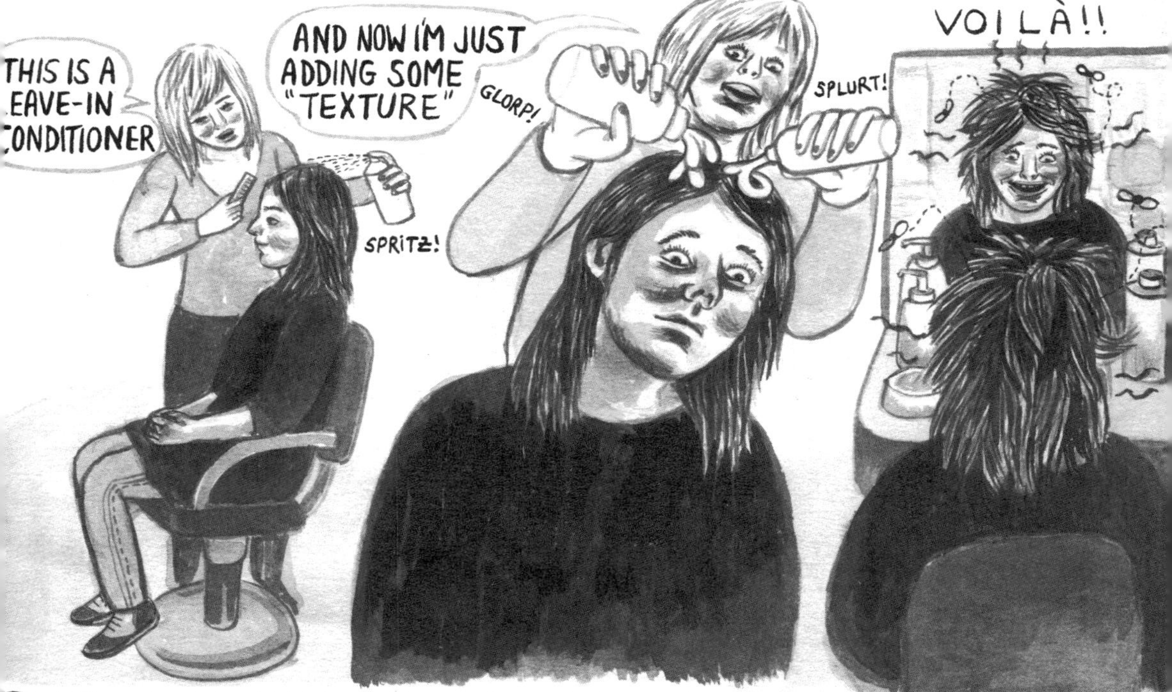
THIS IS A EAVE-IN CONDITIONER
SPRITZ!
AND NOW I'M JUST ADDING SOME "TEXTURE"
GLORP!
SPLURT!
VOILÀ!!

⑩ REVEL IN YOUR GLAMOROUS NEW LOOK!

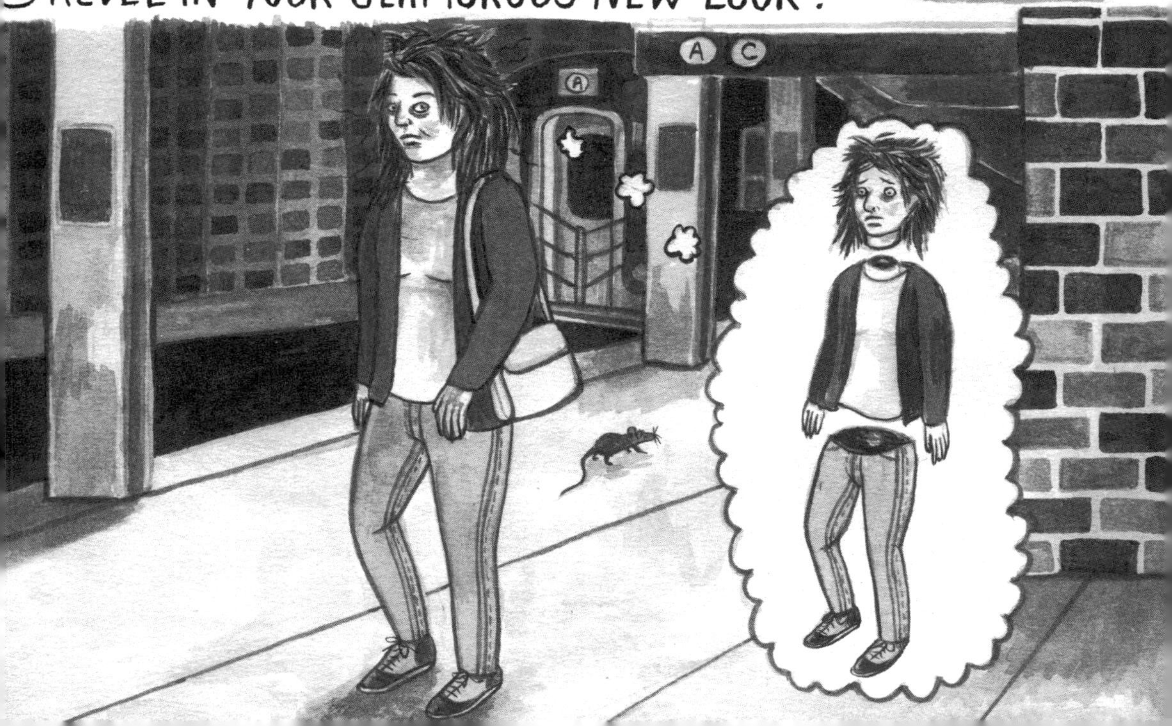
A C
A

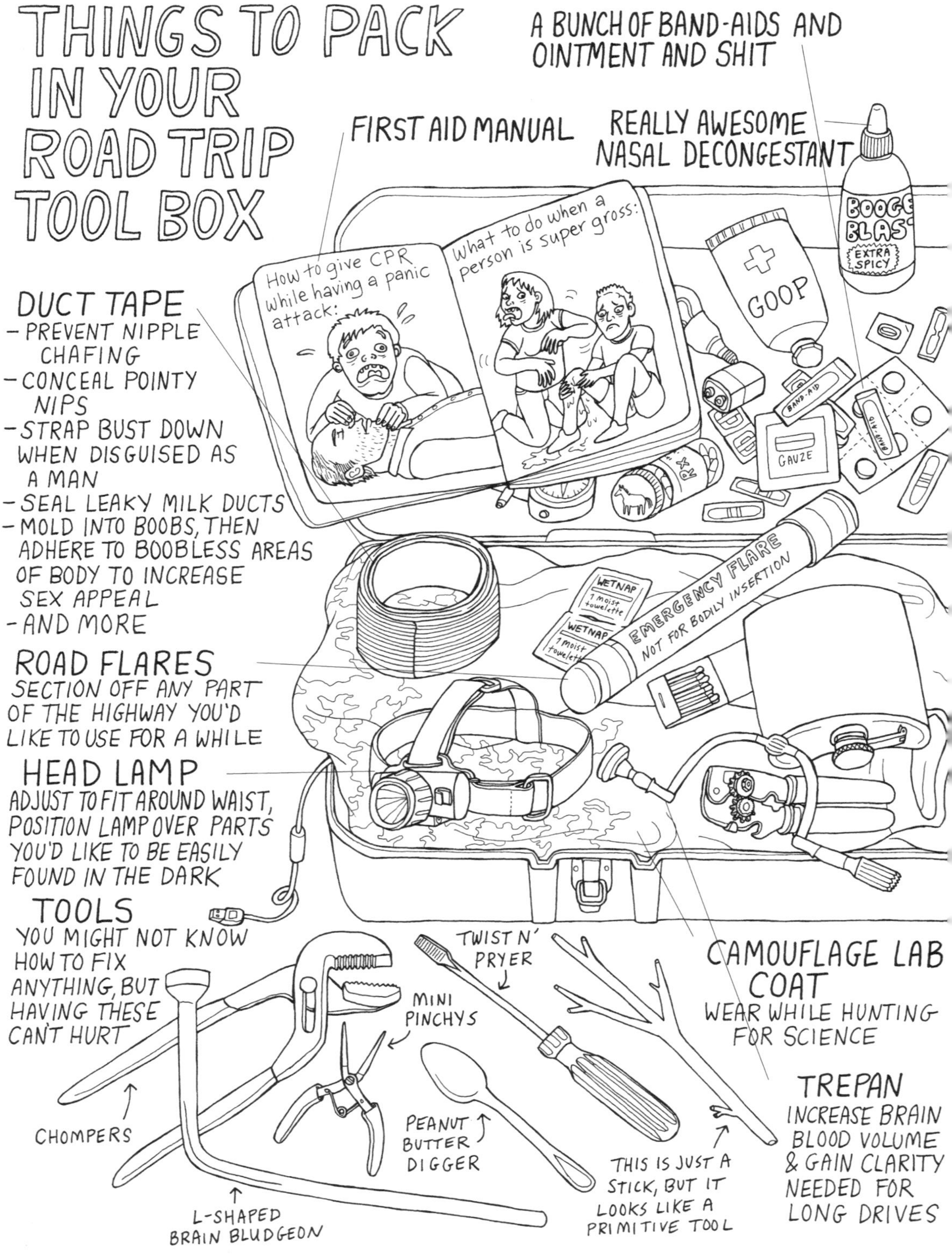
THINGS TO PACK IN YOUR ROAD TRIP TOOL BOX
A BUNCH OF BAND-AIDS AND OINTMENT AND SHIT
FIRST AID MANUAL
REALLY AWESOME NASAL DECONGESTANT
BOOGE BLAST
EXTRA SPICY
How to give CPR while having a panic attack:
What to do when a person is super gross:
GOOP
BAND-AID
BAND-AID
GAUZE
RX
DUCT TAPE
- PREVENT NIPPLE CHAFING
- CONCEAL POINTY NIPS
- STRAP BUST DOWN WHEN DISGUISED AS A MAN
- SEAL LEAKY MILK DUCTS
- MOLD INTO BOOBS, THEN ADHERE TO BOOBLESS AREAS OF BODY TO INCREASE SEX APPEAL
- AND MORE
WETNAP
1 moist towelette
WETNAP
1 moist towelette
EMERGENCY FLARE
NOT FOR BODILY INSERTION
ROAD FLARES
SECTION OFF ANY PART OF THE HIGHWAY YOU'D LIKE TO USE FOR A WHILE
HEAD LAMP
ADJUST TO FIT AROUND WAIST, POSITION LAMP OVER PARTS YOU'D LIKE TO BE EASILY FOUND IN THE DARK
TOOLS
YOU MIGHT NOT KNOW HOW TO FIX ANYTHING, BUT HAVING THESE CAN'T HURT
TWIST N' PRYER
MINI PINCHYS
CHOMPERS
PEANUT BUTTER DIGGER
L-SHAPED BRAIN BLUDGEON
THIS IS JUST A STICK, BUT IT LOOKS LIKE A PRIMITIVE TOOL
CAMOUFLAGE LAB COAT
WEAR WHILE HUNTING FOR SCIENCE
TREPAN
INCREASE BRAIN BLOOD VOLUME & GAIN CLARITY NEEDED FOR LONG DRIVES

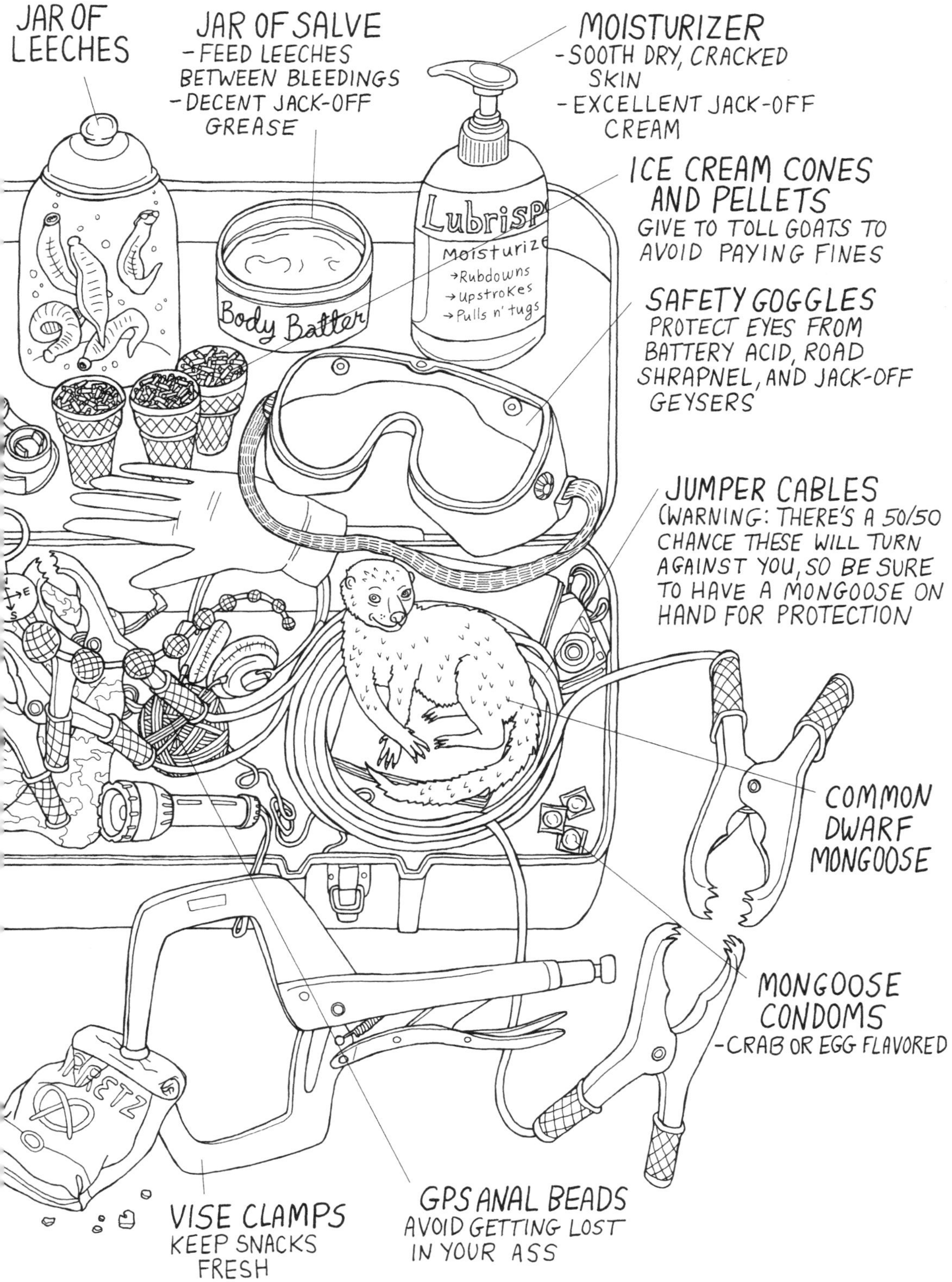
JAR OF LEECHES
JAR OF SALVE
-FEED LEECHES BETWEEN BLEEDINGS
-DECENT JACK-OFF GREASE
MOISTURIZER
-SOOTH DRY, CRACKED SKIN
-EXCELLENT JACK-OFF CREAM
ICE CREAM CONES AND PELLETS
GIVE TO TOLL GOATS TO AVOID PAYING FINES
Body Batter
Lubrisp
Moisturiz
→Rubdowns
→Upstrokes
→Pulls n' tugs
SAFETY GOGGLES
PROTECT EYES FROM BATTERY ACID, ROAD SHRAPNEL, AND JACK-OFF GEYSERS
JUMPER CABLES
(WARNING: THERE'S A 50/50 CHANCE THESE WILL TURN AGAINST YOU, SO BE SURE TO HAVE A MONGOOSE ON HAND FOR PROTECTION
COMMON DWARF MONGOOSE
MONGOOSE CONDOMS
-CRAB OR EGG FLAVORED
PRETZ
VISE CLAMPS
KEEP SNACKS FRESH
GPS ANAL BEADS
AVOID GETTING LOST IN YOUR ASS

HOWTO DRAW HORSES

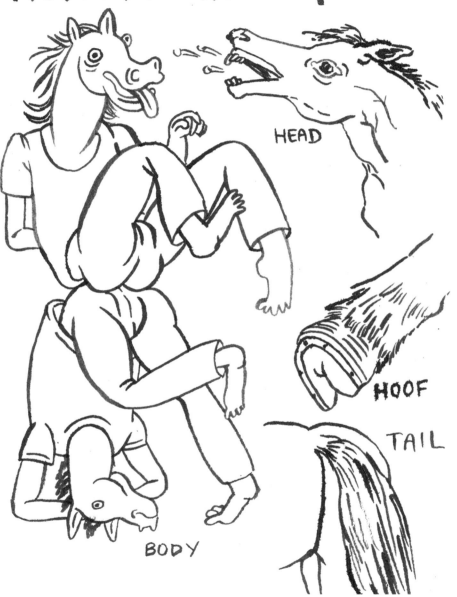

HEAD

HOOF

TAIL

BODY

HOW TO DANCE

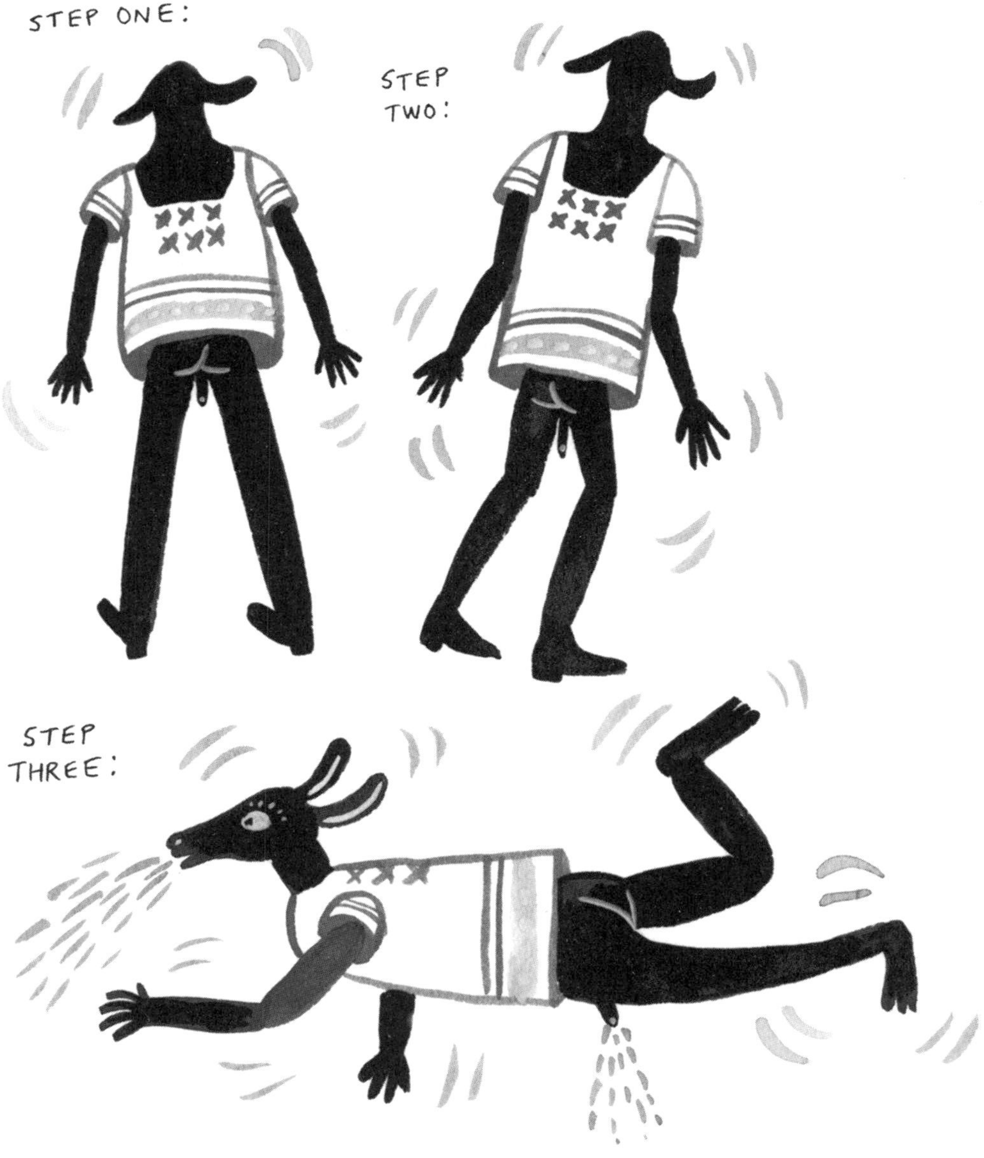
STEP ONE:
STEP TWO:
STEP THREE:

HOW TO FLATTER A PERSON

① COMPLIMENT PART OF THEIR OUTFIT.

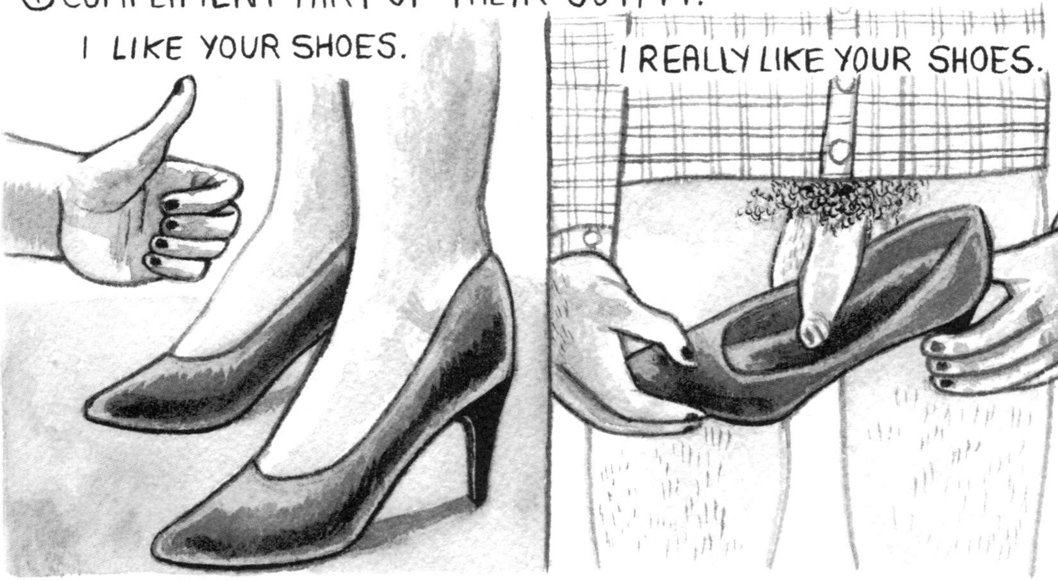
I LIKE YOUR SHOES.
I REALLY LIKE YOUR SHOES.

② GIVE THEM A GIFT THAT TOOK SOME EFFORT TO OBTAIN.

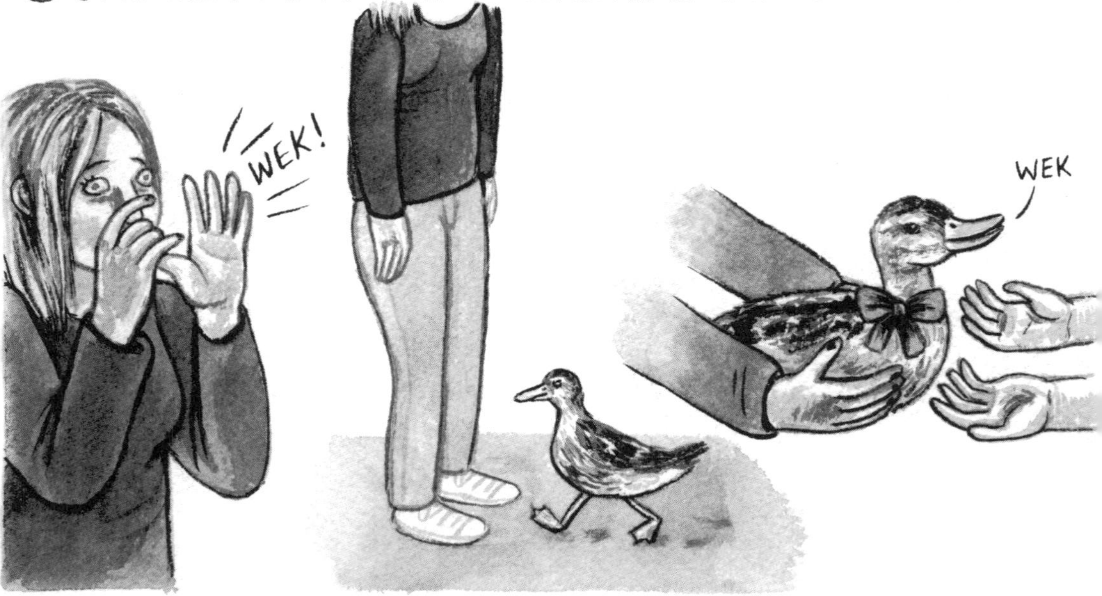
WEK!
WEK

③ ASK THEM TO HELP YOU WITH SOMETHING.

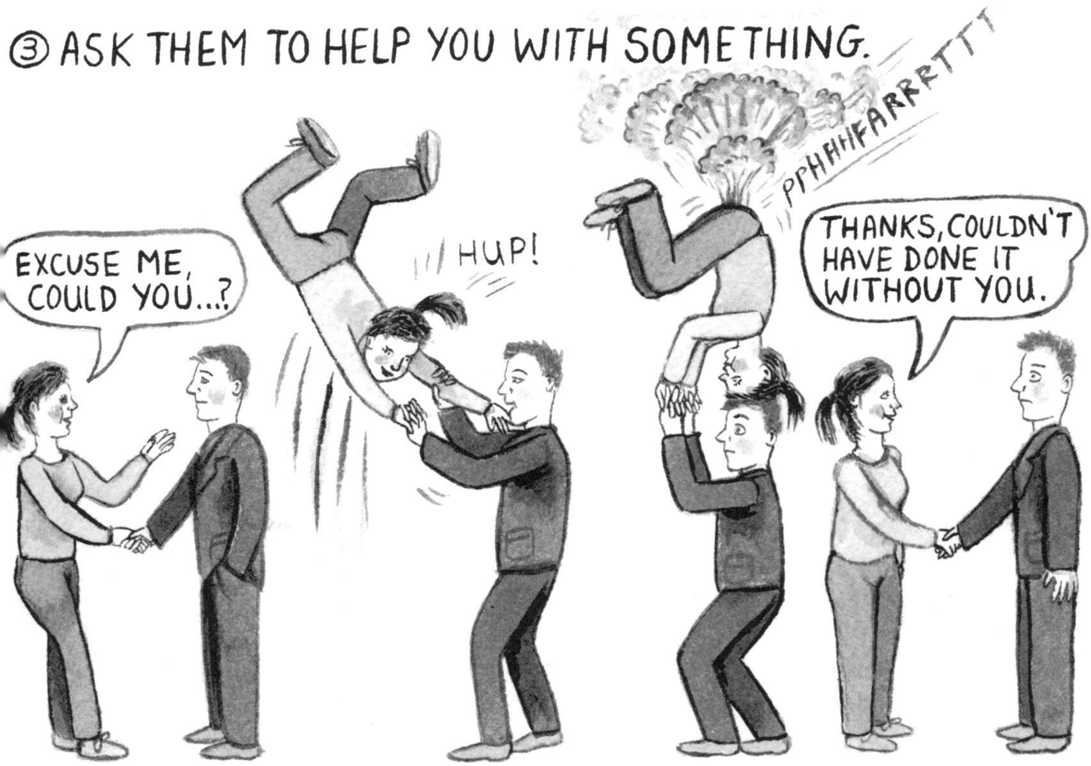
EXCUSE ME, COULD YOU...?
HUP!
PPHHHFARRRTTT
THANKS, COULDN'T HAVE DONE IT WITHOUT YOU.

④ OBJECTIFY THEIR BODY.

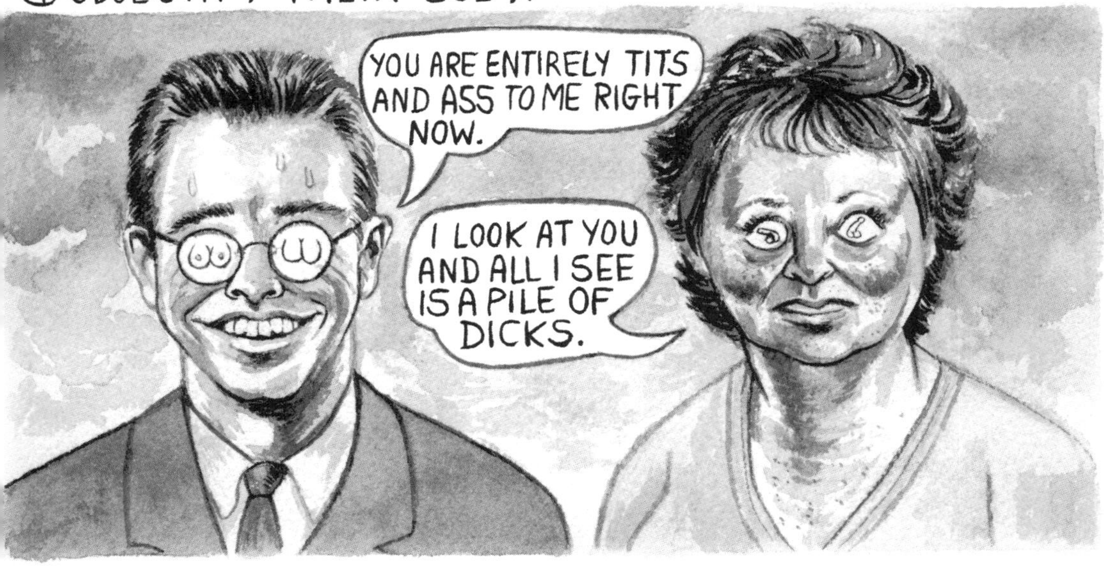
YOU ARE ENTIRELY TITS AND ASS TO ME RIGHT NOW.
I LOOK AT YOU AND ALL I SEE IS A PILE OF DICKS.

⑤ DON'T LET THEIR UNIQUE TALENTS GO UNNOTICED.

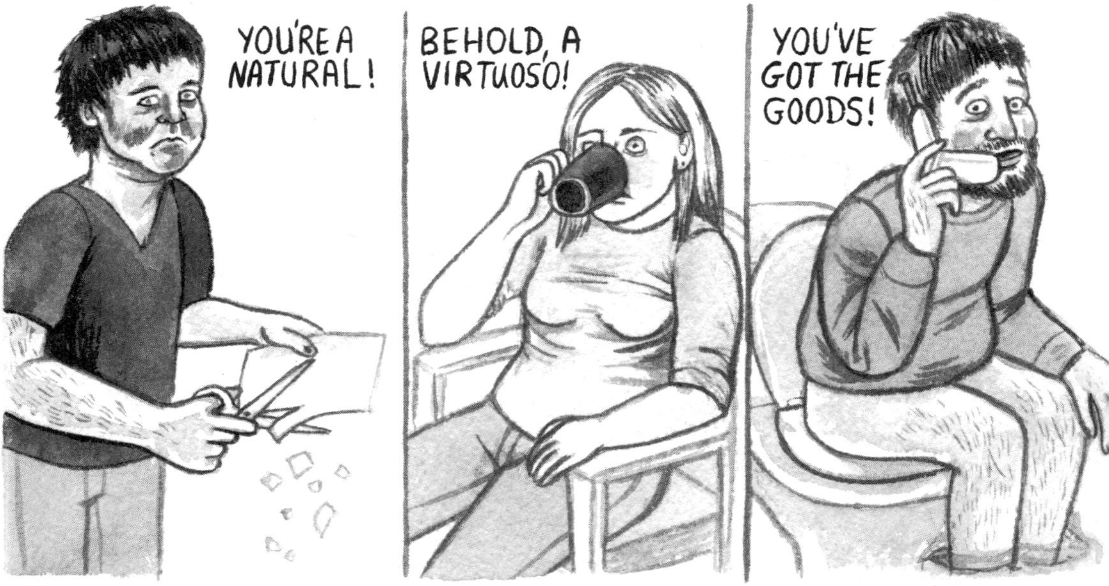
YOU'RE A NATURAL!
BEHOLD, A VIRTUOSO!
YOU'VE GOT THE GOODS!

⑥ TRUST THEM WITH YOUR DEEPEST THOUGHTS & CONCERNS.

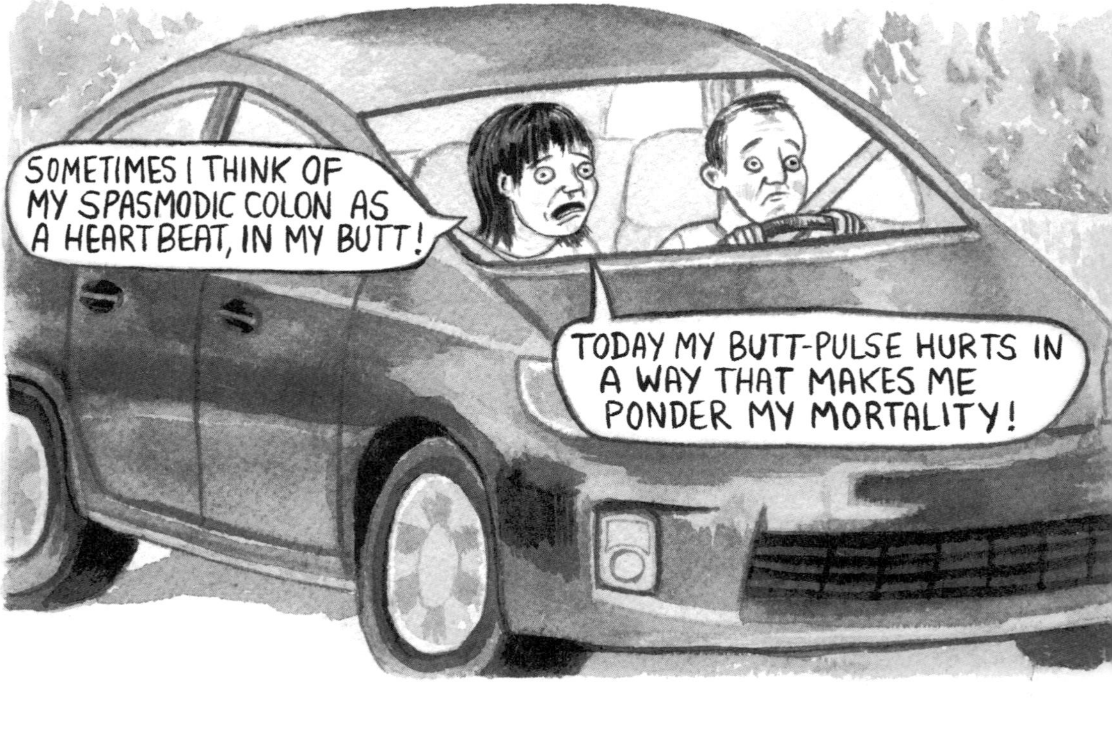
SOMETIMES I THINK OF MY SPASMODIC COLON AS A HEARTBEAT, IN MY BUTT!
TODAY MY BUTT-PULSE HURTS IN A WAY THAT MAKES ME PONDER MY MORTALITY!

(7) CONVINCE THEM THAT THEY'RE DIFFERENT & SPECIAL.

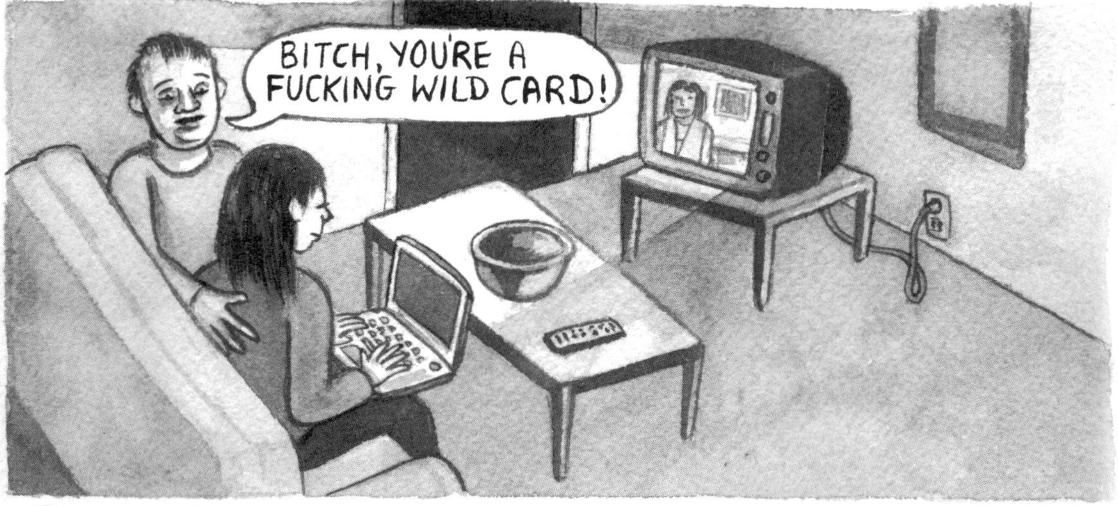
BITCH, YOU'RE A FUCKING WILD CARD!

(8) IF YOU GET TIRED, LET A DOG TAKE OVER THE FLATTERY FOR A WHILE.

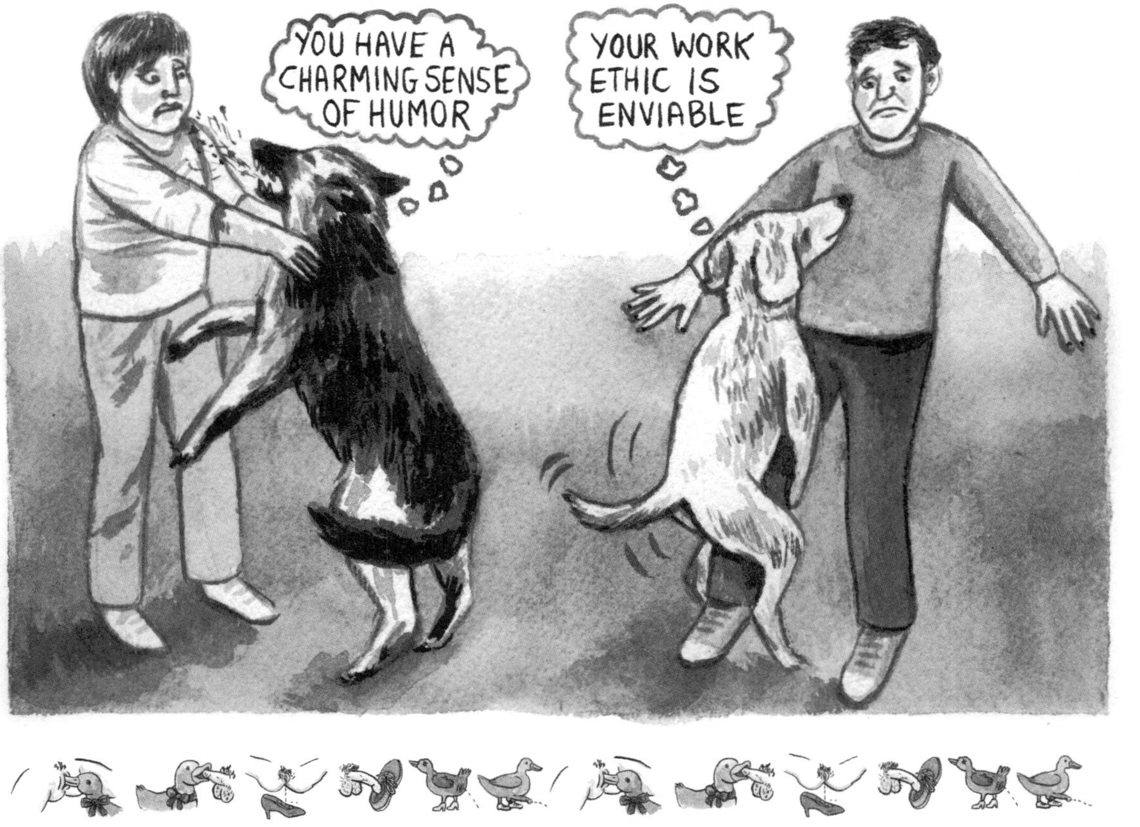
YOU HAVE A CHARMING SENSE OF HUMOR
YOUR WORK ETHIC IS ENVIABLE

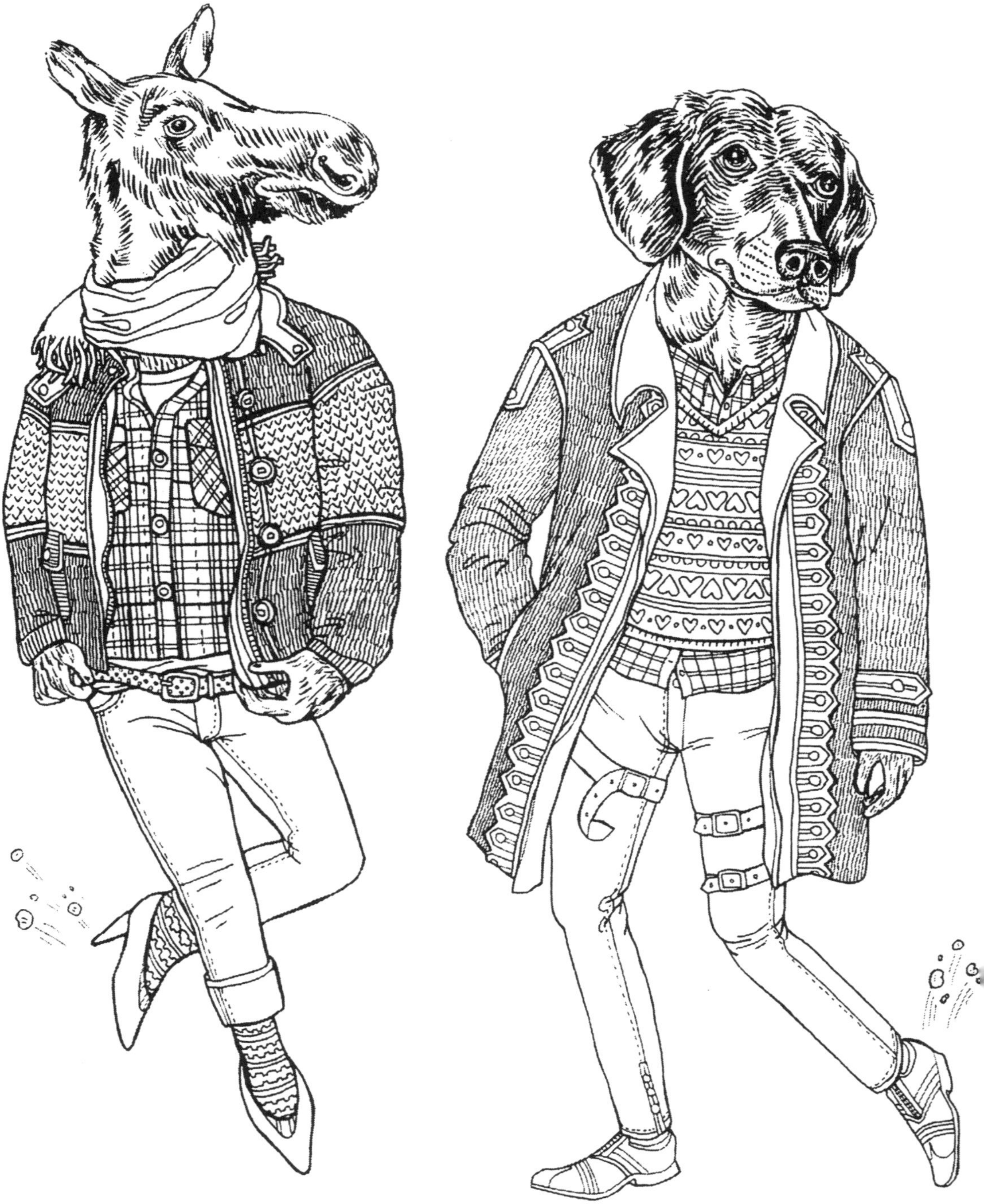

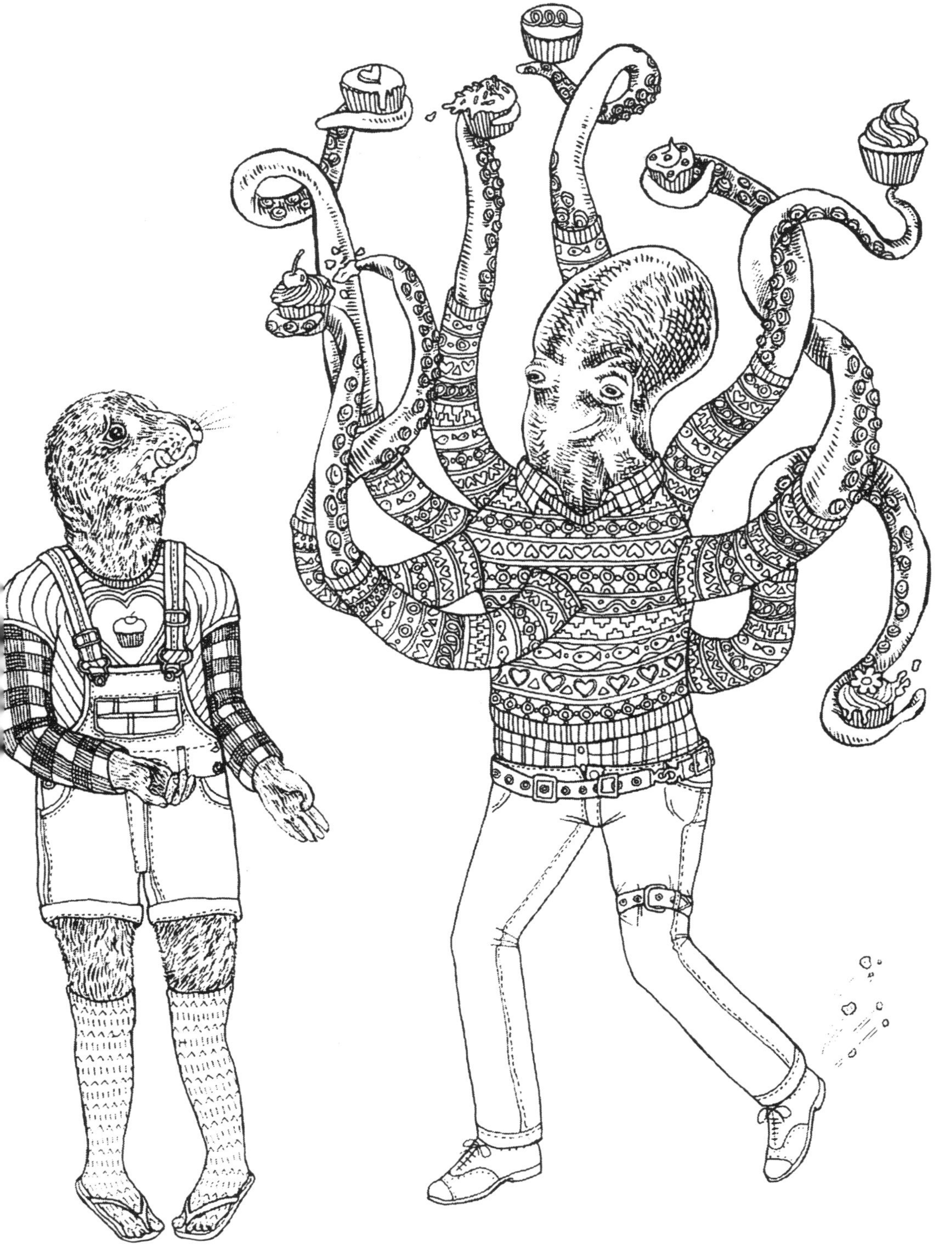

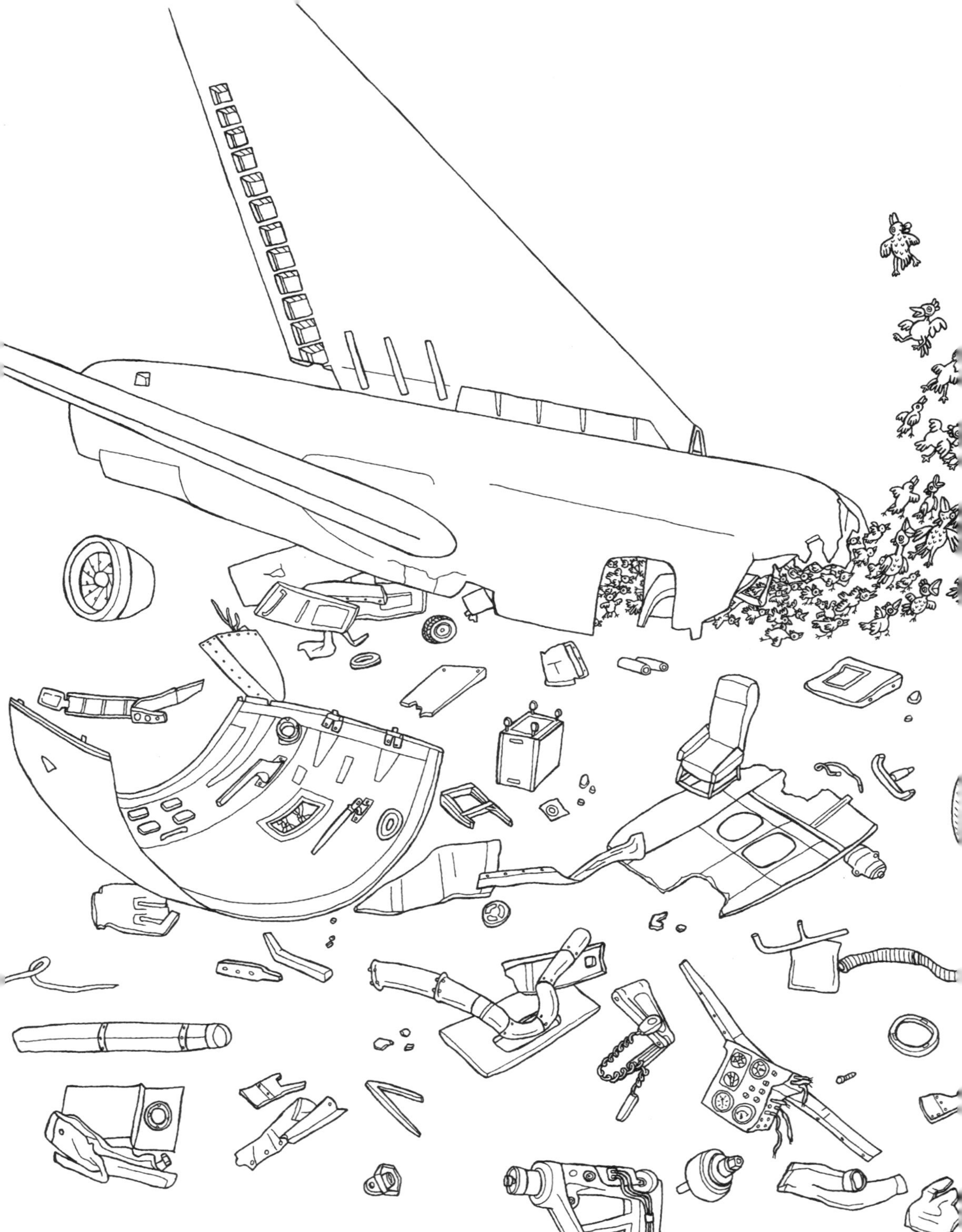

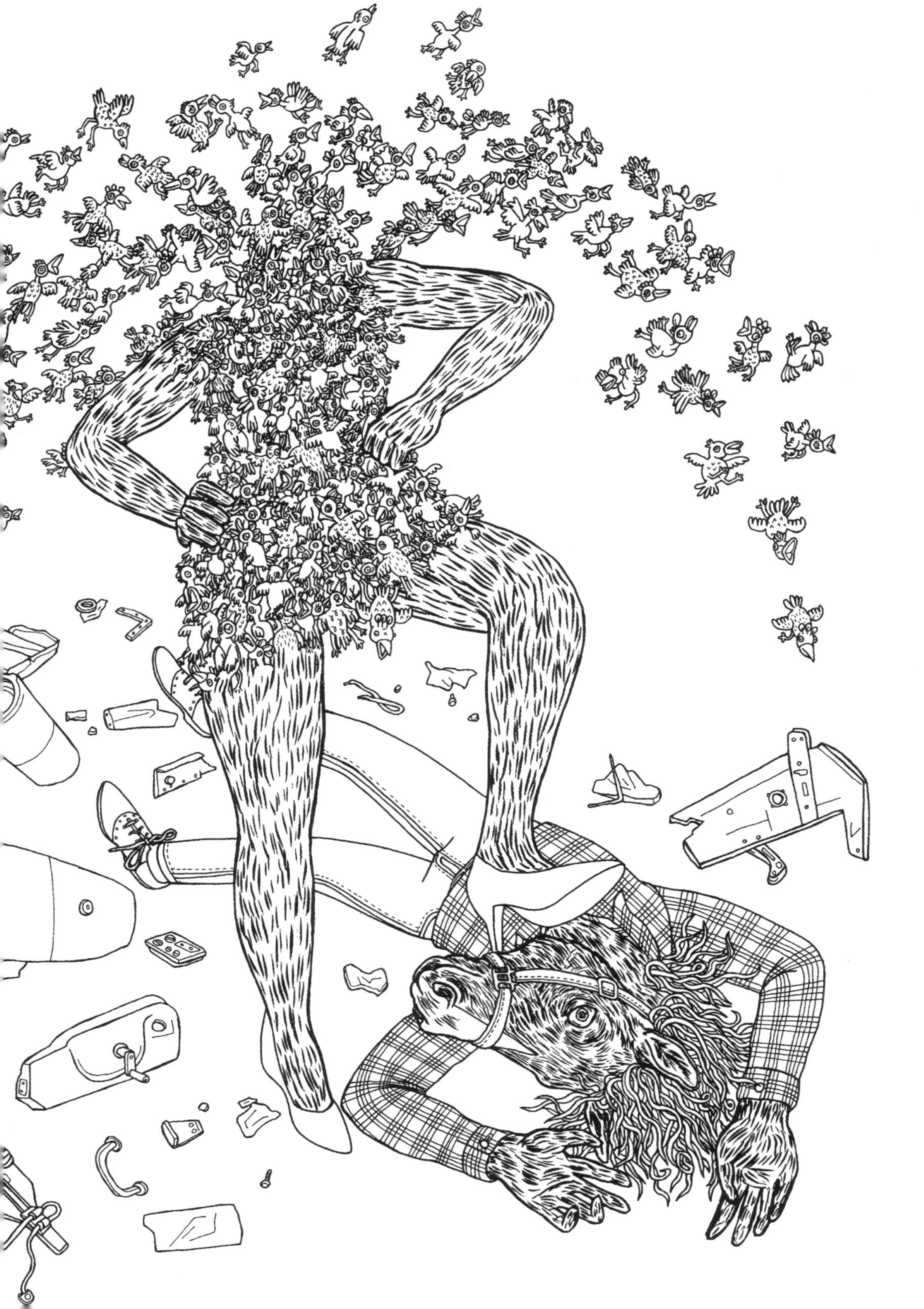